ZHUAN FALUN

Hongzhi Li

The Falun symbol pictured here is a miniature representation of the universe. In all other dimensions it has forms of existence as well, along with processes through which it evolves, and so I consider it a world.

HONGZHI LI

ZHUAN FALUN

轉法輪

Hongzhi Li

2018 ENGLISH EDITION

First printing, October 2019

*Translated by practitioners in the United States and
the United Kingdom, from the original Mandarin text, © 1995*

*Translated and printed with the consent of
the Falun Dafa Association*

*As no single translation can capture all of the depth,
nuances, and intricacies of a spiritual text like Zhuan Falun,
several versions have been made available. These can be found
online at FalunDafa.org and in bookstores.*

*Published by: Yih-Chyun Book Co, Ltd.
No. 229-9. Sec. 2, Chung-Ching North Road, Taipei, Taiwan 10359
Tel. 886-2-255 331 23*

ISBN: 978-957-8632-32-5 (PAPERBACK EDITION)
ISBN: 978-957-8632-33-2 (HARDCOVER EDITION)

Printed in Taiwan, 2020
英文版

CONTENTS

THE FOURTH TALK

THE FIFTH TALK

THE SIXTH TALK

THE SEVENTH TALK

THE EIGHTH TALK

THE NINTH TALK

ON DAFA
(*Lunyu*)

Dafa* is the wisdom of the Creator. It is the bedrock of creation, what the heavens, earth, and universe are built upon. It encompasses all things, from the utmost minuscule to the vastest of the vast, while manifesting differently at each of the cosmic body's planes of existence. Out of the depths of the cosmic body, the tiniest of particles first appear, with layers upon layers of countless particles following, ranging in size from small to great, reaching all the way to the outer planes that humankind knows—those of atoms, molecules, planets, and galaxies—and beyond, to what is still larger. Particles of varying sizes make up lives of varying sizes as well as the worlds of varying sizes that permeate the cosmic body. Lives at any of the various planes of particles perceive the particles of the next larger plane to be planets in their skies, and this is true at each and every plane. To the lives at each plane of the universe, it seems to go on infinitely. It was Dafa that created time and space, the multitude of lives and species, and all of creation; all that exists owes to it, with nothing outside of it. All of these are the tangible expressions, at different planes, of Dafa's qualities: *zhen*, *shan*, and *ren*.*

---

* This and all terms marked with an asterisk appear in the Endnotes at the back of the book.

i

However advanced people's means of exploring space and probing life may be, the knowledge gained is limited to certain parts of this one dimension, where human beings reside, at a low plane of the universe. Other planets were explored before by humans during civilizations predating history. Yet for all the heights and distances achieved, humankind has never managed to depart from the dimension in which it exists. The true picture of the universe will forever elude humankind. If a human being is to understand the mysteries of the universe, space-time, and the human body, he must take up cultivation of a true Way and achieve true enlightenment, raising his plane of being. Through cultivation his moral character will elevate, and once he has learned to discern what is truly good from evil, and virtue from vice, and he goes beyond the human plane, he will see and gain access to the realities of the universe as well as the lives of other planes and dimensions.

While people often claim that their scientific pursuits are to "improve quality of life," it is technological competition that drives them. And in most cases they have come about only after people have pushed out the divine and abandoned moral codes meant to ensure self-restraint. It was for these reasons that civilizations of the past many times met with destruction. People's explorations are necessarily limited to this material world, and the methods are such that only what has been recognized is studied. Meanwhile, things that are intangible or invisible in the human dimension, but that do objectively exist and do reveal themselves in real ways in this immediate world—such as spirituality, faith, divine word, and miracles—are treated as taboo, for people have cast out the divine.

If the human race is able to improve its character, conduct, and thinking by grounding these in moral values, it will be possible for civilization to endure and even for miracles to occur again in the human world. Many times in the past, cultures that were as divine as they were human have appeared in this world and helped people to arrive at a truer understanding of life and the universe. When people show the appropriate respect and reverence toward Dafa as it manifests here in this world, they, their race, or their nation will enjoy blessings or honor. It was Dafa—the Great Way of the universe—that created the cosmic body, the universe, life, and all of creation. Any life that turns away from Dafa is truly corrupt. Any person who can align with Dafa is truly a good person, and will be rewarded and blessed with health and happiness. And any cultivator who is able to become one with Dafa is an enlightened one—divine.

Hongzhi Li
May 24, 2015

THE
FIRST TALK

Truly Taking You to
Greater Spiritual Heights

FROM THE START, I have been teaching in a way that's responsible both to those who want to learn our practice and society. It has gone quite well, and the practice has had a widely positive impact. In recent years there have been many figures teaching energy practices, but their instruction has always been geared toward health and wellness. There's nothing wrong with that, of course. My point is that they haven't taught anything of a more advanced sort. I have a good sense for the state of energy practices in China today, and can say that no one here or abroad is offering a practice like this, which really takes you to greater spiritual heights. As for why that is, there are bigger, and broader, reasons at work, some of which stretch far back into the past and can be controversial. Not just anyone can teach something like this, as it entails dealing with factors from a host of other practices. The problem is especially acute these days, when many people jump from one practice to the next and make a mess of their bodies, ruining any spiritual aspirations they may have had. They go in for all sorts of things, rather than committing to just one solid approach that could take them somewhere, and each new one that they dabble in only conflicts with the last. All of which only dashes their spiritual prospects.

We have to straighten out all of those things for you. What's good will be kept and what's bad disposed of, and this will make spiritual progress possible for you. But there's a stipulation, which is that you have to be serious about this practice. It doesn't work if you are motivated by the wrong things, like attachments, or wanting psychic powers, or healing, or are here out of intellectual curiosity. Remember that what I am doing is unique. Something like this is hard to come by, and I won't be offering instruction* forever. So I think that by being able to sit here and hear my teaching in person, you are really… you will grasp the significance of it later on, and realize how fortunate you were. We subscribe to the idea of destiny, and I would say it is your destiny to be here.

It's worth pausing to consider what it means to be learning a practice that truly takes you to "greater spiritual heights." It means deliverance from this world. So you will need to be doing genuine spiritual practice, and not just involved for health or wellness. It follows, then, that there are high expectations for your personal character. You are here because you want to learn Falun Dafa, so as you sit here you have to really listen with sincere spiritual intent, and let go of whatever things might have initially motivated you. You will get very little out of the practice if there are impure motives still

2

with you as you try to learn it. In truth, the spiritual journey is none other than an ongoing process of learning to let go of the things of this world that we may be attached to. If you are someone who competes fiercely with others, who tries to cheat and outwit people, or who even tramples on others to come out on top, then you really have to change your ways. It's especially imperative for you as someone who is here to learn the practice today.

I won't be teaching you how to heal, as that's not part of our practice. But an ailing body is a real impediment to anyone serious about spiritual practice. And so I will purify your body for you. But I can only do this for whoever is sincere about the practice and the teachings. And so I have to stress that we will be powerless to help you if you are set on getting healed and can't get past that idea. Why, you might ask? It's because the way things work in the universe, according to Buddhist thought, is that everything in a person's life has "causal reasons" behind it, and the ordeals of existence—such as coming into the world, aging, getting ill, and dying—are as they should be. The ailments and miseries that people experience result from their karma, and karma is the product of past wrongdoings. So the ordeals that people face are how they pay for their karma. This means that nobody may change them. Changing them would be like letting people build up debt and never having to pay. So people's lives can't be freely changed, and it would be wrong to do so.

Some people are under the mistaken impression that they are being helpful when healing people. But as I see it, in no case is the person actually getting healed. His ailments are just being postponed or turned into something else, and aren't really removed. To end the person's physical ordeals you have to eliminate the karma involved. And to really, thoroughly do that and heal the person you have to be someone quite spiritually advanced. And anyone like that would be aware that the workings of this human world can't rashly be tinkered with. That said, it *is* allowed for those who are in the process of spiritual development to do a few acts of charity, such as healing someone or helping a person regain his health, if they are moved to do so by compassion. But any healing done wouldn't be thorough. That's because it would not be right to remove the person's ailment at the source, by dissolving his karma, and completely free him of it, since he would still be his same old, worldly, self afterwards and go back to his competitive and self-interested life. So truly healing someone like that is out of the question.

But *purification* can be done for those who engage in sincere spiritual practice. It is because they are valued above all others. The desire to work on yourself and become a better, or more spiritual, person is the greatest aspiration there is. It has long been believed that everyone has divinity within them, and this would be a reflection of it; so higher beings will help you. This takes a little explaining. The practice that I'm teaching is quite advanced, I would say, and so higher matters and bigger things are involved. From a higher vantage point in the universe, it can be seen that the lives of those on this earth didn't come into being here. Their souls were born in the higher realms of the universe. There are many, many things in the universe that can, when working in conjunction, generate life, and so it was in the greater universe that each person's soul first came into existence. The universe is by nature good and kind, and so when a person is first born he shares in its defining qualities: *zhen, shan, ren.* As more

4

lives come about, however, people enter into community with one another, and some grow selfish and no longer worthy of the realms they are in. And so they must fall to a lower plane, since they are not allowed to remain where they are. But then, in that new realm, they may again change for the worse and not be allowed to remain, whereupon they drop again. And the cycle could keep repeating itself until, in the end, they fall to the human plane.

All of humanity is on this one plane. Upon arriving at this level, lives were meant to be, if viewed with higher powers, or as divine beings see it, destroyed. But divine beings, acting out of compassion, decided to give these lives another chance, and created this unique setting, or realm, much as we know it. The lives in this realm are different from those in all other realms of the universe. From here, the lives of other realms cannot be seen, nor can the universe be seen as it really is, and so the lives here are as if under a spell of ignorance. So the only way for someone to be healed, to be free of adversity, and to be unburdened of karma, is to engage in spiritual practice and return, pure as he once was, to his true home. This is a belief common to a range of spiritual traditions. And this is in fact the meaning of life. And it explains why the wish to become a better, or more spiritual, person is considered divine and is prized; it means that the person wants to become pure again and return to his true, heavenly abode, and be freed of this world.

In Buddhism there has long been a belief that when one's divinity shines through, it is moving to higher beings throughout the many planes of the universe. All who behold it will wish to provide help, and will do so unconditionally. Buddhists believe that higher beings expect nothing in return when they save someone from this world; they don't affix any price, and their help is always unconditional. And it is on these grounds that we can do much for anyone who takes up our practice. By contrast, little can be done for the average person, who just wishes to keep going through life as he has and perhaps be healed. Some only want to do this practice if it will heal them. But your interest shouldn't be conditional. Just start practicing if you are inclined to. Naturally, there will be some who come to the practice with ailing bodies, with bodily energies all out of sorts, or with no prior experience with energy practices; and even those who *have* done them, and even for decades, usually haven't moved past the most basic stages of energy practice to actual spiritual progress.

So what do we do? We cleanse their bodies for them so that progress in our practice will be possible. The first, most basic stage of the spiritual journey involves thoroughly and completely cleansing your body, as well as clearing out all of the bad things in your head, the cloud of karma engulfing your body, and the factors compromising your health. Without this cleansing it would be hard for you to make spiritual progress, plagued as it were by a body dark and foul, and a mind that unclean. Our practice doesn't work on the basic kind of energy known as *chi*.* You needn't work on such basic things with our practice. We boost you past that stage, so that you begin with a body free of ailment. But at the same time, we still provide you with everything that one would normally develop as a foundation at the basic stage of practice, ready-made. This means you start right off at an advanced stage.

In Asian spiritual practice there are said to be three stages of practice, if the beginning one, which involves *chi* energy, is included. But true practice only begins after *chi*, so there are just two main phases: that of the human realm, and that of beyond the human realm. These shouldn't be confused with the religious concepts of renouncing the world or returning to secular life, which might sound similar. The two terms we are using refer to the two main stages of bodily change that occur in true spiritual practices with a physical component. In the first stage, of practicing within the human realm, the body is being purified constantly, again and again, until ultimately the body has been fully remade with high-energy matter. The second stage, of practicing beyond the human realm, is essentially practice that's done with a divine body. It is a body made of high-energy matter, and it will now be developing all powers anew. These are the two stages of practice that we will be referring to.

We believe in destiny. So by virtue of your coming to this class, I can do what I've described for you. And I could still do what I said even if we had not just two thousand people, like we have in attendance today, but even several thousand, or over ten thousand. So none of you need to worry about practicing for the basics, as I said. I will purify your body and advance you past the basic stage, and provide everything you need to make spiritual progress. So you are starting right off at an advanced stage of practice. But this is only true for those of you who are sincere about the practice and about making spiritual progress. It's not enough just to be here, enrolled in the class; that doesn't make you a practitioner. There may have to be a deep and dramatic change in your way of thinking before you get the benefits I've described. And there are more in store, in fact, as you will find out later on. While we don't do healing here, what we will do, to use our term for it, is bring your entire body into balance. Doing this will make it possible for you to do our practice. If you were trying to do the practice with a disease-ridden body, you really wouldn't be able to develop higher energy, or *gong*, as it's called. So don't ask me to heal you; I don't do that. I made this practice public because I want to really, truly bring you to greater spiritual heights.

The Many Levels of the Way

Chinese energy practices, known by names like *chi-gong* and *tai-chi*, have taught that there are three phases of practice—beginning, intermediate, and advanced. But as it turns out, all of those phases are at a basic stage since they work on the lower form of energy known as *chi*. Most who are involved in those practices have little to no idea about higher stages and what they entail. By contrast, right from day one all of what we will be teaching will be the higher Way (*fa*) of advanced practice. Along the way I hope to help give spiritual practice the status it deserves. This means that I'm going to have to shine a light on some of the questionable things that are happening out there, and explain the right way to look at them. And by teaching a higher Way, as we are, bigger and broader things are going to be hit on, some of which are quite controversial. But I am going to address them all the same. Some of the things troubling this world, and in particular the spiritual arena, trace back to other dimensions, and these need to be laid bare and remedied for our students, which I will do. Your practice would be doomed from the start if I didn't address these issues. But to deal with them on a fundamental level means that I have to regard you as true practitioners.

Of course, you might not be able to change your way of looking at things right from day one. But I think you will in the days to come, and I hope you can listen attentively. I teach in a different way from others in this field, who typically just run through the basics of their practices, impart energies to you, and teach you their exercises. And this is what many people have come to expect.

But real guidance takes more than that: there needs to be a moral component, or Way, to the teaching. And that is what I will be providing over the course of our ten sessions. We will teach the deeper workings of spiritual practice in great detail, and this will be what makes your spiritual growth possible. Without this, you really wouldn't be able to get very far. The instruction offered in most other settings is simply about healing and physical well-being, and doesn't provide a higher Way or teaching that could guide you to advanced stages of spiritual practice. It's analogous to trying to go through college by studying primary school texts: you would come out with an elementary level of education. There are people who have studied all kinds of practices and have a stack of certificates to show for it, but it hasn't taken them anywhere. And yet they think that they've learned the true meaning of practice and all that there is to it; they don't realize that they have only scratched the surface and gained just a small, partial picture of it. But there is much more to traditional practices like *chi-gong* and *tai-chi*. They are forms of *spiritual practice*, and are far-reaching and profound. And it's important to know that the Way and its guidance are different at different stages of practice. It's not like what most people imagine—that the more one learns the merrier. To give an analogy, you could toil away studying textbooks gathered from around the globe—from England, from America, from Japan, from China—and if they were all just elementary school books, you would only come out of it with an elementary level of education. And in the case of energy practices, you're even worse off: the more instruction you take in of a lower sort, the more harm it will do. Your body will pay for it.

I want to emphasize, then, that as ours is a spiritual practice, it is vital that we teach a higher Way. This doesn't sit very well with some monastic Buddhists, particularly those who are Zen, and they turn a deaf ear to us. The reason is, in Zen Buddhism it's believed that higher, spiritual truth, or *dharma*,* is not something that can be taught, or it's no longer truth. They believe there is nothing to be taught, and that any higher truths are just to be intuited on one's own. And so as it now stands, the *dharma* is no longer taught in Zen. This traces back to Zen's founder, Bodhidharma, who based his ideas on one line from the Buddha, Shakyamuni,* who had said: "No *dharma* is definitive." So the discipline of Zen was built around a single sentence. To us it seems that the discipline has essentially revolved around splitting hairs, and gone down a dead end. I say that because it has found itself in more and more of a predicament with each successive generation, going from having an idea that seemed quite deep at first and allowed ample room for reflection, when Bodhidharma began things, to one that was less so by Zen's second patriarch, that still had a little to it by the third, barely any left by the fourth, and that had basically bottomed out by the fifth. By the sixth patriarch, Hui-neng, the original idea had been mined to the point that nothing was left. Today, if you go to a Zen temple in hopes of understanding the *dharma*, you'd best not ask any questions or you might just get rapped on the head with that "waking stick" of theirs—since you're supposed to just intuit the truth yourself. But that's pretty confusing, as the whole point of going there would be to learn something, and now you're supposed to figure things out for yourself—or otherwise get whacked with a stick! This suggests that Zen really has reached a dead end, and has nothing left to teach. Bodhidharma himself had said that his teachings would only survive down to the sixth patriarch, which was hundreds of years ago. But there are now people who just insist on the wisdom of Zen and stick with it. Yet we should think about what might have been the true meaning of the Buddha's statement that, "No *dharma* is definitive." Very few people since the Buddha, and that includes the monks who followed in his footsteps, have achieved the divine rank that he ultimately had, known as *tathagata*; nor have many attained the same degree of enlightenment or realm of mind. So it has been hard for them to know the true meaning of his *dharma* teachings or what he said. And this accounts for the wide and confusing array of interpretations that you see of his statement—including, even, Zen's belief that spiritual truth shouldn't be taught and that whatever is, isn't valid. But that wasn't what the Buddha meant. When the Buddha became enlightened and his powers came to him under the Bodhi tree, his awakening was not yet at its highest point of *tathagata*, which he ultimately achieved. He continued to make regular spiritual progress throughout the forty-nine years of his ministry. And with each successive breakthrough he would find, looking back, that what he had previously taught wasn't quite right. This continued to happen again and again, with each new spiritual breakthrough being followed by a re-evaluation of what he had taught before. And this went on for forty-nine years as he kept progressing; he kept finding that what he taught before was incomplete. He came to realize that the spiritual insights from the Way that he was perceiving at each new level of attainment were specific to those realms, with different truths existing at each realm, but with none of them being the ultimate Truth of the universe. However, he could see that at each progressively higher realm that he reached, the Way [he had awakened to] grew closer to the true qualities of the universe. And so this was what led him to proclaim that no *dharma* is definitive.

In the end, the Buddha also remarked that he had "never taught the *dharma*." And this was taken by Zen to mean that higher truth cannot be taught. When the Buddha remarked as he did, he would have been in his later years and had in fact achieved the divine state of *tathagata*, so it's worth reconsidering what he meant. What he meant was that he could not make out, at his stage of spiritual achievement, what the ultimate Truth or Way of the universe was. And so he didn't want those who came after him to take what he had said as absolute or final Truth, lest his words limit people to his degree of achievement or lower, and prevent higher breakthroughs. Later generations misunderstood his remarks, taking them to mean that no teaching could reveal the Way. But what he meant was that the Way differs across levels of existence, with no instance of it being the ultimate Truth of the universe, though each would serve to govern its own level. So now you know what the Buddha was getting at.

Many people have had a radical take like Zen has, and been wrongly biased against the idea of teaching a higher Way or *dharma*. But how are you to make progress in spiritual practice without instruction or anything to guide you?

A Buddhist tale comes to mind, which you might have read; it's one of many in the Buddhist tradition. It tells of a person who ascended to a heavenly realm, where he saw a well-known Buddhist text called the *Diamond Sutra*. Yet this version of the sutra was completely different from the one in the human realm, from the words of the text to the insights it contained. This might seem puzzling, then. It has likewise been said that the scriptures in the Pure Land paradise have no similarity to their counterparts on earth, with everything being different—from their words and insights to the ideas they contain. What accounts for this is the fact that the Way differs, in both form and substance, at each plane of existence. And so it can always provide guidance to believers, at whatever stage they may be, in their spiritual journey.

Similarly, there is a Buddhist booklet that some of you might be familiar with, titled *A Journey to the Pure Land*. It tells of a monk whose soul left his body while he was meditating and went to this fabled paradise and beheld what was there. His soul spent a day there, only to find, upon returning to the human world, that six years had passed. He did really go there, in case you're wondering. But he didn't see the paradise as it truly was, because his realm of spiritual attainment didn't qualify him to. So what he beheld was only one expression of the paradise, provided by the Way, as befitting his level of attainment. A paradise like that is an embodiment of the Way, and so he was not allowed to see it as it truly is. The above conveys what I believe the Buddha really meant by saying that no spiritual truths, or *dharma*, are definitive.

The Sole Measure of Goodness: Zhen, Shan, Ren

The "Way" has long been the subject of religious discussion and inquiry. But that doesn't mean that all that can be known about the Way has already been revealed by past teachings and scriptures. When the Buddha gave his teachings twenty-five hundred years ago, they were meant for the relatively simple people of his day whose civilization was still in its earliest stages, and whose understanding of the world was quite rudimentary. And he spoke of a future time, or "latter day," when his teachings would no longer be able to guide people's spiritual development. That time is in fact our day. He indicated that in the latter day it would be hard even for dedicated monastics to free themselves from this world, let alone laypeople. So what he taught was geared towards the people of his day, and didn't include all of the insights he had gained into the Way at his stage of attainment. And there would have been no way to keep his teachings from being altered in the centuries that would follow.

People's minds have grown increasingly complicated as civilization has developed, and it has become harder to progress spiritually by following the old ways of devotion. It should also be said that the spiritual truths of any one tradition are only one small part of the Way, and couldn't possibly capture all of it. And there are still many other, lesser-known practices that similarly follow the Way and that have been passed down outside of any religious institutions, such as in a private lineage. Truths differ from one plane of existence to the next and from dimension to dimension, since the Way is revealed uniquely at different planes of existence and in different realms. All told, there are only a dozen or so Buddhist disciplines that are well known—such as Zen, Pure Land, Tiantai, Flower Garland, and Tantric—and yet the Buddha indicated that there are *eighty-four thousand* avenues to enlightenment, or divinity. So the few that we know of couldn't possibly represent the full array of spiritual insights that exist. And this is on top of the fact that, as I just mentioned, the Buddha didn't teach all that he had come to know of the Way, but rather, only what was suitable for his audience at the time.

Then just what exactly is the Way? Its highest expression is the fundamental qualities that underlie all of existence: *zhen, shan, ren.* These are the essence of the Way. The Way is expressed differently at different levels of existence, and serves to govern each accordingly, with its expression becoming increasingly intricate at lower planes. The qualities of *zhen, shan, ren* are imbued in all of creation, from particles of air to stones, wood, earth, metal, and the human body. And so too are these qualities found in the "five elements" of classical Chinese thought, which are believed to make up all of existence. Those who engage in spiritual practice will only come to know the expression of the Way unique to the realm that their attainment has brought them to; its revelations reflect the success of one's spiritual efforts, or realm of attainment. When looked at in its entirety, the Way is enormous. But in the highest of realms it is quite simple, for its structure can be likened to that of a pyramid whereby at the very top everything can be summed up in just three words—*zhen*, *shan*, *ren*—while as you go downward toward the base, things get increasingly complex. A parallel can be drawn between man and the universe, as ancient Daoist thought has done. While you may be endowed with a physical body, that alone isn't enough to make you a complete person. You also must have other invisible elements such as disposition, temperament, personality, as well as a spirit, or soul, to be a complete and independent individual. By the same token, the universe has a Milky Way as well as other galaxies, living creatures, and water—with all such tangible facets of creation being its physical side. Yet at the same time, behind it all, it has the invisible qualities, or spirit, of *zhen, shan, ren*. So these qualities are imbued in the particles of anything and everything that exists, down to the very smallest of particles.

And it is these qualities that act as the measure of good and evil in this universe. They are what define good and evil, as well as what has traditionally counted as virtuous. People's values have undergone a change, however, and many people's moral compasses are now askew. For instance, many would now think it's silly for someone to try to learn from the example of selfless figures from the past, like Lei Feng.* But it wasn't like that back in the 1950s or '60s. People's values are eroding at a dramatic rate, and getting worse by the day. Many people now put their own gain before all else, even at others' expense, and will do whatever it takes to come out on top. But what will become of our world if it goes on like this? There are people who won't even listen if you try to point out the error in their ways; and they really can't see what's wrong on their part. Some even think that they are better than others, since they see themselves through the distorted lens of modern values, which has altered their sense of right and wrong. But however much people's values may change, the qualities that define this universe *will not*, and they are the sole measure of your person. It is these—and not the values now in vogue—that must be what you live by as someone who does spiritual practice. If you would like to regain the purity you once had, and return to your true home, if you would like to develop spiritually, then you must live by the cosmic qualities of *zhen, shan, ren*. Anyone who abides by these is a good person, while anyone who lives a life contrary to them is a bad person. And so how well someone regards you at your workplace or in whatever setting may not reflect how you really are. Yours is a spiritual life, and you must embody these qualities if you hope to become a spiritually realized being. It's rather simple, in fact.

In the Daoist tradition, practice focuses on the *zhen* of *zhen, shan, ren*. And so it teaches followers to engage in spiritual discipline, speak and act honestly, be genuine, return to one's true state of purity, and ultimately become an enlightened being. *Ren* and *shan* do feature in their practice, but the focus is upon *zhen*. In the Buddhist tradition, meanwhile, practice focuses on the *shan* of *zhen, shan, ren*. By cultivating *shan,* great compassion develops in one's heart, and one becomes sensitive to the suffering of others; and this, in turn, gives rise in oneself to a wish to deliver people from suffering. *Zhen* and *ren* also appear in their practice, but the focus is upon *shan*. What makes Falun Dafa so powerful is that we integrate all three of the universe's highest qualities—*zhen, shan,* and *ren*—and work on them all together.

Energy Practices Predate History

Many instructors of energy practices have sought to explain what these are all about. My take is quite different from theirs, which tend to be narrow in scope; I look at the practices from a higher, more spiritual, vantage point. Some instructors might date them back two or three thousand years in China, or as far as five thousand years—which is roughly as old as Chinese civilization. But even the furthest proposed dates, which are based on archaeological findings and put the figure at seven thousand years back—and which would predate Chinese civilization by quite a bit—don't go much beyond human civilization. And going by the calculations of those who subscribe to Darwin's evolutionary theory, civilization in any form wouldn't really have begun earlier than ten thousand years ago, when people with the thought and culture of modern man are believed to have come about; and this would be after his evolutionary journey from aquatic plant life, to aquatic animal, to land and eventually tree dweller, and then finally, once settled on land again, to ape. With the idea being that before the advent of civilization, people would have had no written record of any sort and lived a supposedly wild and savage existence, covering themselves with things like leaves, eating raw meat, and with no knowledge of fire.

But there are problems with this view. There are many artifacts around the world that far predate the earliest era of civilization now known. Many of the remains display a sophisticated level of craftsmanship and artistry. The arts of the past had a high aesthetic value and almost give the sense that modern man was just following in their footsteps. And yet some of these remains date back hundreds of thousands or millions of years, with some even exceeding 100 million. It would seem to radically challenge current views of history, wouldn't it? But there is nothing inherently radical about it. People always try to push the boundaries of what is humanly possible, and keep arriving at new insights about themselves and their past. So people's initial findings and views about things aren't always right.

This leads to the topic of prehistoric civilizations, or prehistoric cultures, which you might be familiar with. In the world today we have Asia, Africa, North America, South America, Antarctica, Europe, and Oceania, which are all considered in geology to be continental land masses. These settled in their current configuration tens of millions of years ago. So some land masses emerged from the ocean floor, while others, now no longer with us, became submerged under the ocean's waters. The current land masses have been in place for tens of millions of years. Yet discoveries have yielded ancient megastructures at the bottoms of several oceans. And these structures are covered in intricate carvings bearing no resemblance to the works of any civilization today. Yet they must have been built *before* having sunk to the bottom of the sea—many millions of years ago. But then who would have built them, if man, supposedly, wasn't even a monkey yet? Such sophisticated things wouldn't have been possible. Another enigma surrounds the discovery by archaeologists of a certain trilobite fossil. This is a creature that dates back some 260 to 600 million years, and has long been extinct. Yet an American scientist discovered a trilobite fossil with a human footprint on it—the footprint of someone wearing shoes. And the print was unmistakable. For many, it's an embarrassing challenge to established views about the past. Darwin's evolutionary model can't explain the existence of human beings that long ago.

Another telling case is a rock in the museum of a national university in Peru that has a human figure carved on it. An analysis determined that the person was carved on it thirty thousand years ago. But the person wears clothes and a hat, has shoes on, and is holding a telescope and observing the stars. And while it might be hard for us to imagine people weaving clothes like those back then, it's even harder to fathom the presence of a telescope and the possibility that they knew something of astronomy. People have always thought that it was a European, Galileo, who invented the telescope, some three hundred years ago. So we are left to wonder how a telescope came about thirty thousand years ago. And there are many unsolved mysteries like this. Another is the cave murals that have been found in various countries including France and South Africa, as well as in the Alps. These were painted skillfully, in a very lifelike and vivid way, with the use of mineral pigments. But what's striking is that the figures depicted in them are dressed like people from modern times, with European-style clothes, like breeches. And some are holding what look to be tobacco pipes, while others have canes or wear hats. Art of that quality is hardly what you'd expect from our supposedly primitive ancestors.

Another example goes further back. Uranium ore is present in the African country of Gabon, but the country is not very developed and hasn't the means to refine it, and so they have exported the ore to more developed nations. When a plant in France imported some of it in 1972, they were surprised to find, after chemical analysis, that the uranium had already been processed and depleted. They thought it was rather strange, and sent over scientific and technical personnel to investigate onsite. And eventually scientists from many other countries went as well. Ultimately, what they determined was that what was thought to be the uranium mine was in fact a well-designed, large-scale nuclear reactor—one built better than could be made today. And yet the reactor was built 2 billion years ago and had operated for around five hundred thousand years. That's an extremely long time ago, and makes no sense within an evolutionary framework. And there are many anomalies like this, in fact. There have been more than enough scientific discoveries to rewrite the books. It's hard for people to be receptive to new ideas or findings if their views on things are set and have formed into a mode of operating and thinking. So they will shy away from the truth, even when it comes to light, or instinctively reject it. Owing to longstanding biases, hardly anyone in the sciences is systematically reviewing or trying to make sense of these anomalous findings. And so the theoretical frameworks aren't keeping pace. New findings continue to be written off as "pseudoscience," even if they are valid, though not well-publicized.

A number of scientists in other countries who are a bit more courageous have openly voiced their opinion that these finds do bespeak of earlier cultures prior to written history or civilization as we know it. So this would mean that they did indeed exist, and it's believed that there was more than one—judging from the artifacts that have been unearthed so far. It is now believed that on multiple occasions something catastrophic befell civilization and left the population decimated. The few people that survived would have lived a most basic existence at first, until, with time, the population had grown again and civilization developed anew. And this cycle would have repeated itself many times, with phases of destruction and renewal. All changes throughout creation follow patterns, much like how in physics the motion of matter follows patterns.

It would be hard to imagine that things have always gone smoothly for this Earth as it moves within the vast universe and within this turning Milky Way, and chances are it has collided with another planet or object at some point or experienced some type of catastrophic event. But we can tell, by way of extrasensory powers, that these events are part of larger designs. I once looked into it in some detail and saw that humanity was nearly destroyed eighty-one times. In each episode little of civilization and very few people remained, and they would then enter a new phase, and live primitively, before the population recovered and a new civilization emerged. So while I observed eighty-one cycles of this, there were still more to look into. There is a longstanding Chinese belief about the importance of "timing, location, and togetherness"—and there is something to it. The state of the world is indeed brought about by larger, cosmic forces that are at work, and there is a timing to everything. Just as how physics holds that the motion of matter follows patterns, the way that things unfold in the universe does as well.

The reason I've delved into all of this is because energy practices like *chi-gong* trace back to cultures predating history, rather than this civilization. And they were each transmitted in unbroken lineages of considerable length. We can see hints of this in certain religious scriptures. The Buddha, for instance, indicated that he had completed his spiritual journey and gained enlightenment "many eons ago." This amounts to a mind-boggling figure; in Buddhist terminology one eon is equivalent to hundreds of millions of years. Then assuming what he said was true, all of this would be plausible in light of the larger history of civilizations and earth that I've been describing. The Buddha also remarked that there were six earlier Buddhas before him, each of whom themselves had teachers, and so on, with all of their spiritual enlightenments having taken place hundreds of millions of years earlier. Then if that's so, you might wonder whether authentic spiritual practices like those, with such an ancient pedigree, still exist in the world today. I can answer in the affirmative, that they do, for sure. But they are rare, and their number is dwarfed by that of the false masters and charlatans, who have entities attached to them and invent things at will. And it's hard to tell which category a practice falls into. The true practices aren't easy to identify or find.

There are other things that date far back, similar to how energy practices do. Examples include the *tai-chi* symbol, the mystical *he-tu* and *luo-shu* diagrams, the *Book of Changes*, and the Eight Trigrams. All of these were handed down from before this civilization. And that is why each has proven hard for regular scholarship to make sense of. Their secrets won't be revealed to those whose thinking or perspectives are steeped in a secular worldview.

Energy Practices Are for Spiritual Development

So if energy practices have such a long history, you might be wondering just what exactly they're for. I can tell you that ours is an advanced Buddhist method of spiritual practice, and so it seeks to bring you to divinity, or what's known as "Buddhahood." And Daoist methods, similarly, seek to foster enlightenment, or enable you to "attain the Way," as it's called.

The idea of becoming divine shouldn't seem absurd, or far out, as it may to some. For example, take the concept of Buddha. It's a term from the ancient Indian language known as Sanskrit. The term has undergone various permutations in China since arriving there long ago, being translated phonetically as *foah-toah, foo-too*, and eventually just *foah*. Translated into our own language today, the term simply means "one who has awakened," and refers to any being who has gained a state of awakening through spiritual discipline. So it shouldn't seem that far-fetched.

Consider that extraordinary powers can come to those who engage in spiritual discipline. While six types of powers are now generally recognized, there are in fact a myriad number that exist. There are individuals who can, just while sitting in place, do things that normally even physical action couldn't accomplish; or they might be able to see the true workings of the universe in multiple dimensions, and how it really is, and see things that are invisible to others. I think you would have to agree, then, that they have attained a higher state of awakening, or spiritual attainment, and are no longer mere mortals. So it's only fitting to call them spiritually awakened, holy, or divine—or in ancient Indian terms, a "Buddha." And this is what these practices are in fact meant to achieve.

Some people can't imagine why anyone would want to do practices like *chi-gong* or *tai-chi* for anything other than health. The implication being that that's all they are for. But that's a very shallow view of these. People can't be faulted for thinking that way, though, because many instructors of these practices *are* only focused on health, and nobody is offering guidance of a higher, more spiritual sort. I don't mean to imply anything bad about what they're teaching. That's the role that they are meant to play—to keep it at the level of health and popularize these arts. But many people are looking for something more, for something spiritual, that can take them further. Yet without a true spiritual teaching to guide them, it's going to be hard and they are apt to get into trouble. Instruction of a higher sort involves bigger things, naturally enough, and so you really have to go about it in a way that's responsible to people, or the world. And that is why we have had good results all around. Some of what we talk about is a bit lofty, for sure, and to some people it might sound hard to believe. So I'll do my best to draw scientific parallels to help make sense of things.

Some of the things we'll be discussing provoke strong reactions from people, who quickly dismiss them. They think that anything that isn't known to science, that they haven't personally experienced, or that seems impossible to them must be nonsense and divorced from reality. But is that the right way to look at the world?—to write off anything not known to science, even if it's because of science's limitations? It seems to me that this line of thinking puts a little too much faith in science, and is itself divorced from reality. If everyone had this mindset it would utterly stifle any scientific progress or innovation. And you would see few developments in the world, more broadly. Every technological development represents a step beyond what was formerly known. If the world's innovators had treated the unknown as "nonsense," we wouldn't be where we are today. Many people simply don't understand practices like *chi-gong* or *tai-chi*, and think they are nonsense. But that's not the case. Consider that scientific instruments have detected that the bodies of true masters of these practices emit everything from infrasonic waves to ultrasonic and electromagnetic waves, to infrared rays, ultraviolet rays, gamma rays, neutrons, atoms, and trace metal elements. All of these are very much real and physically exist. There is a physical basis to everything. And the same would certainly hold true for the other dimensions and realms that we discuss. So there are no grounds for writing them off as nonsense. Since these practices are meant to make us divine, any discussion of them is naturally going to touch upon a lot of deep things, and we won't shy away from them.

It's curious that practices like these, which have such a profound purpose, sometimes have very ordinary-sounding names. For example, *chi-gong** simply means "energy practice." But they are more properly referred to as spiritual practice— or in traditional Chinese culture, as self-cultivation. For that is their purpose. Of course, there are many individual names for such practices, but as a whole they should be referred to as spiritual practices. The case of how *chi-gong* got its name is telling. It has to do with the state of affairs in China some twenty years ago, when these practices first started to gain in popularity. China was in the middle of the Cultural Revolution at the time, and there was a strong stigma and hostility surrounding traditional thought and culture; only later did interest in these practices peak. Without getting into the earlier spiritual names for *chi-gong*, which predate known history, we can see just from the names it's had in this cycle of civilization what the issue would have been: they were very much religious, owing to the times they date back to, and often had what people would have considered "feudal," or backward, overtones. Examples included the Great Way of Practicing the Dao, Vajra Meditation, Way of the Buddhist Saints, The Dafa of Buddhahood, and The Nine-Cycle Method of the Golden

26

Elixir. Naming your practice something like that during the Cultural Revolution would have gotten you denounced and attacked—even if you were sharing the practice with people out of good intentions, like to promote better health. And so nobody dared to use traditional-sounding names. What most instructors did, instead, was to adopt two non-contro-versial terms—*chi* and *gong* ("energy" and "practice")—from traditional Chinese spiritual texts to refer to their practices. So even though you now see some people researching the history of "*chi-gong*," there's not much to it. It would have just been referred to as spiritual practice, or self-cultivation, before. So the term *chi-gong* is just a recent invention that was meant to suit a modern, secular sensibility.

When Practicing Doesn't Bring Results

When doing an energy practice doesn't bring the results that one would hope for, people typically attribute it to not having been taught "the genuine stuff." They tend to think that they would see their energy levels shooting up if they could just get in on the best techniques or learn "the secret." Around ninety-five percent of people think this way. But that line of thinking is funny to me. That's because these practices are not some worldly skill, but go fully beyond the ordinary. And so it takes a different, and higher, logic to make sense of them. I can share with you that when people don't see the results they hope for, it's because they are overemphasizing the *physical* aspect of practice, to the neglect of its *spiritual* component. The keys to success do not lie in outward, or physical, techniques. It's a stretch to think that you could develop the kind of higher energy you seek just by the power of your own human hands, body, or thoughts—as those techniques would have you believe. That's what strikes me as funny about it. It's never going to work out if you are pinning your hopes on superficial things.

Spiritual practice doesn't work like worldly skills, where you can pay some fee to learn a technique and then it's yours. It's something altogether different, as it operates on a plane beyond the ordinary, and thus has higher demands. I'll explain. With this kind of practice you have to work *on yourself,* not on anything else. And yet many people are doing just the opposite, trying to learn one thing after another and even harboring attachments to psychic powers. You see all kinds of motives. Some even want to become energy healers so that they can make money from it! But true spiritual practice is about working on the mind, or character. For example, it entails learning to worry less about the disputes that might surround you, and value less the worldly things that people normally want and feel strongly about. You shouldn't expect many results from your practice if instead you are all caught up in competition with others and pushing hard to come out on top. In that case you are just like everyone else, and shouldn't expect to get any higher energy from it. This is why you need to put *character* at the heart of your practice. And if you can do that, you will find yourself elevating spiritually and your energy growing.

What does character consist of, then? It includes being virtuous (as virtue is physically real), practicing self-restraint, having faith and discernment, letting go of what others normally desire and hold onto, and being able to suffer gracefully. So there is a lot to it. We should strive to perfect every facet of our character. And by doing so you will make real spiritual progress. It is one of the keys to developing powerful, higher energy.

Some people have objected that character is just a moral concept, and something theoretical, whereas what they are interested in is getting real energy, which it has no bearing on. But that's just not true. There have long been philosophical debates in China about whether reality is fundamentally something material, or mentally constructed. But ultimately, I would say, material and mental phenomena are the same in nature. Scientists have found that there are physical properties to the thoughts that take place in the brain. So this means that thoughts *materially* exist, yet at the same time they are certainly *mental* phenomena. This would suggest, then, that the two are actually the same. It's similar to what I said about the universe: that it is something physical but which has its own qualities. The qualities of *zhen, shan, ren* that are imbued throughout all of creation aren't perceptible to the average person, who dwells on the plane of ordinary existence. They only become perceptible to those who rise above the ordinary. Let me explain. Every single thing that makes up creation, wherever it may be in the universe, is alive and has thinking, and whatever it does, no matter the level that it exists at, is an embodiment of the Way of the universe. And so you will not be able to progress to higher levels of existence, or attainment, if they do not agree to it. Their reason would be that your character has not grown sufficiently. There is a standard for each level of existence, and you must meet it—by ridding yourself of bad thoughts and intentions and whatever is unclean in you—if you are to go there.

With a change in character will come a significant change in your body; physical changes in your body are guaranteed to accompany positive changes in your mind. What will happen is that the bad things that have led you to form attachments will be cast away. To help you picture what happens, imagine that there is a bottle filled with dirt and that's capped tightly. If the bottle is tossed into water it will sink to the bottom. But if you pour out some of its dirt, and toss it into the water again, it will float up this time; and the more that's poured out, the more it will float. Pour out all of it and the bottle will float all the way up. And that is what we try to do in the process of spiritual refinement: to rid ourselves of all that is bad within us, so that we may rise up. And it is the qualities of the universe that act as the gatekeeper. If you don't work on your character, become a more moral person, and remove the bad material and thoughts in you, then those qualities won't let you progress. I think you would have to agree, then, that mental and material phenomena are the same. Here's a funny scenario to imagine, which makes the point. Just try to picture what a mess it would be if a regular, average guy who was still brimming with human desires and emotions were allowed to go up and join the ranks of the divine. Upon beholding the beauty of the angels he would probably start having indecent thoughts. And because he would still be prone to jealousy, he might make trouble for the divine beings there. It's a scenario that would absolutely never happen. And so a person must rid himself of all bad thoughts and intents while he is still in this world, before possibly being allowed to ascend.

What this means, then, is that you need to make a focus of perfecting your character, ground your practice in the cosmic qualities of *zhen*, *shan*, *ren*, and rid yourself of any worldly desires, bad thoughts, or wrongful intents. Just by elevating your realm of thought ever so slightly, the bad things in your body will have been purged to some degree. You also must go through some painful things and experience a bit of adversity in order to eliminate some of your karma. And by doing so, your level of attainment will rise somewhat, for the qualities of the universe will no longer be holding you back as before. You put in the effort and your teacher will handle the rest. What he will do is to provide you with a mechanism for developing higher energy. The mechanism will then do the work for you of transforming your virtue into a higher energy around your body. And as you continue to progress and elevate in your practice, the column of energy that you have will continue developing upward to new heights. So the task for you, as someone doing spiritual practice, is this: to work on yourself spiritually; to perfect yourself as you go through difficult things; and to constantly work to weed out any attachments or wants that you have, all while a part of this human world. Often what is considered good or desirable in this world is seen as *bad* at higher planes. Most people think that the more that you gain materially in life through trying, the better. But in the eyes of higher beings above, you are worse off for it. In what sense? Your material abundance may come at other people's expense, and not all be rightfully yours; and it might only make you more attached to worldly things like status and wealth. And all of this would be at the expense of your virtue. So you must make a focus of perfecting your character if you want to earn the higher energy we seek.

People of faith have long believed that the soul is immortal. The idea of "the soul" has met with suspicion in certain circles of late, but consider the following. The insights of physics have revealed that the body is made up of molecules, protons, electrons, and at deeper levels, quarks, neutrinos, and so on. At that point the body's composition is beyond the powers of microscopy to behold. And yet it is still far removed from the plane that is the ultimate source of matter, or of your life. You may be aware that it requires a powerful collision or extraordinarily high heat to trigger nuclear change. So do you think that when a person dies, the atomic nuclei in his body would simply perish along with his death? And this explains why we have found that when a person dies, it is merely that his body at the molecular layer—the layer of the largest particles in this dimension—has been shed. His bodies in other dimensions have not in fact perished. Just consider what the human body looks like under magnification. Even if a person is just sitting still, all of his body is found to be in motion. The cells of the molecular level are moving, and all of the body seems to be loosely composed, as if it were granular. So the body under magnification looks nothing like what it seems to the naked eye. So our eyes play tricks on us, in a sense, and don't allow us to see the body or physical things as they really are. The inner eye, however, *can* see in a magnified way once it has opened. This is an innate ability, even if it's now thought of as an extrasensory power. To gain powers like these you have to recover, via spiritual practice, the purity you once had.

Let's turn our attention to virtue now, and see how it's related to what we have been discussing so far. I'll explain it in some detail. Each individual has multiple bodies that exist across many dimensions. The largest component of the body that the eyes can see is the cell, and cells make up the physical body. But if you were to enter into the space between cells and molecules, or one molecule and another, you would experience what it's like to enter another dimension. To go there, however, your body would have to first meet the requirements for existence there. But the concepts we have here wouldn't enable you to understand the very different bodies you saw there—bodies that can expand or shrink. And those are unimaginably vast realms. But I am just describing one simple form of parallel dimension, which exists in the same place and at the same time as ours. A person has a different body in each of various dimensions, and in one particular dimension he has a body that is surrounded by a field filled with virtue. Virtue is actually a white material, and not just a moral or theoretical concept. It is very much physical. And this would explain the old sayings in China about "accumulating" or "losing" virtue. There was really something to them. Virtue surrounds a person's body and forms a field. And so in the Daoist tradition the common practice is for masters to seek out disciples, rather than vice versa, since they can see how much virtue someone's body has and what his spiritual prospects thus are. Someone with much virtue would have good prospects, while someone with little would not, and it would be hard for him to develop higher energy.

At the same time, there is also a black form of matter on the body, which we call karma, or which in Buddhism is referred to as "the karma from evil deeds." So both a white and black matter exist at the same time. I'll explain the dynamics between the two. The white one, virtue, comes to us when we suffer, are dealt a blow, or do something meritorious. While the black one, karma, comes from doing evil or wrongful things, or mistreating people. Nowadays some people will do anything for their own gain, including all manner of evil. People will stoop to just about anything for money, they even commit murder or hire others to kill for them, and both homosexuality and drug abuse are now common. All kinds of things are now done. But doing wrong costs a person virtue. I can explain. When a person speaks abusively to someone he might think that he's the better for it and has let out his frustrations. But as the universe works, everything comes at a cost. You can't get something for nothing, and if you don't personally pay, you will be forced to. And by whom, you ask? It will be enforced by the underlying qualities of the universe. So you can't get away with not paying, wish as you may. Here's what happens in a scenario like I was just describing. When one person speaks abusively to another, or pushes someone around, he will give his virtue to the other party. It is given to him as compensation, since he counts as the party that's been hurt or wronged in this circumstance, given that he suffered to some degree and it was at his expense. So while the one person is hurling abusive words in this dimension, in another, a portion of his virtue is sent over from his expanse to the other person and lands on his body. And the amount of virtue sent over will be proportionate to the severity of the abuse. The same happens with physical altercations as well. If one person strikes or kicks someone else, his virtue will go over to the other party according to the severity of it. The average person can't perceive the workings of all this. And so he might be incensed by the abuse, and fight right back. But if he punches back, he will be returning the virtue that he had just been given, and as a result, neither one gains or loses anything from it. But then suppose the second person won't feel avenged unless he lands one more punch in return.

Well, if he punches again, another portion of virtue will fly over from his body to the other party.

To appreciate why we value virtue so much, just pause to consider what becomes of it in spiritual development. There is a longstanding religious belief that blessings will come to the virtuous, in the next life if not in this. The blessings, for the very virtuous, might take the form of a coveted position of office, great wealth, or having their wishes in life fulfilled. All of these would come to them by cashing in their virtue, so to speak. Another belief is that a person who is devoid of all virtue faces the extinction of both body and soul. It means that his soul (*yuan-shen*) will be destroyed at the time of his passing, and nothing of him will remain. For those of us engaged in spiritual practice, however, virtue has a different value: it can be remade straight into higher energy.

Let's look more closely at how virtue is rendered into higher energy. There is a saying in spiritual practice, that, "One only needs to worry about putting in the effort of practice, and the rest is in the hands of one's teacher." This contrasts with the approaches that some take or consider important, such as doing elaborate visualizations of alchemical processes within the body. But I would say that those really aren't what is important, and in fact, they might become an attachment if they occupy the mind too much. If it weighs heavily in your thinking it would seem to be an attachment. So just put in the effort needed and leave the rest to your teacher. The intent that you have to develop higher energy and make progress will suffice. It will be your teacher that does the real work, and it will be beyond anything you could possibly do. There is simply no way that you, with your ordinary body, could possibly fashion for yourself a supernatural body made of high-energy matter. Just the thought of it is humorous. The processes involved in transforming one's body in other dimensions are highly mysterious and intricate, and by no means something you could do yourself.

What your teacher will do is give you a mechanism that develops higher energy. The true higher energy that you develop will be born from virtue, which resides outside of your body. So it is ultimately virtue that's responsible for your degree of spiritual attainment and spiritual power. The mechanism I just mentioned transforms your virtue into higher energy, which grows upward in a spiraling manner. This higher energy in fact determines your level, and it develops on the outside of your body; it spirals around it, upward, until it reaches the top of your head, where it forms into a column of energy. Just by glancing at the column's height one can see how much higher energy a person has, and it indicates his degree of spiritual attainment—or divine rank, in religious terms. And this explains how it is that some people's souls can travel to certain heights as they meditate, but at a certain point go no further, and wouldn't venture to try. What allows them to reach the heights that they do is that they are boosted there by their energy column. And this explains why they can't climb further; they have reached their column's limits. So this sheds light on the religious concept of having "divine standing."

There is also a measuring stick that gauges one's character. This stick and the column I was just describing are not to be found in the same dimension, though they exist concurrently. Let's look at what happens when you improve your character. Suppose someone out in the world swears at you or berates you, yet you manage not to say a word in reply, and keep calm.

Or suppose someone hits you, and you don't say anything and just shrug it off with a smile. In either event it would mean that you have made progress with your character, which is excellent now. Then what's in store for you, as a practitioner? You will get higher energy for it. The level of your energy will rise in proportion to your character. It will always be capped by your character, however, and there are no exceptions to the rule. And this explains why some people, who were at one time devout about whatever energy practice they did, never had higher energy to show for it or were never freed of illness. They might put in great efforts and do well at their exercises wherever they did them, be it outdoors or at home, but afterwards they would turn around and go back to their ordinary ways, contending with people over worldly things. So that's why they never got the health benefits they hoped for in spite of their sustained efforts. Energy exercises are meant for *spiritual* development, which is something higher. They aren't just another routine form of fitness. And so character has to feature prominently in one's practice for there to be any healing or higher energy.

There are some who believe that forming a concentrated cluster of energy (*dan*) is a way of developing higher energy, but it is not. As part of their practices, they do elaborate visualizations of alchemical changes in their bodies to form this energy cluster. But this cluster only contains a certain range of energy from throughout the spectrum, and not all of it. Let me put it into context. You're now aware that our practice has a physical component to it, and this enables practitioners to develop higher powers and many abilities in their bodies. In all practices, the majority of powers like these will be sealed up and not available to the person. As each of the many, myriad powers develop in the practitioner they will most likely be sealed up as they are formed. The purpose is to prevent the person from using them freely out in the world and impacting it, or rashly showing them off. Doing so would disrupt the designs of this world. Many a person's spiritual journey depends on the exercise of *faith*, and it would be a problem were a practitioner to start unveiling his powers around others. Who wouldn't believe or want to practice if they saw such miraculous things. Even the most wicked of people would get interested. All of which would be a problem. So no one is allowed to display them. Another factor is that people would be apt to misuse them if they had free rein over them, since people can't perceive the deeper causes or karmic reasons behind things, or their core. What's taken to be a good deed could turn out to be the opposite. And with any misuse of powers, a person's level of attainment will fall, undoing his spiritual efforts. So for this reason many powers are sealed up and unavailable to the practitioner. Then what becomes of the energy cluster? When the day arrives for the person's enlightenment and the freeing of his powers, the cluster is used like a bomb. It is used to blast open all of the powers in the person's body that have been sealed up, as well as its acupuncture points, for that is its purpose. Sometimes when the bodies of deceased Buddhist monks are cremated, they are found to have small, beaded, crystal-like relics known as *śarīra*. Skeptics have tried to dismiss them as just being bones or teeth. But that would just raise another question: why aren't these seen when others are cremated? What they are, in fact, are the remnants of an energy cluster after it was ruptured and its powerful energy released. The energy cluster was every bit physical; it consisted of a large amount of matter from other dimensions. But these don't have any purpose beyond what I've described. People now consider these objects to be precious, and they do have energy, are luminous, and hard. So this gives you a sense for what they are.

Then there is another reason why people might not get the results, or higher energy, they expect from their practice: they haven't any higher teachings to guide them. Spiritual progress isn't possible when that is the case. To understand, recall the analogy that I made earlier. I explained that learning a large variety of practices doesn't do a person any good. That's because if all that someone learns are just basic things, he will still be just a kid in terms of spiritual practice. Basic, beginner teachings aren't able to guide a person to higher stages of spiritual practice. And as I said, if you try to go through college by studying books from elementary school, you won't get a college education—no matter how many of them you study. And it will only make things worse. The Way offers different spiritual truths to guide you at different levels, and these truths each govern practice in their respective realms. And so the insights of a lower plane can't guide you to higher ones. The insights we will be offering here are all of what you need for spiritual practice of a higher order. I am building into my instruction insights spanning many planes, and so the teachings will always be able to guide your practice from here on out. I have several books as well as audio and video recordings of my teachings. You will find that after you finish them and return to them again, you will continue to get new insights from them. I guarantee it. And they will keep providing you with new insights and direction as you keep progressing. That is the nature of a genuine spiritual teaching. So now you know the two reasons why people might not get results with their practice: one is that they can't make spiritual progress if they don't have the higher guidance of the Way; and the other is that they won't get higher energy if they don't work on themselves or strive to perfect their character. These two reasons sum it up.

What Sets Falun Dafa Apart

Our practice of Falun Dafa is one of the eighty-four thousand avenues to enlightenment spoken of in Buddhist thought. And while it hasn't been taught publicly during this cycle of civilization, it was in a previous one, and was then a widespread means of deliverance from this world. In these final times I am making it public again and available to all, so it is something to treasure. I have disclosed the means by which virtue gets rendered straight into higher energy. And now you know that this energy does not come from exercises, but from spiritual development. Many people are looking to build up this energy, but are focusing solely on energy exercises to the neglect of the spirit. And yet higher energy is always the product of working on your moral character. We do, however, have a place for energy exercises in our practice, and I'll explain why. But first it's worth considering why no such exercises feature in the Buddhist monastic tradition. Its monks mainly focus on meditation, recitation of scripture, and working on the mind, and yet they do manage to develop higher energy—a form of it that determines one's level of spiritual attainment. The reason they don't make use of any bodily exercises is that the Buddha taught his followers to forsake all that is of this world, including even one's own body. Circumstances are very different in the Daoist tradition, however, where they don't aspire to benefit all of humankind, [as Buddhists do]—and thus won't find themselves in the situation of having to deal with people from all walks of life with all sorts of attitudes toward practice, different degrees of spiritual understanding, and varying degrees of selfishness. Daoists are selective about who they take on as students, and it's no surprise, for example, if only one of the three students they select ever receives the true teaching. And so they are assured that whoever is taught will be a good and virtuous person, and not apt to run into trouble. Bodily practices are thus used in Daoist practice, and feature prominently, since they seek to extend one's life and develop supernatural powers, which requires this approach.

Falun Dafa is a practice of mind and body, and so there is an exercise component to it. One purpose of the exercises is to increase your spiritual power, which, in turn, serves to strengthen the powers of your body. Another purpose is to develop a number of supernatural beings in your body. And this is what, at higher stages of practice, Daoists describe as the "birth of the immortal infant" and Buddhists the "developing of an incorruptible body." Many special powers are to be developed in the body as well. Physical movements and techniques are needed to develop all of these, and our exercises serve this purpose. For a practice to really be considered one of mind *and* body, there has to be both a spiritual and a physical component to it. I think you're now aware that the kind of higher energy that decides your level of attainment is ultimately not the product of exercises, but of spiritual development. Your ascension to higher realms comes from working on your character while in this world and embodying the

41

qualities of the universe, such that they no longer hold you back. Your virtue will be transformed into higher energy as this happens, and this energy will only continue to grow as you raise the bar for your moral character. So all of these go together.

Ours is genuinely a practice for mind and body. The higher energy that it develops will be stored in the cells throughout your body, reaching all the way to your particles in the tiniest and most invisible of realms where your physical existence begins from. Your energy will increase in both density and might as your spiritual power grows. It will be a high-energy matter that is alive and that has its own intelligence. And because it is stored in the cells of your body all the way down to the starting point of your life, it will, over time, assume the same shape and appearance as your cells and nuclei, with the same molecular arrangement. So your cells will undergo a change in substance; you will no longer be composed of the same physical material as you once were. And so you will transcend the five elements, naturally enough. Of course, that doesn't mean that your spiritual journey will be done. You will still have further spiritual refinement to undergo while a part of this world. So your appearance will still be normal. The only difference will be that you look young for your age. For all of this to happen, however, your body first needs to be cleansed of the bad things it contains, including any diseases. We will *not* be healing you though, but rather, cleansing your body. We avoid using the word "healing" and simply refer to it as "cleansing." This is something we do for whoever is sincere about our practice. It's not done for those who come just for healing. People with serious medical conditions are not allowed to enroll in our classes, because their minds are going to be occupied with thoughts of getting healed; they won't be able to let it go, understandably, since their condition is serious and causing them pain. That makes it very hard to engage in spiritual practice. And so we have always maintained a strict policy that the seriously ill may not take our classes. Our classes are about spiritual practice, which is something far from their minds. They might be able to find others who will heal them, but that's not our approach. That said, there are many people with normal ailments who are sincere about learning our practice, and we can cleanse their bodies.

After practicing Falun Dafa for some time, the changes in your appearance might be dramatic. Common ones include the skin becoming soft and fair, with a rosy glow, and a lessening of wrinkles—sometimes quite dramatic—among those who are older. And I'm not making outlandish claims, as many who are seated here and who have been practicing a while will attest to. Another change that will happen is that older women will have their menstrual period return, since there is an essential energy involved in this blood that's needed in mind-body practice. So while their period will start up again, it won't be heavy; it will be just enough to serve the purpose for this stage of practice. And this too is common, since the development of your body would be impeded without it. Meanwhile men, both young and old, will experience changes as well, such as a feeling that your entire body is becoming lighter. The changes that I've described will come to you if you are sincere in your practice.

Our practice is based on something big—something simply enormous, in fact. This contrasts with the many practices that base their exercises on the movements of wild animals.

The teachings given by the Buddha and the Daoist sage Lao-tzu were informed by the workings of the Milky Way. But the practice of Falun Dafa is informed by the processes that underlie transformation throughout the universe, and it is based on its highest expression: the qualities of *zhen*, *shan*, *ren*. And it is this standard that guides us in practice. So the scale of our practice is so big, you could call it cosmic.

Then there is another feature of Falun Dafa that's incredibly unique and that truly sets it apart. All of the energy practices currently in this world and that are available to the public take the approach of developing an energy cluster, like I described. But with that approach it's awfully difficult for someone to achieve enlightenment and the realization of his powers while still part of the secular world. We take a different approach in Falun Dafa. In our practice you develop a *falun** at the position of your lower abdomen, and I personally bestow it during our classes. As I teach the practice we systematically provide it to each of you, whether you can sense it or not. Most people can, but the qualities of people's bodies vary. So our practice develops the *falun*, not an energy cluster. The *falun* is essentially a miniature universe and is capable of all that the universe is, and so it can turn automatically of its own accord. It will forever turn in the area of your lower abdomen, once provided to you, and continue to do so without ceasing, year in and year out. When it turns clockwise it automatically draws in energy from the universe, transforms it for you, and delivers it to whatever parts of your body may need this energy for development. When it reverses direction (turning counterclockwise), it sends out whatever matter is no longer needed by your body, in the form of energy, which disperses once it has been sent far away from you. New energy is then taken in again, thereafter. And I should add that the energy sent out will be of benefit to whomever is nearby you. This is in keeping with the Buddhist belief in helping all of humanity, in saving all life—not just oneself. And so others might benefit in any of various ways, such as by having their bodies put into balance or healed, even though you didn't intend it. But you won't be losing energy when it's sent out. New energy will be brought in again when the *falun* turns clockwise. And this is sure to happen, since it turns perpetually.

Some people find it hard to imagine how the *falun* could manage to turn, or keep doing so. It's hard for them to make sense of, even though they might be accustomed to the idea that energy can be condensed into a cluster, as in other practices. A parallel might help to explain it. The universe is moving, as are all of the Milky Ways and galaxies; the nine planets of our solar system are orbiting the sun; and the earth itself is constantly rotating. But you wouldn't be able to make sense of how they move or what drives them if you were to try to do so with the common logic of our world. There is simply a mechanism at work behind it. The same holds true for our *falun*. It simply turns. And by doing so, it extends the time that your practice sessions go for and resolves the challenge of finding enough time to practice while still living a normal life. How so? By turning constantly, it allows you to continually be drawing in energy from the universe and transforming it. So when you go off to work, for example, it will be doing the work of practicing on your behalf. And this is true not only for the *falun*, of course, but also for the many mechanisms and capabilities that we provide to your body, which will be automatically operating and moving in connection with the *falun*. So this is a practice that automatically transforms you, leading us to say that "the mechanisms are practicing for you," and that "the Way is working on your behalf." Even when you aren't doing the exercises, the mechanisms will be working on you, just as when you *are* doing the exercises. And these mechanisms will be working to transform your body even as you are eating, sleeping, or doing your job. This might lead you to wonder what need there is for doing them, then. Doing them serves to strengthen the *falun* as well as the many capabilities and mechanisms that I give you. And this is characteristic of spiritual practice at higher stages, which is done without active intent; you needn't direct or will things with your mind, or via breathing techniques, and the physical movements that you do will simply be following along with the mechanisms that are in place.

In our practice you also don't need to worry about the time or location that you do the exercises at. I am sometimes asked what phase of the day is optimal for doing them—such as late night, early morning, or midday. The phases of the day don't matter in our practice. The mechanisms you have will always be at work, practicing on your behalf, whether it's at night or in the morning, and no matter whether you are sleeping, walking somewhere, or at work. So this greatly cuts down on the time you need to spend exercising, as you'd imagine. Many people come to our practice with a sincere wish to gain enlightenment, and that's of course the goal of spiritual practice—to ultimately become enlightened, or divine. But some of these individuals might be faced with a challenge, which is, that there aren't many years left in their lives, and so normally they might not have sufficient time to achieve that goal. Falun Dafa can solve this issue by shortening the course of spiritual practice for them. And along with that, ours is a practice of mind and body, and so a person's life will be pro-longed as he or she continues to practice. This means there should be enough time for those who are older and who have good innate foundations. But there's one condition, in this scenario: the days that you may gain beyond those originally allotted to you, are only provided so that you may continue to practice. And so you may be at risk if your thinking gets off track, for your life was supposed to have already ended. The exception to this rule is when someone progresses in prac-tice to the stage where he is no longer subject to the laws of the human realm, which is a different matter.

You also don't need to concern yourself with things like which direction you face while doing the exercises or how to "close" each session, as in other practices. That's because our *falun* turns constantly and never needs to be "closed." In our practice you can stop abruptly if you need to, as when you have to take a phone call or answer the door. That's because when you switch gears like that, the *falun* will promptly respond by turning clockwise and drawing back in any energy that may have been scattered around your body at the moment. By contrast, in other practices that involve things like direct-ing energy into the crown of the head, the energy would be lost if you stopped abruptly, no matter how long your ses-sion had gone for. The difference is that the *falun* has its own intelligence and will know what needs to be done. Facing in certain directions isn't a concern for us, meanwhile, because our practice is attuned to the workings of the greater uni-verse. Even if you wanted to pinpoint north, south, east, or west, you couldn't with the scale we are working at, since all of the universe is in motion, the Milky Way is in motion, the planets of the solar system are orbiting the Sun, and Earth itself is revolving. So whichever way you face as you exercise amounts to facing every way, to all four of the cardinal directions at once. Another feature of Falun Dafa is that our students will be protected. This takes some explaining. The *falun* will protect those who genuinely do our practice. My roots are planted in this universe, and so someone would have to be able to harm me in order to harm you, which means that they would have to have the power to harm this universe. Don't worry if this sounds a bit far out. It will make sense later on as you come to understand the practice better. I could say more, but I don't want to divulge things that are too advanced for you right now. What we will do is to systematically explain the higher insights of the Way to you, going from the simple to the profound. But things might not work out well for you if something isn't right on your part, and you have other agendas mixed in. I've seen many students who have practiced for a while but who now have deformed *falun*. But how could that be? They have added things in from other practices, which they like. The *falun* didn't protect them from those things since it had been given to them and was theirs, and so it heeded their will. It's a principle in this universe that *you* are the one who decides what you want. So if you don't really want to practice, nobody is going to force you to; it would be wrong to, in fact. Nobody can force someone to have a change of heart, after all. You are the one who sets the bar for yourself. When you start "drawing on the strengths" of other practices, and learning all sorts of things from others, it's usually driven by a wish to get healed. But it never works out in the end. At most it will only serve to postpone your condition. With advanced practice you have to commit to one discipline and devote your heart to it. It's only acceptable for you to learn something else after you have gained enlightenment and all possible powers in one practice, as you would be dealing with a whole new system then. Any authentic spiritual practice will have been carefully passed down over many centuries, and the means by which it transforms one's body will be highly complex. And so it's foolish to think that you could combine sophisticated practices like these and figure out something new just going by what feels right to you. The real changes that one's body goes through in spiritual practice take place in other dimensions, and are exceptionally intricate and profound, with no margin for error. The processes are no less exacting than assembling a precision instrument, where adding even just one wrong component would result in a breakdown. With our practice your bodies in multiple dimensions are undergoing changes, and it's incredibly profound, and here too there is no margin for error. What I said earlier applies here as well: you only need to do your part practicing, and your teacher will handle the rest. If you freely add in other people's things, the energies they carry will disrupt our practice's workings, you will be heading off course, and the problems that result will manifest themselves in your regular life and be similar to the kinds of problems that non-practitioners have. But as I said, you are the one who decides what you want. If that is what you want, then I can only say there's a problem with your judgment. Whatever you add into the practice will foul up the mechanisms I gave you and ruin your spiritual prospects. But I have never said that anyone has to practice Falun Dafa. I'm not opposed to your learning some other, true practice if you don't do Falun Dafa. But I would just remind you that you must commit to one practice if you want to ever make significant spiritual progress and reach a higher realm. And there's something else I should share. Currently there is nobody else offering instruction like this that truly brings people to greater spiritual heights. You will one day realize what I am doing. So I hope that you make the right choice. Many people have longed to become better, more spiritual people, and to go to a higher place. I am now laying this out right before you, offering what I have—only you might not realize it. You could spend a fortune traveling the world to study under spiritual mentors far and wide but never find something like this. And today I am delivering it right to your door. I just hope you can realize what this is! Ultimately, whether you can be saved from this world is up to you, and it begins with your discernment.

THE
SECOND TALK

The Inner Eye*

THE INNER EYE (*tian-mu*) is something that many spiritual teachers have spoken of. However, it should be remembered that the Way reveals itself according to each person's level of spiritual attainment. And so any individual will only be able to see things that correspond to his stage of progress; higher realities will neither be visible to him nor believable. And so he may think that what *he* sees, at his level, is absolutely true. And until he has reached higher realms himself, through practice, it will be hard for him to imagine that still higher things exist or are possible. So his level of attainment acts as a limiting factor, as it limits his realm of thought. And this accounts for why there are such widely divergent explanations of the inner eye, which makes things confusing. And so far nobody has explained it very well. This shouldn't be surprising, though, because the inner eye isn't something that can be explained well by those at a low stage of attainment. The structure of the inner eye used to be considered the secret of secrets and not something to disclose to the uninitiated, so little has been revealed about it throughout history. I am not going to go into past ideas about it, but instead, will use modern science and the simplest, current language possible to explain it. I will get to the heart of it.

When we use the term "inner eye," we are actually referring to the spot a little bit higher than the midpoint between your eyebrows, which is connected to your pineal gland. This is its main channel. There are many eyes throughout the body, and in Daoist thought it's believed that each aperture of the body can be an eye. Daoists call the acupuncture points of the body apertures, while in Chinese medicine they're called acupuncture points, or "acupoints" for short. Buddhist thought holds that each pore of the skin can be an eye. And this would help explain why there have been people who could decipher words with their ears, hands, the back of the head, or even their feet or stomachs. All of these are possible.

Before going into the inner eye further, let's first talk about the pair of physical eyes that we as humans have. Nowadays there are people who believe that their eyes can see all that there is to this objective, material world. And so some people stubbornly believe that only what the naked eye can see is real. They don't believe in the unseen. People like this used to be regarded as "having little faith," though now people might have a hard time explaining exactly what faith has to do with it. After all, it sounds sensible enough—not believing in the invisible. But it doesn't seem very sensible to the beings at even just the next higher plane of existence. Other worlds of existence are just as material and real as this one, only their physical makeup and how lives appear there are different.

Let me illustrate it. Spiritual traditions have taught that the phenomena of the human world are illusory, or not real. But how so, one might wonder? Who would say that a solid object right in front of you is not real? The way that objects appear is different from how they actually are. But our eyes have the ability to stabilize the appearance of objects in this dimension so that they look as they do. But that isn't in fact their true state, not even in this dimension. For example, what would a person look like under magnification? The whole body would seem loosely comprised, with molecules moving all about that are small and round, like grains of sand. Electrons would be orbiting around atomic nuclei and in motion, with the entire body pulsing and moving. And the surface of the body would be irregular, not smooth. The same holds true for any object in the universe—even iron, steel, and stone. The molecules that make up all things are moving, only you can't see the full picture. Nothing is in fact static. Even this table before me is moving, only our eyes can't perceive the reality of it. Our eyes can mislead us.

It's not that we cannot see what is invisible, that we are incapable of it. We have an innate ability to perceive realms invisible to the naked eye, up to a certain point. But precisely because of our eyes from this physical dimension, we are given a false picture of reality and unable to see beyond. And so, traditionally, it's been said that those who don't believe in the invisible have, as religious believers put it, "little faith"—for they have been misled by the false appearances of this world and become lost here. People of faith have long seen it this way, and it makes sense from our perspective.

Yet these eyes serve to do little more than stabilize the things in this physical dimension so that they appear as they do. The images that we see don't actually take shape in our eyes. Rather, our eyes are just like a piece of equipment, similar to a camera lens. When a camera is used to capture a distant image, the lens will extend, just as our eyes will adjust for distances; or our pupils will dilate under dark conditions, similar to how the aperture of a camera expands in poor lighting to ensure adequate exposure. And conversely, our pupils shrink when we walk outside into bright light so that we won't experience a blinding glare. And the principle is the same for a camera, as the aperture has to similarly contract when flooded with light. So a camera merely captures the image of an object. It's just a tool. When we see the form of a person or an object, it is actually in the brain that the image takes shape. The image merely enters through the eyes and then is relayed by the optic nerve to the pineal gland, in the rear part of the brain. And it is in this area that it is rendered into an image. This suggests that when an image is rendered and we see something, it actually happens in the region of the pineal gland. Modern medical science has also come to realize this.

We believe that opening the inner eye is a matter of bypassing the optic nerve and opening up a channel between the eyebrows that allows the pineal gland to see outward directly. Some people may think this isn't realistic, and will object that the physical eyes play an important role, since they capture the images of things, and we couldn't get by without them. But the medical sciences have discovered through dissection that the frontal portion of the pineal gland has the full structure of the human eye. They take it to be a vestigial eye since it grows inside the skull. Those of us engaged in spiritual practice may have reservations about that interpretation, but, whatever the case, the sciences have come to understand that in the center of the cranium there is an eye. The channel that we open goes precisely to that location. So this is anatomically consistent. And this eye won't present you with a false picture of reality, as our normal eyes do. It can see past the appearances of things and affairs to perceive them as they really are. Someone whose inner eye has opened at a high level can see beyond this dimension into other space-times, and perceive what is invisible to ordinary people. And if the eye is at a level not that high, it may still have powers like the ability to see through walls and into the body.

Buddhist thought holds that there are five levels of mastery in this regard, namely, mastery of the naked eye, the celestial eye, the wisdom eye, the *dharma* eye, and the divine eye. These are the five major levels of the inner eye, and each is additionally divided into upper, middle, and lower levels. In Daoist thought there are nine times nine, or eighty-one, levels of spiritual vision. While we will open the inner eye for all of you here, we won't open it to the plane of celestial eye or below. The reason is, though you have begun spiritual refinement as you sit here, you have only just begun to leave your ordinary self behind, and still have many worldly attachments to let go. Were your eye to be opened at the level of celestial eye or below, you would have what are commonly known as psychic powers and would be able to see through walls or see inside people's bodies. It would seriously disrupt this world and its ways if we were to impart such powers on a large scale, opening the eye like that for everyone. State secrets might be at risk; clothes would do little to cover people; you could observe people inside their own homes from outside their walls; and you could spot the winning ticket in any prize drawing. These things would really be a problem. It would change the face of this world if everyone were to enjoy celestial vision, wouldn't it? Anything that seriously disrupts the human world is strictly prohibited, however. Were I to indeed open your eye like that, you might turn right into a *chi-gong* "master"—something that you might have once longed for. And with your open inner eye you would now be in perfect position to do healings. I would be leading you down the road to ruin, in that case.

Then to what level will I open the eye for you? Straight to the level of wisdom eye. Were it opened higher, your character wouldn't suffice; were it opened lower, it might severely impact the way of the world. But by opening it to wisdom eye there is no risk of your seeing through walls or into people's bodies, since it hasn't that capacity. You will be able to see things in other dimensions, however. The benefit of this is that it can strengthen your faith in the practice. You will actually be seeing things that are invisible to others, and will be able to sense that they are real. So whether you have clear visions or not, your eye is being opened to the wisdom level, to the benefit of your spiritual development. Those who are sincere in their practice of Dafa and strict about bettering their character will experience what I've described by reading this book.

So what determines the level of someone's inner eye normally? Not everything becomes visible to the inner eye once it is opened. Rather, it depends on what the eye's level is. Three factors determine this. The first factor is what we refer to as an essential energy. This energy fills the range of space spanning from the inside of the inner eye to the outside, and it is needed for the eye to see. Its function is similar to that of the screen in a television set: the screen, which has phosphors on it, is what allows the television to display images; without it the television would amount to little more than a light bulb. It is the phosphors that make pictures possible. The analogy isn't perfect, of course. We see things directly, while the images on a television are mediated by a screen. You can get the general idea, though. The essential energy I'm describing is exceptionally valuable, as it is refined from virtue and something of utmost quality. Most everyone has a different amount of it; only two out of every ten thousand people might have equal amounts of it.

The level of your inner eye is a direct result of the workings of the Way. It has a spiritual dimension to it and is closely connected to one's character. Someone of poorer character will have a lower level of inner eye. That's because his poor character will have cost him more of his essential energy. By contrast, someone of excellent character will go through life without getting caught up in worldly things like status and money, interpersonal disputes, self-interest, or feelings and desires, and so his essential energy is likely to have been preserved better. So once his inner eye is opened he will see with greater clarity. Children who are six or younger have lucid visions after their eyes are opened, which is easily done. One sentence is all it takes.

✕ The human world has a strong corrupting influence on people, and its powerful currents are hard to resist. Under its sway, people often confuse right and wrong. It's natural to want to have a good life, but that tendency can lead one to deprive others or become more selfish; and one might gain at other people's expense, take advantage of them, or harm them. But vying and fighting for one's own gain surely goes against the nature of the universe. So, what people consider right isn't necessarily right. Parents often teach their kids to "be a little smarter" so that they will make it in life, in a worldly sense. But being "smart" like that is wrong in view of the universe. We believe in letting things take their course and worrying little about how things will turn out for us, whereas someone who has learned to really be clever will always try to come out on top. He might have been taught [to not let things go, and] that if any kid crosses him, to "get them in trouble" with teachers or parents, and to "pocket any money" he sees lying around. And the more he learns such things growing up, the more selfish he becomes in life. And his mistreatment of people will cost him virtue.

When virtue, which is physical, is lost, it doesn't simply dissolve. It undergoes a transformation and is given to the party that was wronged; one's essential energy, however, *does* dissolve in such cases. Someone who is cunning from his childhood up into adulthood, and is very selfish and always puts himself first, will usually find that his inner eye doesn't work, or work well, after it is opened. But that doesn't mean it will never work. That's because we seek to return to our original state of purity through spiritual practice, and the essential energy will be constantly replenished and restored for us as we keep practicing. So your character is vital to all of this, and we stress that your entire person must improve and elevate. As your character is perfected, all things will improve in kind. But if your character doesn't change for the better, your essential energy, which powers your inner eye, won't be replenished. You should be able to see the connection now.

There is also a second factor to explore. Some people might find, if their innate foundation is good, that their eye opens when they are practicing, even if on their own. It's often fright-ening when the inner eye first opens. The reason is, people usually choose to meditate or do energy exercises late at night, when all is still. They will be practicing away when suddenly a large eye appears before them, out of nowhere, giving them a scare. It's frightening enough that it scares them away from practicing again. It's incredibly unsettling—such a large eye, blinking and looking at them, and all of it so vivid. This has led to its being called by some "the Devil's eye," though others call it "the Divine eye." But this eye, in fact, belongs to you. Remember that one only needs to worry about putting in the effort of spiritual practice, and the rest is in the hands of one's teacher. The elaborate process of developing higher energy for a practitioner all takes place in other dimensions. And not just in one dimension, but in all dimensions asso-ciated with the person; his body will be undergoing changes in each. That's obviously not something you could do. These things are in the hands of one's teacher; it is he who does them. And this is why it's said that one only needs to focus on practicing and one's teacher will handle the rest. It is actu-ally he who handles things, whatever you might hope or try to accomplish.

So some people experience the opening of the inner eye while practicing on their own. While we do consider it to be an eye that belongs to them, it's not something a person can develop himself. What happens is that a person's teacher, for those who have one, will develop for them something called a "true eye" once he sees that their inner eye is open. Or in other cases, as you might imagine, the person may not have a permanent master but one in passing. There is a religious belief that higher beings are so abundant as to be omnipresent, or everywhere. It has also been thought that spirits are so numerous as to be right beside you. So a passing-by master might take an interest in someone after seeing that he has practiced well and has an open inner eye, but just lacks a true eye. And so a true eye gained in this fashion does count as a result of the person's own practice. Beings like these are far superior to any worldly role models or heroes, for they are motivated solely by compassion and a wish to save people from this world; so they give of themselves freely, without terms, and have no thought of being rewarded or recognized for it.

The first time someone's inner eye opens, his human eyes may be overwhelmed by light and bothered by it. Yet it's not the eyes that are finding it harsh, but the pineal gland. It only *feels* as though it's the eyes that are bothered. This happens when the person doesn't yet have the true eye; the eyes won't be bothered by light once the true eye has been bestowed. A portion of us will be able to sense or see the true eye. Its nature is the same as the universe's, and so it is innocent and inquisitive, and will look inward to see whether your inner eye has opened and can be used to see. It will stare inward at you. If your inner eye has opened, you might unexpectedly catch sight of the true eye staring at you, and be startled by it. But it is actually a part of you now. And it will be this eye that enables you to see into other realms thereafter. Without it you would have no visions, even with an opened inner eye.

Then there is a third factor, which really makes a difference in which level your inner eye is working at; namely, the changes that take place in you across dimensions as you progress in spiritual attainment. When people see through their inner eye, they make use of not only a primary passageway, but also many sub-passageways. Buddhist thought holds that each pore of the body can be an eye, just as Daoist thought believes that each aperture, or acupuncture point, of the body can be an eye. What they mean is that this is possible with a kind of altered bodily state brought about by the Way, where one can see from anywhere in the body.

But we hold that there is still more to the inner eye's level. There are also several major sub-passageways in addition to the main passageway I mentioned, and these are above the eyebrows, above and below the eyelids, and at the Mountain Root acupoint at the bridge of the nose. Breakthroughs in inner eye level are a matter of whether these passageways can be used. For a regular believer to be able to make use of these passageways is quite an achievement, of course. There are people who can use even their naked eyes to see realms beyond this one, after having developed various powers in them via spiritual practice. But if these powers aren't utilized skillfully, the person will only see objects in one dimension but not in others, or only in other dimensions but not in ours, which isn't ideal. And so some people will be using one eye for this dimension and the other eye for a dimension beyond this one. Now, this eye (the right eye) doesn't have a sub-passageway beneath it, for reasons directly related to the Way: people tend to use the right eye for doing wrongful things. My remarks so far are about the main sub-passageways that people develop while at a point in their practice where they are still subject to the laws of the human realm.

At a highly advanced stage of practice, where one has gone beyond the human realm, a person can also develop a type of eye that resembles a compound eye. A large eye that spans the top half of the face can develop, with countless smaller eyes within it. And some divine ones who have reached very high planes have developed so many eyes that they are all throughout their faces. All of these eyes will see via the one, larger eye, and anything that is willed can be seen; all planes of existence can be seen with one look through this eye. The zoologists and entomologists who research flies have found, through microscopy, that flies have large eyes that are made up of countless smaller ones. And these are referred to as compound eyes. Something like this may come about when someone achieves an extremely high level of spiritual attainment, but it must be a level far surpassing that of *tathagata*. Regular people won't be able to see these eyes, however, and nor will the typical practitioner be able to. Everything here will appear as normal, for the eyes are in another dimension. This should offer a sense for what happens when higher levels, or other dimensions, are broken through to.

For the most part I have explained the structure of the inner eye for you. We use an external force to open your inner eye, so it happens rather quickly and easily. Each of you should feel a tightening at your forehead as I explain the inner eye, as if the flesh there were pinching together and burrowing inward. You are sure to feel it. Each of you will sense it as long as you can really set your attachments aside and learn Falun Dafa. And the force that you will feel pushing inward should be strong. We are sending out an energy meant specifically to open your inner eye, and it is doing just that, while we also send out *falun* to repair it. While I teach about the inner eye we will open it for each of you, as long as you are practicing Falun Dafa. Not everyone will necessarily have clear visions, if any at all. This owes to things on your part. You needn't be anxious, though. It's not a big issue if you can't see right now; it will gradually come with spiritual refinement. Visions will gradually come to you as you steadily progress, and they will evolve from being hazy to clear. As long as you go about the practice with a sincere commitment, all of what you may have lost before will be replenished.

It's rather challenging for a person to open the inner eye on his own, by contrast. Let's talk about the ways that it happens. One way involves gazing at the forehead, where the inner eye is, while meditating. At first the forehead will be dark for someone who does this, with nothing there. With time, however, the color will gradually become less dark. And as more time goes into the practice, the forehead gradually brightens until ultimately it takes on a red glow. At this time it will seem as if the forehead is blossoming, with a scene similar to how flower buds open almost instantly in nature films. The red part of the forehead, which originally appeared flat, will bulge suddenly in the center and bloom, again and again. If a person tries to work through this process all on his own, even eight or ten years might not be enough, for his entire inner eye would have started out being completely blocked up.

Some people's inner eyes are not completely blocked and the person has an open passageway, but no energy is present there since they haven't ever done spiritual exercises. So when they first start, something dark and round will suddenly appear before their eyes. With continued practice, it will gradually turn white, and grow progressively brighter, to the point that the eyes might be bothered by it. Some people may think that they've seen the sun or the moon. But what they saw was neither, in fact; it was actually their own passageway. Some individuals can see other realms as soon as they are given a true eye, as they make quick breakthroughs to new levels. But for others, seeing may prove to be difficult.

As they move through the passageway they find that it's like a tunnel, or perhaps a well, which they rush outward through whenever they do their exercises, or even as they sleep. The experience varies from person to person, and it could seem like anything from riding a horse to flying, running, or speeding along in a vehicle. But it will always seem as if the end can't be reached. That owes to the fact that it's really hard to open the inner eye on one's own. Daoist thought [can help shed light on this, as it] considers the human body to be a micro universe, and if the body really is like that, then we can just imagine how far of a distance it would be from the forehead to the pineal gland. That would explain why some people feel as if they are always rushing forward along a passageway but never reaching the end.

The Daoist idea that the human body is a miniature universe is quite sound. The concept isn't that the body's composition and structure are like those of the universe; it's not about the body in this physical dimension. To understand it, we should consider what the sciences now know the body to be like at a level beneath cells. They have found that there are a variety of molecules there, and smaller than molecules are atoms, protons, atomic nuclei, electrons, quarks, and neutrinos—with the latter being the smallest particles researched so far. But what is the smallest particle, ultimately? It's really not something research can answer. The Buddha once remarked in his later years that the universe is both "infinitely large and infinitely small." This suggests that even to a divine being such as he, the universe is at once so large that its perimeter can't be seen, and so small that its tiniest particles can't be made out. And this would be what led to his statement.

The Buddha described the vastness of the universe through

his teaching about multiple worlds. He explained that within the Milky Way galaxy of this universe there exist three thousand planets with beings who have carnal bodies similar to ours, and that even in a single grain of sand there exist a great many worlds. This would mean that a grain of sand is like a universe, with intelligent beings like man and worlds like ours, with mountains and rivers. This might sound rather far-fetched, I realize. But assuming it's valid, you would expect to find sand once again in those smaller worlds, and then inside of it you would again expect to find still more worlds. And then in those worlds you would again expect to find sand, inside of which there would again be multiple worlds. It appeared endless even to the Buddha, with his level of spiritual attainment.

What was said about sand could also be said of people's cells and their molecules. People wonder how large the universe is. I can tell you that this universe does have a boundary, though to a being at the Buddha's level it would seem to go on forever, and be incomparably large. Although it may be hard to fathom, the interior of the human body, which spans from the molecular level to that of the tiniest of invisible particles that make up the body, is in fact equal to the universe in size. At the time of a person's, or any life's, creation, a composition unique to his being and his innate qualities will be formed in the most micro of realms. These sorts of things are well beyond the reach of modern science—a science which pales in comparison to that of the advanced life forms found on planets throughout the universe. Our science can't even break through to other dimensions that exist at the same time and place as us, while the spacecraft of other planets can readily travel through different dimensions. Space and time are altogether different there from how we know them, and so those entities can come and go instantly—so fast that it's hard for people to believe.

I am talking about this in conjunction with the inner eye because you might have had the sense, as you were rushing outward down your own passageway, that it stretched on forever. Some of you might have seen something different. You might have had the impression that you were not going down a tunnel but instead a road that is broad and never-ending, with mountains, waters, and cityscapes off to the sides. It sounds hard to imagine, I realize. The words of one master come to mind: that within just a single pore of your body a city may be found, with trains and vehicles moving about. Some people who heard this were taken aback, as it didn't seem very believable to them. But consider this: what if research were to go further than just studying particles like molecules, atoms, and protons, and to reveal for us the *plane* of each such level, and not just any isolated particle—if we could see the plane of the molecular level, the atomic level, the proton level, and the atomic nucleus level—we would see how things really are in other dimensions. Any physical thing, including our bodies, exists in parallel to, and in connection with, various planes of other dimensions in the universe. The research done in modern particle physics merely studies particles in isolation by splitting them through fission, after which it looks to see what matter results from the breaking of the nucleus. If instead there were an instrument that could reveal to us all that exists at the plane of atoms or molecules, and give the entire picture, it would represent a breakthrough to another dimension, and we would be seeing the reality of that world. People's bodies correspond to other dimensions, which are like I just described.

There are other things that might be experienced when a person opens the inner eye on his own. So far I've been discussing the fairly common ones. It's less common for people to see that their inner eye is turning, but it does happen. This is most frequent in Daoist energy practices, where there is a *tai-chi* disc that has to be split open before the adherent can see things. But it's not that the person had a *tai-chi* in his head. Rather, it was that his master, right at the outset, installed things for him that would make his practice possible, one of which was the *tai-chi*. His master would seal up his inner eye using the *tai-chi*. Then, when the time came for the inner eye to open, the *tai-chi* disc would be split apart. So, having it was part of his master's designs for him, and it was not something originally in his head.

There is also a small segment of people who want to open their inner eye, but who only make it less likely the more they try. Yet they aren't aware of what is happening. It doesn't work out mainly because the inner eye isn't something you should yearn for, and doing so will only make it less likely to open. Your inner eye won't open if you long to have it. Instead, a certain greyish material will ooze out of the inner eye and cover it. And if it goes on for long, more and more of this material will leak out, covering a large area. And if you keep wanting the inner eye, even as it fails to open, more of this material will leak out, such that it might encase your entire body. It could even become dense and have a large presence to it. Even if you were to open your inner eye at that point, you still wouldn't be able to see anything, since your eye would have become sealed up as a result of your attachment. That material will only start to break up and dissolve once you stop thinking about the inner eye and get rid of the attachment entirely. But you will have to go through a long and painful phase of practice to remove that material—a situation that never should have come about in the first place. Some people don't realize any of this, though, and they repeatedly ignore warnings from their master to stop trying for the inner eye, and end up with the opposite of what they hoped for.

The Power of Clairvoyance

One extrasensory power that's directly connected with the inner eye is clairvoyance. There is a person who has claimed that while seated in one location he could perceive things in Beijing, the United States, or on the other side of the world. It's hard for people to know what to make of such claims, since there's no science to support it. So they are left to wonder if it's possible. There is no shortage of theories for it, but none are that convincing. Part of the problem is that they've been working under the assumption that it's a superpower, which is not the case. People who are in the stage of spiritual practice where they are still subject to the laws of the human realm don't have truly superhuman powers. What they see through clairvoyance or other powers occurs only within a certain dimension. The furthest reach of their abilities doesn't exceed this physical dimension where we exist, and usually they don't go beyond the dimensions associated with their own bodies.

One's body has a field in a designated dimension. This field is not the same as that of virtue. They don't occupy the same dimension, though their reach is the same. This field corresponds to the universe, so a mirror image of anything that exists in the universe could appear in it. But these are merely reflections of the real thing. For example, on this earth there is an America and a Washington, D.C., and so a mirror image of either could appear in your field, but they wouldn't be the real thing. Still, though, these mirror images do physically exist. What appears in your field will change in keeping with what happens in the universe, since the two correspond. So what people call clairvoyance is a matter of viewing things that are present in the dimensions associated with one's own body. But you won't see in this manner once you have reached a stage in your practice that is beyond the human realm. You will perceive things directly then, and that is in fact a divine ability that is incomparably powerful.

Let's take a look at how clairvoyance works during the stage of practice within the human realm. In the dimension where your field exists, there is a mirror at the position of the forehead. It is face-down for those who don't practice, and turned over for those who do. When a person is about to gain clairvoyance the mirror starts to spin. As you may know, motion picture film looks fluid when viewed at a rate of twenty-four frames per second, while anything less than that gives a choppy feel. The mirror spins at a speed faster than twenty-four frames per second, capturing on its surface the images of whatever is in its trajectory, and turning over to let you see them. As it turns over again, any images that it had captured are erased. It does it again and again, non-stop—capturing images, turning, and erasing. And this is why what you see appears to be in motion. It allows you to see the things that it picks up from the dimensions associated with your body, and the images will be counterparts to actual things in the larger universe outside.

You might be wondering whether such a small mirror could manage to capture everything around one's body. As we've established, when a person's inner eye is open at a level beyond celestial vision and is about to attain wisdom vision, it is going to surpass this dimension. Right when the full breakthrough is imminent, a change will occur with the inner eye: it will no longer see the physical things of this dimension, be they objects, people, or even walls; they will all be gone. What happens, more specifically, is that when you probe more deeply with your vision in that other, designated dimension, your body will no longer be visible there. Only a mirror will be there, positioned in the space associated with your dimension. And this mirror, while in that space, will fill completely the space associated with your dimension. And that is why there is nothing that it can't capture as it turns there. As long as what is in the space associated with your dimension corresponds to the universe, the mirror can capture it and reveal it fully to you. This is our take on clairvoyance.

Scientists who research extrasensory powers have a hard time verifying this ability. Here's why. Suppose they want a clairvoyant to try to tell them what a certain person's relative is doing while at home in Beijing. They provide the clairvoyant with the relative's name and some general facts, and soon he begins to have a vision. He provides a description of the building, the path leading to the door, and how the room inside is furnished. And all of it is accurate. Then the researchers ask what the relative is doing, and the clairvoyant responds that the person is currently writing. To verify it, they pick up the phone and call the relative to find out. But he informs them that he had just been eating, which contradicts what the clairvoyant saw. Scenarios like this one have led people to dismiss the ability. But what's confusing is that the clairvoyant's account of the physical setting was flawless. All of this can be explained by the fact that there is a discrepancy in time between this dimension, or "space-time," and the one where this power is. Time as we know it is different in the two places. In the scenario I described, as it turns out, the person's relative *was* writing earlier, but was eating at the time of the call. So there was a time lag. If psi researchers keep basing their ideas and research on conventional theories, or current science, they aren't going to get very far anytime soon. These phenomena reach beyond this world, and so there needs to be a change in thinking in order to understand them. People shouldn't keep interpreting them as they have.

The Power of Knowing Fate

There is another power that shares a direct connection with the inner eye, which has been termed "the power of knowing fate." Six extrasensory powers are now generally acknowledged in the world, among which are the inner eye, clairvoyance, and knowing fate. What the power of knowing fate refers to is the ability to know another person's past or future. Someone whose power is well-developed may be able to foresee the rise and fall of a society; or if it's particularly advanced, the laws of change governing all of the cosmos. All of this is possible with the power of knowing fate. That's because there are certain principles at work regarding the movement of matter, and so objects that exist in a given dimension also exist simultaneously, in various forms, in many other dimensions. We can illustrate this by looking at what happens when a person moves his body. All of the cells of his body move when he does, and in invisible, micro realms, all of his molecules, protons, electrons, as well as the tiniest of his particles—all that he is made up of—move as well. Although each particle exists independently, the movement of each that happens here is reflected in his bodies in those other dimensions and realms.

Remember the law of the conservation of matter. Whatever a person does in this world has a physical reality in another, designated dimension; and this is true for even a simple gesture, like a swiping motion. Whatever one does will leave an image and information there. They are conserved in that dimension and will exist there forever. Those with psychic powers can know what took place in the past just by looking at the corresponding scenes that are still present there. One day, if you yourself have the power of knowing fate, you will be able to see the class we are holding here today, as it will still exist there; it is already there now. Right from the moment of birth, your entire life already exists elsewhere, in a special dimension where time as we know it doesn't exist. And for some people more than one lifetime is there.

It might be hard for some people to come to terms with this, as it would mean that their striving to achieve things and to change their lives for the better amount to little. But indeed, the hard work that people put in can only change minor or little things in their lives. And in fact, it is precisely on account of all those efforts to change things that you may have made karma for yourself. If people's efforts truly didn't impact anything, there would be no chance of doing wrong in life, and it would be impossible to incur karma. When you force things to go your way it will be at someone else's expense, and so you will have done wrong. This is why in spiritual practice it is always stressed that you should let things unfold naturally. You might end up harming people if it takes effort to get your way. You will incur a debt to them if you, through your efforts, end up seizing what was meant to be theirs.

Ordinary people can't change their lives in any significant way, try as they may. The only exception is if they do nothing but evil and have no moral boundaries. But while that can change one's life, what lies ahead is utter destruction. We can see from higher realms that the soul doesn't perish when a person dies. How is that? Here's what we have observed. The body of the deceased that's placed in the morgue consists only of the cells of this dimension. The entire body, including all of its organs and tissues—that is, all of the cells in this dimension—has been shed. Yet in another dimension this person has a body made of particles smaller than molecules, atoms, or protons that is very much alive, and it lives on there, in that invisible and micro dimension. But what lies ahead for those who do relentless evil is the total disintegration of their cells on all levels, or what Buddhism has called "the perdition of body and soul."

There is another way to change your life, and it is really the only way to go: to take up spiritual practice. But why would this enable your life to be changed? And who would have the power to do that? What makes it possible is that your intention to practice shines like gold and resonates with higher lives throughout the universe—or what in Buddhist thought is referred to as "ten directions of worlds." This happens because being human, in the eyes of higher beings, is not the goal of human life. As they see it, your life originated in one of the dimensions out there in the universe, and shared in its qualities; it was good and kind, and imbued with the physical properties of *zhen, shan, ren*. It is only that as lives like these enter into community and interact with others, they might change for the worse and fall. And upon falling to a lower plane of existence, they might again change for the worse and be unable to stay, and so they fall to a plane still lower. This process of falling can repeat itself again and again, until ultimately they fall to this human world.

Any being that falls to this plane should have been destroyed or annihilated. Yet they have been spared by higher divinities who created this special dimension and human world, out of a great sense of compassion. Here, beings are given an additional, mortal body, along with a pair of eyes that are limited to seeing only this material world. So it's as if these beings are put under a spell of ignorance that prevents them from seeing the universe as it truly is—which is not the case in any other dimension. By being put into this state of ignorance, they are given an opportunity, however. It is extremely painful here, while lost and confused, and the human body is fashioned to suffer. Yet if a person in this setting wants to find his way back to his true, heavenly home, or return to his original state of purity, as Daoists put it, if he wants to dedicate himself to spiritual practice, it means his innate divinity has shone through, and higher beings will help him, for they value that intention above all others. It would mean that this person hasn't lost his way, even in such a trying setting, since he wants to go back. And so higher beings will help him unconditionally and in every way possible. And so this is why we can do so much for those who practice, but not others.

We can't help you, then, if you are just a regular person who is looking for healing. There is nothing exceptional about a regular, worldly person, and he is supposed to experience the human condition. Many people believe that it is Divine Will to help humanity and be merciful to all. But that shouldn't be equated with doing healings for people, and there is no scriptural basis for it. It is false energy healers who have confused people about this in recent times. The authentic teachers of energy practices in China, who paved the way, never suggested doing healings for others. They simply taught people how to do energy exercises and improve their own, personal health. It's really a stretch to think that you, as a regular person, could do healings for people after learning how for just a few days. If you were to try to heal, you would be misleading people. And it would only make you more attached. You would be trying to use higher powers to promote yourself and gain from it, which would never succeed. So this explains why some people never get the powers they hope for; were they to get them, it would undermine the human condition.

A principle of this universe is that if you wish to return to your true home, higher beings will help you. As they see it, your soul is not meant to stay in this world, but to go back. Yet if someone were to free you of sickness and life was all good, then the idea of going to heaven would lose its appeal. You might think it would be great to be free of illness and suffering, and have everything go your way, leading a charmed life. But it was because you turned bad that you fell this far, so it's not supposed to be pleasant. People, in their state of ignorance, are apt to do wrong here, and for their transgressions there will be what Buddhism calls "karmic retribution." The ordeals that people go through or the misfortunes they experience are often cases of them paying off karma. People often wonder how come the divine, which some religions believe to be all around us, doesn't heal all of humanity—especially when doing so would, in fact, take but a wave of the hand. Well, it's because the ordeals people face trace back to their own misdeeds and debts. So if someone then heals them with supernatural means, it amounts to undermining the laws of the universe. It would mean that they could do wrongful things and rack up debts without paying for them, which is not allowed. Higher beings all try to preserve the human condition, not violate it. If you want to truly enjoy a pleasant, illness-free existence, and finally be freed of the human condition, there is only one way: through spiritual practice! Getting people to do real spiritual practice is something that truly benefits all of humanity.

Then what explains all of the energy healing that's being done and taught out there? In most cases it's that the people involved have gone down the wrong road. True masters of energy practices like *chi-gong*, by contrast, develop compassion in the course of their spiritual progress, and become sensitive to people's suffering. And so it is allowed, when that's the case, for a master to help someone if he feels moved to do so. But what he does won't cure the person. He can only mitigate the ailment for the time being, or push it off to a later date in the future; or he might transfer it to someone else in the person's family. He can't thoroughly dissolve the karma for the person. You can't freely do that for a regular person; it can only be done for people engaged in spiritual practice. So there are principles at work in all of this.

The Buddhist teachings about "saving all living things" are actually about taking people to higher planes, where they will be outside of the human condition and its pain, liberated and free of suffering. And this is what the Buddha's remarks about "crossing over" to *nirvana* referred to. But you wouldn't be interested in such a spiritually elevated existence if your life on earth were full of joy, overflowing with wealth, and free of all adversity. So the course of your life *can* be changed, if you are someone doing spiritual practice—but for this reason alone.

The power of knowing fate involves having a small screen, much like that of a television, at the position of the forehead. For some people it is on the forehead, for some at a slight distance from it, and for others inside of it. Some people will be able to see it only with their eyes closed, while some, if the power is strong, will be able to see it with their eyes still open. It won't be visible to other people, though, since it exists in another dimension that is associated with your body. Another power is still needed, then, to act as a carrier and allow the images that are captured from other dimensions to be reflected onto this screen and seen by your inner eye. With the power of knowing fate you will be able to see people's pasts and futures, and with great accuracy. Fortune-tellers can't make out the details of what they see, no matter how skilled they are. But with this power, you will be able to see things with great clarity, including even the time period and the details of how things change. This is possible because what you see will be accurate reflections of persons or things in other dimensions.

I open the inner eye for every practitioner of Falun Dafa. However, I won't make available to you the other powers we've discussed. The power of knowing fate will naturally come to you as you advance in practice; it will be something that you experience down the road. And that's why I have given this teaching now—so that you will know what's happening when the power comes to you.

Surpassing This Material and Mortal Realm

It's somewhat delicate to discuss spiritual concepts such as surpassing this material and mortal realm, or [as Chinese thought calls it,] "surpassing the five elements" and "three realms." Many teachers of energy practices who have broached these topics have had a hard time responding to skeptics. They often get hit with tricky questions like, "Who can you name that's achieved these things?" Some of these teachers have not been masters, however, even if they fancy themselves so. But they would try to respond to the questions when they should have just kept quiet; they were in no position to answer them. And so they would get tongue-tied. This has hurt the credibility of spiritual practices in general and muddied the waters. And people have used episodes like these as a pretext for discrediting these practices. Terms related to surpassing the five elements and three realms are spiritual in nature and have religious origins; they came out of a religious context. So it's important for people to be aware of the historical background of the terms.

So what does it mean to surpass the five elements of this material world? The physics of ancient China, much as with physics today, believed that the theory of five elements was valid. And it is indeed the case that the five elements of metal, wood, water, fire, and earth give rise to all of creation, so we subscribe to the theory. For someone to surpass the five elements means, in contemporary terms, to transcend the physical world that we know. I realize it might sound a bit hard to believe. But bear in mind that true spiritual teachers carry a higher energy, known as *gong*. I have undergone testing to assess my energy, as have many teachers of *chi-gong*. There are many instruments now that can detect the material elements of higher energy, which these teachers emit; all it takes is the right instruments. Instruments can now detect radiation including infrared, ultraviolet, ultrasound, infrasound, electricity, magnetism, and gamma rays, as well as atoms and neutrons. True *chi-gong* teachers emit all of these, and more— only they are things that instruments can't yet detect. So all it takes is the right instruments, and it's now established that these teachers emit many types of matter.

True spiritual teachers exude a powerful and beautiful aura, which can be seen with the right kind of electromagnetic field. The stronger someone's energy is, the larger the aura that he emanates. Ordinary people have auras as well, only they're really quite small. From research in high-energy physics we know that energy is in fact things like neutrons or atoms. Many *chi-gong* teachers have had their energy assessed, and that's the case for most of those who are renowned. I too have been assessed, and it was found that the amount of gamma rays and thermal neutrons I released was eighty to one hundred and seventy times greater than what matter normally emits. And that was only what the equipment could measure, as the indicator had reached its limit. The researchers found it hard to believe—neutrons that powerful. It shouldn't be humanly possible. So we can say that it has been scientifically affirmed that masters of energy practices do have higher energy.

It takes a practice of both mind and body to transcend the five elements. Practices that don't involve the body will develop the kind of energy that facilitates spiritual attainment only, and aren't concerned with surpassing the five elements.

Practices of mind and body, by contrast, store up energy in every cell of your body. When most adherents first develop higher energy, the particles of energy that they give off are coarse and low in density, with gaps between them. That makes it not very powerful. At a more advanced stage of practice, the density of energy might be greater than even that of water at the molecular level, by a factor of a hundred, a thousand, or even 100 million. It's all possible, because your energy becomes more dense, more fine and smooth, and more powerful as you progress. The energy is stored in every cell of your body. And not just your body in this dimension, but your bodies in other dimensions, too. The energy will fill your cells, from the plane of molecules to atoms, to neutrons, to electrons, all the way to the cells at an extremely subatomic level, and over time your body will come to be brimming with higher energy.

This higher energy has intelligence and is quite capable. As you gain more of it and it grows denser, it will fill all of your body's cells and easily inhibit them, since they are weak in comparison. And as this happens, the process whereby old cells are shed and replaced by new ones will cease, since high-energy matter will replace the matter originally making up your cells. While it's easy to describe, reaching that point of spiritual refinement is a long process. But when it does happen, your entire body will have been remade at the cellular level with high-energy matter. Then it would no longer be the five elements that make up your body. It would instead be material from beyond this world that forms you—you would have a body of high-energy matter harvested from other dimensions. On another note, virtue, similarly, is made up of matter from other dimensions and not subject to the time of this dimension.

The sciences now hold that time has a field, and that time's influence cannot extend beyond it. It's not possible for time, in one dimension, to have influence over things in other dimensions which are ruled by altogether different laws of time and space. So time, here, would have simply no impact on matter of other dimensions. And the same would be true for your body, which would no longer be mortal in any sense. It would have, as the ancients put it, "surpassed the five elements." But your body would look no different to people than before. That's because, despite the dramatic changes in you, your practice wouldn't be done. You would still have breakthroughs to higher realms to make. And to do that you would need to keep practicing in this world. Being invisible to people wouldn't do you much good.

So what comes next, then? By this point in your practice your cells at the molecular level will have all been reconstituted with high-energy matter. But the atoms one level down have a specific configuration, just as do molecules and atomic nuclei; the configuration doesn't change for any of them. The molecular configuration of cells makes one's flesh soft to the touch; the molecules of bone are configured with a greater density, and so they are hard to the touch; while the density of the molecules of blood is very low, so it's liquid. Others won't be able to tell from your appearance what a change you've undergone, however, since at the molecular level your cells will retain their original structure and configuration. So the energy inside of you will have changed, even if your cellular structure hasn't. This means that you will no longer be subject to aging. Your cells will no longer decay and die, and you will forever stay young. So spiritual practice can bring you a youthful look that never fades.

It's only natural that a body like this might still suffer a fracture if hit by a car or bleed if cut by a knife. That's because its molecular configuration hasn't changed, even if it is free of aging or metabolic processes. So this is our take on surpassing the five elements. It's well-founded and can be explained scientifically. It's unfortunate that terms like this get a bad rap as being religious imaginings when they are carelessly used by people who don't know what they are talking about. People aren't familiar with the terms since these have an older, religious background, and aren't necessarily in the idiom of our day.

Next let's look at what it means to "surpass this mortal realm"—or the "three realms," as it's also known. As I explained the other day, perfecting your character is the key to developing higher energy. The qualities of the universe will no longer limit you as they come to define your character. And as your mind elevates, your material virtue will be transformed into higher energy. Eventually this energy will form into a column as it grows and climbs higher. The higher that the column is, the greater your energy. We like to say that "anything is possible through Dafa." It all comes down to how sincere and committed you are. Any height is possible if you have the grit and tenacity that it takes. And even if you one day have converted all of your white matter, more can still be had by reworking your black matter through suffering. And if that's still not enough, you can take on the sins of your close friends or family who don't practice, and increase your energy that way. But, this only applies to you if you have progressed to an extremely advanced stage. You shouldn't even think of assuming others' sins when you only recently came into the practice as an ordinary person. That much karma would doom most people's practice. The guidance I am giving here applies to different stages of practice.

"Three realms" is a religious term that describes three hierarchical realms of existence—namely, the "realms" of minor deities, this world, and the underworld. Within these three there are nine major planes of existence, and a total of thirty-three planes in all. An accompanying belief is that all things within the three realms, no matter the plane, reincarnate cyclically and may be reborn on any of several possible tracks. So someone who is a human in this life might become something else, such as an animal, in the next. And so Buddhism has taught that you should really make the most of your life as a human being, for the chance to do spiritual practice might not come again. They say this because animals are forbidden from practicing or hearing the Way. Or if an animal did learn to practice, it would never reap the divine rewards of spiritual effort; higher beings would slay it once it built up much energy. You may have waited hundreds of years, or more, for a human body, only to not cherish it now, when you finally have one. If you reincarnate as a rock, it might be eons before you are freed—if ever. You would never be freed if it didn't break, crumble, or erode away. Human bodies are *not* easily come by! A person who truly learns Dafa, the "Great Way," is incomparably fortunate. This should give you a sense for how hard it is to get a human body.

There is such a thing as "levels" of attainment in spiritual practice, and they are simply the outcome of how well you do. If you want to enjoy eternal life, keep on practicing, and when your column of energy reaches to a great height, you will be outside of [the cycle of reincarnation]—or the "three realms." There are people whose souls leave their bodies when they meditate, and rise to a higher point. One of my students did a write-up about his progress in the practice and described visiting heavenly realms and what he saw there. I told him to try going higher. But he said that he couldn't go further, and indeed, he wasn't able to at that point. Why would that be the case, though? It was because he had visited those realms by riding atop his column of energy; it was as high as he could go at the time. Ascending to greater heights, as I had suggested, would mean that he had achieved, to use a religious term for it, "divine standing." But greater things are still possible for a practitioner. Whatever height you have reached, you can still continue to perfect yourself and advance in your practice. And if, in the process, your energy column breaks through the outer limits of the three realms, then you will have indeed "surpassed" them. We measured it once and determined that the three realms described in some religions lie within the scope of the nine planets; and I should add here that there is no basis for the claim that there are ten planets. I have seen that the energy columns of some past masters had reached great heights and broken through the boundary of the Milky Way, which means that they very much had surpassed the three realms. So it should be clear now that doing so is a matter of spiritual attainment.

The Problem with Having Intentions

There are many who come to the practice with intentions. We see all sorts of motives, from wanting psychic powers to hoping to hear new theories, to getting healed, or getting a *falun*. People have even offered to pay our class fee to get a *falun* for someone in their family who didn't attend. Imagine that, expecting to buy a *falun*—something born of generations of effort over a staggering number of years—with a little cash. But if it's that valuable, why do we give it to *you* at no charge? Because you are someone who wants to lead a spiritual existence, and that aspiration is worth more than any sum of money. A *falun* can only be given in cases like this, where your innate divinity has shown itself.

You should ask yourself whether you are here because of something you hope to get out of it. Whatever thoughts you have are known to my spiritual bodies* in another dimension. Space and time are different there, and so your thoughts, as my spiritual bodies behold them, are extremely slow to form. And so those bodies of mine know your thoughts even before you could. The point is that you should change any thoughts that aren't appropriate. Since ours is a Buddhist discipline, we believe in destiny, and I would say that it is the workings of destiny that have brought you to the practice. It could be that you are meant to learn it. So I would suggest that you cherish it and get rid of any worldly intentions that might have initially motivated you.

In religious practice, Buddhists have traditionally stressed the concept of "emptiness," teaching adherents to keep the mind free of thoughts and to shun the secular world. And Daoists, likewise, have stressed the idea of "nothingness," asking followers to forgo material possessions and to not want or try to get them. This is similar to how in energy practice you are taught to put your mind on practicing, not on the energy you will get from it. If you can be free of intent as you practice and simply focus on perfecting your character, you will make spiritual breakthroughs and naturally come to have whatever is meant to be. It's only fitting to call whatever occupies your mind, or that you cling to, an "attachment." The teachings I offer are quite advanced, right from day one, so I have high expectations for you in terms of character, and this includes my hope that you are here free of intentions.

I feel a sense of responsibility to guide you in the right direction, and that means I need to spell out my teachings in full. As I mentioned, some people have the intention of getting their inner eyes opened, but it only results in their eyes getting blocked up and sealed off. And as I indicated, any powers that come to people while they are still practicing at the human level are no more than innate abilities, even if they are now called things like "psychic powers." They can only do things in this dimension and affect regular people. So I don't see any point in wanting or trying for those lesser things. If one day your practice reaches a higher level beyond this world, you will see that they don't do anything there and aren't worth all the trouble. At that stage any lesser powers like those will have to be disposed of by removing them to a deeper space, where they will be stored and serve only as a memento of your spiritual journey.

When you progress to a higher stage of practice, beyond this world, your journey begins anew. Your body will be one that has transcended this material world, or "five elements," as we just discussed, and it will only be fitting to call it holy. Your holy body will need to be cultivated anew and develop new powers, only now they should be referred to as sacred powers of the Way. Their strength is truly extraordinary and they can work in multiple dimensions. And *these* do have impact. Lesser, worldly abilities should have little appeal next to these. What attracts people to them is always the prospect of using them to build oneself up in this world, or show what one is capable of, as they don't offer much benefit otherwise. And besides, they're even less useful than, say, a nice object, which at least could be used for decoration purposes, since it'd be tangible and visible. I can guarantee that if you want them, on some level, it's to use them for something. And remember that they aren't like normal skills in this world that you can work honestly towards. Rather, psychic powers are something higher altogether, and are not meant for you to show off with in front of people. Wanting to show off is a strong attachment, a bad intention, and one that someone with spiritual aspirations should break. And it's all the worse if you want to use these powers to make money or get wealthy, or to achieve some worldly goal that you're after. You would be disrupting the designs for this world by using those higher means, and that's an even worse idea than showing off. So for these reasons nobody is allowed to use higher powers freely in this world.

Extrasensory powers usually come to those at two ends of the life spectrum, children and older folk. They are most common among older women, who tend to be of solid character and less attached to this world than others are. When powers come to them they are apt to handle it well, since they're not looking to show off and promote themselves. Younger people, by contrast, are less apt to develop higher powers—especially young guys. That's because they still want to work hard towards their goals in life, and they would use any powers they gained to these ends, as if they were tools for achieving things. But it is forbidden to use them like that, and so no powers will come to those people.

Spiritual things like these are sacred, and not to be treated like toys or normal skills. Your mind needs to dwell on a higher plane if you want to get anywhere in spiritual practice. You can just imagine what a mess it would be if someone who didn't understand these things managed to get the powers he was craving. Spiritual progress would be the last thing on his mind, and there's no telling what evil he might do, since his thoughts would be wed to this world and his powers would have come to him in the wrong way. He might magically remove money from the bank or hit the jackpot in a lottery. Yet things like that never happen, and it's worth considering why. I don't agree with the teachers who claim that unvirtuous people are prone to doing wrongful things when they get supernormal powers. That's not the case at all. Those who are unvirtuous or don't try to become better people will never gain such powers. The closest thing to it would be cases where someone with good character gets powers somewhere along the way but doesn't handle it well, and does something inappropriate. But his powers will be weakened or even lost if he abuses them. And any such loss would be permanent. Yet the more serious risk is that he would get attached to them.

Some teachers have claimed that people can do healings after just three to five days of learning their energy practices. It's like marketing—as if they were in the business of energy. But let's pause to think: could the average person heal someone's ailment just by sending out a little basic energy, [like they advertise]? Both parties, in this case, merely have the basic energy known as *chi,* with the only difference being that one of them has just started practicing and can take in or project energy since the Palace of Toil acupuncture point on his hand is open. So if one of the two tries to heal the other, there's no telling who might heal who, since both just have *chi*!

There's no reason that one of these people's energy should be more powerful than the other's. Energy like *chi* does not heal. And another thing is, a person will be connected with whoever he tries to heal, and it's possible that the sick energy in the recipient's body will come over to the healer's, such that he ends up with just as much of it. Though the root of the person's ailment won't be transferred, the healer might still become ill if he takes on too much of it. And it's easy for a person to get attached once he believes that he can heal. He might set up a practice and welcome all who come. And how happy he'll be about it—being able to heal! But he hasn't given thought to what makes it possible. It turns out that false healers like these are getting their energy from entities that have attached to them. And then they turn around and share a little of that energy with those who take their classes, to win their confidence. But these students' energy will disappear for good after they've treated a handful of people. What little energy they had will be gone, since doing that consumes it. It wouldn't be a higher energy that they were using since they wouldn't have had any in the first place. A master such as myself will have gone through decades of practice, and it really wasn't easy in the past. Spiritual progress is very difficult for those who haven't found a true practice, and it's hard to get very far in a lesser one.

The well-established masters of energy practices each had to practice for decades to get the higher energy that they have, however little. So it's a bit naive for people to think that they could get it by attending a brief class and without ever engaging in spiritual practice. And they come out of those healing classes attached. And then, when their attempts at healing don't work, they get anxious. Some people are so concerned about their reputations when they do healings that, would you believe, they even think about taking on the person's illness so that he or she can get well. But this isn't coming from compassion. Compassion can hardly arise in a mind that's occupied with things like money and reputation. To want to take on someone's illness just to protect your reputation indicates that there is a *serious* attachment! And so they get what they asked for. It really can result in the illness being transferred to their own body, and then it sets in. So while the ill person may now be well, those who do the healing will end up suffering for it afterward. And yet they might be pleased with themselves, and delighted about it. They think that they've healed someone and people start calling them a "master." But it should be obvious that it's an attachment. The fact that they get visibly dejected when it doesn't go well is a telltale sign that ego and money are motivating them. And as if that weren't bad enough, as I indicated, they are bringing sickly energy from people onto their own bodies. The pseudo master who supposedly taught them how to heal might have claimed that they could learn to "dispel" any sick energy, but I know for a fact that people can't do that, since the average person doesn't have the ability to tell good energy from bad. And over time the insides of their bodies will turn dark from karma.

If that kind of person wants to do genuine spiritual practice at some point, he will really be in a difficult spot, with no simple solution. It's going to be awfully tough—and painful—for him to rework all of that karma into white matter. Those who have a better innate foundation are more susceptible to landing in this predicament. Some people are just insistent about wanting to do healing. Animal spirits can see that kind of intent and will affix themselves to the person's body, which is called entity attachment. They see that the person wants to do healing, and they will help out. But they don't help for nothing, as everything comes at a cost. And this makes it dangerous. You can just imagine how hard it would be to make spiritual progress after bringing animals onto yourself. All of your spiritual efforts would have been for naught.

Some people exchange their good innate foundations for others' karma, by healing them. Yet people with medical conditions have large amounts of karma. Someone who heals people like that is going to feel wretched afterwards. Many who heal have had that experience; the other party gets well, while they themselves get seriously ill afterwards. And if they keep at it, significant amounts of karma will be transferred to them, at the cost of their virtue. But that would be the price they pay. Even though it's sickness they want, the laws of exchange still hold: even to get karma, virtue has to be paid. That's how the universe works. If that's what you want to do, it's up to you, and nobody is going to intervene—though it doesn't necessarily mean they approve. There is something that has been decided in this universe: whoever has a lot of karma is a bad person. Yet the people I just described are trading their own virtuous foundations for karma. It's going to be very hard to do spiritual practice then, with all that karma. They will have ruined their own foundations. What a horrible prospect. While the people they healed may feel fine now, they themselves have to suffer. And just imagine how dangerous it would be if they healed a couple of cancer patients—the healers might have to die in their place. Most people don't realize how these things work.

However well-known some false masters may be, it

doesn't necessarily mean they know much. Most people easily fall for hype. Though it might seem like everything is going fine for these false masters, they are not only harming others but also themselves. You will see what becomes of them in a year or two. Nobody is allowed to abuse things like these that are meant for purposes of spiritual refinement. And while spiritual refinement can bring healing powers, that is not what it's meant for. It is something higher and not an ordinary human endeavor. So it is strictly forbidden to use such powers haphazardly, in ways that undermine spiritual practice. Some pseudo masters are creating a tremendous mess now, using energy work as a way to build a following and make money. These nefarious groups that they've formed are constantly expanding in influence, and the so-called masters involved now outnumber the genuine ones by a wide margin. It's a mistake to think that *chi-gong* or energy healing is how they portray it—even if others, who don't know better, are taken in by it. Now you know what's really going on.

For selfish reasons the average person will do wrongful things in his dealings with others in this world and incur debts to people, which he will have to suffer the consequences of and pay for. Then even if someone did indeed have the ability to heal whoever he wanted to, it surely wouldn't be allowed. Higher beings are all around us, and yet they don't do that, do they? You would think it would be wonderful of them to bestow wellness upon all of humanity. And yet they don't. That's because people must pay off their own karma, and no beings dare to violate this law. It might be fine for someone who is still developing spiritually to help a person out by alleviating his suffering a little, out of compassion. But even then he is merely postponing the ailment until later. So the person may feel well now, but will have to suffer later; or instead of sickness it might take the form of losing money or some other mishap. A person's karma has to be purged in one shot if he is to be genuinely healed. And it can only be done for those engaged in spiritual practice, not just anyone. What I am explaining here isn't true for just our practice, but is applicable to the entire universe. This should give you a sense for what's really involved in many spiritual matters.

We won't teach you how to heal here, but we will guide you to something greater—to the great Way, a true path—and raise you up. And that is why I always say in my classes that practitioners of Falun Dafa are not allowed to do healings. You aren't one of us if you heal people. We are showing you the virtuous course to take, and I am purifying your body again and again. And I will keep doing so while you practice in this world, all the way until you have been completely transfigured by high-energy matter. But if you are always getting dark things on your body, how are you going to get anywhere? That's karma! You will have no hope of spiritual progress. You wouldn't be able to bear all that karma, and the pain would prove too much for your practice. So there's a reason for our rule. You might not have realized how special this practice is, given how public I've made it. But I have ways to protect it, even so. If you do healings, my spiritual bodies will take back all of what your body was given for your spiritual refinement. We can't let you rashly ruin such valuable gifts while you chase after worldly goals. You are not one of us if you don't follow what Falun Dafa teaches. So your body will be reset to an ordinary state and all of the bad things it once carried will be returned to you, since you are choosing to be an ordinary person.

Beginning yesterday, after class, many of you began to experience a lightness to your bodies. But a few individuals who have serious medical conditions became the first to feel unwell. The majority of you felt wonderful yesterday and completely unburdened after I took the bad things out of your bodies. But there is a law in this universe, that anything comes at a cost, and so we couldn't remove everything for you; you definitely have to bear something. What we have done is to remove the root causes of any ailments or poor health. But a cloud of sickness will still remain. If your inner eye is open, even at a lower level, you might see lumps of dark, turbid, sick energy inside your body, which are concentrated masses of dense, dark energy. If let loose, this energy would spread throughout your body.

Some of you will find, starting today, that your whole body feels chilly, as if you've come down with a heavy cold, and your bones might even ache. Most of you will find that some part of you doesn't feel good; it could be an aching leg or a dizzy head. Or you might seem to have a relapse of some issue that you thought you'd resolved through an energy practice or healing. That's because it didn't actually heal your condition. It had merely been postponed, and was still lodged in its original spot, ready to relapse at a later date. So we have to make it surface and drive it out of you, and remove the whole thing from its root. This might make you think that you're having a relapse, but what's happening is that the karma at the root of it is being purged. And so you will have reactions. They could be in any part of your body and could take any form. But it's all normal. I would encourage you to really try to keep coming to the class, however unwell you might feel. Your symptoms will vanish once you get to class, and you won't be at risk. A true spiritual teaching is hard to come by, so don't let whatever you might be going through physically get to you. The worse you might feel, the closer you are to the turning point, and your entire body will be, *and must be*, fully cleansed. The roots of any ailments that you had, have been taken out, and all that remains is some dark energy that is coming out on its own and causing you a little misery or trouble, since you can't get off completely scot-free.

You might be living a very competitive life, trying to build a name for yourself or make a good living, and your body might be paying the price for your seldom eating properly or sleeping well; in other dimensions even your bones may have become dark. A body like that can't help but have reactions when it's swiftly purified, like we do. So reactions should be expected. For some of you it may take the form of vomiting or loose bowels. Students everywhere have told me in written accounts about having to look for a bathroom all the way home from our classes. That happens because your internal organs need to be purified. A few of you might fall asleep during the class, only to wake up after I finish my talk. That happens because there was something wrong with your head, and it needed to be put right. You needed to be anesthetized so that you wouldn't feel anything. Yet in some cases the faculty of hearing isn't affected, and you won't have missed a word even if you were sound asleep. Afterwards you will feel invigorated, and you might even go on for a couple of days without needing sleep. You might be coming here with any of various conditions. But whatever they may be, they all need to be dealt with since your whole body must be purified.

If you are sincere about practicing Falun Dafa, you will, starting today, experience physical reactions when you leave attachments behind. Some people aren't able to leave them behind, even if they may tell others that they have, and in that case it's hard to purify their bodies. There might also be people who come to understand things only at the end of the classes and then get over their attachments, at which point their bodies will be cleansed. Others will have already experienced their bodies lightening, while this group will only then begin to have their ailments removed and feel unwell. In each class there are some who don't catch on as quickly and who lag behind. So whatever you experience is normal. Wherever I've taught, I have always found that there are some who feel so ill that they stay in their seats, hunched over and not wanting to leave. They hope that when I come down from the stage I might heal them. But I won't do that. If you can't overcome even this hurdle, I worry what will become of your practice when you meet with serious ordeals down the road. That little bit of discomfort really shouldn't be a big deal, and surely you can get through it. So please don't come to me for healing anymore. It's not something I do, and I'd prefer not to even hear the word "illness."

It's hard to save people from this world. In every class there are always around five to ten percent who fall behind. Not everyone can attain enlightenment. It remains to be seen whether those who stick with the practice can keep up their commitment to spiritual development and succeed at it. Divinity isn't possible for all. You will experience the same benefits from reading this book as you would attending a class, and not miss out on anything, as long as you are sincere about practicing Dafa.

THE
THIRD TALK

I Regard All Who Learn as My Students

THOUGH MANY don't realize it, I regard everyone who learns our practice as a student to guide, and this even applies to those who are sincere about it but are learning on their own. It would actually be irresponsible, and risky, for me to do anything less, since these are teachings that take people to greater spiritual heights. We give so much to you and disclose so many things that the average person isn't suited to know. I am teaching you the Way, and much will be given to you. And I purify your bodies as well as deal with other matters. So it would really be a problem if I didn't take you as my students; it would amount to freely revealing so many secrets to non-practitioners, which is forbidden. But with that said, times have changed and we needn't use initiation rituals involving things like prostrating and bowing to me. We don't perform those rites. They don't serve any purpose for us and would look overly religious. And besides, they would be pointless if afterwards you lapsed into your old, worldly ways, vying for things like status and wealth. The ceremony wouldn't have served any purpose, then. And you might even err further and hurt Dafa's image by doing wrongful things while claiming to be associated with me.

In true spiritual practice everything comes down to how sincere you are about working on yourself. As long as you are able to practice, and do so with a sure footing and commitment, I will take you as my student; it wouldn't be right to do otherwise. Yet some people won't really see themselves as practitioners and keep up the practice—it's just not possible for some. But many of you will, and I will regard those who can as my students and guide you in the practice.

Then what about those who just do our exercises each day—do they count as students of Falun Dafa? Not necessarily, because it's not genuine practice unless someone strives to develop his or her character as we've taught, and does so in earnest. If you just do those exercises without working on your character, there won't be powerful energy to strengthen everything, and it won't amount to spiritual practice. So we can't consider you a student of Falun Dafa in that case. And if you carried on like that, doing the exercises but not working on your character as Falun Dafa teaches, and stuck to your old ways with people, you might run into added trouble. Worse yet, you might even claim that Falun Dafa brought you those troubles. This could very well happen to you. You are a true practitioner only when you sincerely work on your character, as we've taught. Now that I have spelled this out, I hope that you won't come looking for me anymore for student-initiation ceremonies. I will regard you as my student as long as you are practicing in earnest. And you can rest assured that you will be under my care, however many learners we have, since I have countless spiritual bodies that can help.

Buddhist Energy Practices and Religious Buddhism

My remarks should make clear that Buddhist energy practices are not the same as religious Buddhism, and Daoist energy practices are not the same as religious Daoism. Some of our practitioners often conflate the two. Some Buddhist monks, or even lay Buddhists, consider themselves knowledgeable about Buddhism and have been busy promoting it among our community of learners. But they should not do that, for these are different disciplines and should remain distinct. What I am now teaching is the part of our discipline related to one's own, personal spiritual development, and so there are no religious trappings, as a formal religion might have. The only ones who should be engaging in any religious rites are the adherents of Falun Dafa who are monastics or have been religiously ordained. So our practice shouldn't be mistaken for latter day Buddhism.

The teachings of Buddhism are but one small part of the greater Way of the universe. Many other profound teachings exist as well, with there being different truths and insights at each and every plane of existence. The Buddha indicated that there are eighty-four thousand avenues to enlightenment, yet only a handful are to be found in Buddhism, such as Tiantai, Flower Garland, Zen, Pure Land, and Tantric. The number hardly adds up to anything. So Buddhism's teachings don't encompass all of the Way and are but a small part of it. Our Falun Dafa is one path among the eighty-four thousand mentioned, but has never been connected to religious Buddhism at any point in time, from Buddhism's earliest days on up to its latter days, and nor does ours have anything to do with today's religions.

The Buddha began what's known as Buddhism twenty-five hundred years ago in ancient India. Upon reaching enlightenment and having his powers freed, he recalled what he had practiced previously and made it public in order to save people. His practice can be summarized in just three words, even if there are thousands of Buddhist sutras: precept, concentration, wisdom. In Buddhism, precepts are meant to put an end to all the desires people normally experience, and it has prohibitions for monks that cut them off from all that is secular, and that are meant to end their selfish longings, among other things. The adherent's mind thus becomes empty, and deep meditative concentration becomes possible. So precepts and concentration go hand in hand. The heart of the practice is carried out while immersed in deep concentration, meditating; progress is dependent on a still mind. So this is where the real spiritual labors take place in their practice. They don't teach anything involving physical movements or techniques, or transform the person's innate body; they just practice for the type of higher energy that is connected to one's spiritual attainment. So they work solely on character, rather than the body, and don't concern themselves with developing higher energy for the body. Through meditation the practitioner of Buddhism can increase his powers of concentration, and in the process work off his karma by suffering. The term wisdom, meanwhile, is about becoming enlightened and gaining a greater intelligence and spiritual insight. With enlightenment, the workings of the universe will be revealed to the believer and its many dimensions will be seen in full. Miraculous powers will also come about. This process of coming to a greater wisdom, or becoming enlightened, is also referred to as the freeing of one's powers.

Back when the Buddha founded his discipline, there were eight religions active in India. One of them, called Brahmanism, was well established. Throughout his life the Buddha battled with these religions on doctrinal grounds. The *dharma* that he taught was a genuine embodiment of the Way, so it grew ever stronger and more prosperous over the course of his ministry. The other religions of his day steadily declined and weakened, by contrast, with even Brahmanism, despite its strong foothold in India, ending up on the verge of extinction. After the Buddha's *nirvana*, however, the other religions enjoyed renewed popularity, especially Brahmanism. So what exactly happened to Buddhism, then? Certain monks experienced the freeing of their powers and enlightenment to differing degrees, but none were very advanced. Many monks never achieved the status of *tathagata* as the Buddha had.

The Way manifests itself differently at each plane of existence, with higher planes being progressively closer to its truest form and lower planes further from it. After the monks I described gained enlightenment and had powers freed, at lower stages of attainment, they went and interpreted the Buddha's words in light of their own limited visions of the universe or realizations about it. And so there were widely ranging understandings of the Buddha's teachings. Some monks preached their own interpretations to people while attributing them to the Buddha, rather than conveying what he originally had said. In this manner his teachings were altered beyond recognition, and became something altogether different from what the Buddha had once taught. This ultimately led to his teachings dying out in India. It is a serious lesson left to us from history, and explains why Buddhism later disappeared from the face of India. It also underwent multiple reforms before dying out, with it ultimately being mixed with doctrines from Brahmanism, becoming a new religious movement in India known as Hinduism. Faith is no longer placed in the Buddha there, or even any Buddha; other entities are now enshrined instead. This is what has taken place with Hinduism.

Buddhism has gone through several major reforms. One happened not long after the Buddha's passing. This was the creation of Mahayana, or "Greater Vehicle," Buddhism, which was based on the Buddha's more advanced teachings. Its founders held that the *dharma* that the Buddha taught publicly was meant for merely the average listener and could lead only to self-liberation, i.e., attaining the heavenly rank known as *arhat*, since it didn't advocate the salvation of all living things. They thus referred to this publicly taught *dharma* as Hinayana, or "Lesser Vehicle," Buddhism. But that was the original practice from the Buddha's days, and is in fact the form that Southeast Asian monks still observe today. In China people have likewise referred to it as Hinayana Buddhism. Of course, Southeast Asian monks don't think of it that way—i.e., as being "Lesser"—since they believe that they've carried on the Buddha's original practices. And they're correct in thinking that. For the most part they have preserved the forms of practice from his day.

Mahayana's reformed version of Buddhism assumed a set form after spreading to China, and it is the Buddhism seen there today. But it is nothing like the one from the Buddha's day. Everything has changed, from the monastic garb to how people study for and gain enlightenment, to the means of spiritual practice. Buddhism originally enshrined and venerated only Shakyamuni as its founder, yet now it has come to have a plethora of Buddhas and *bodhisattvas*; it's now a polytheistic faith. People place faith in many *tathagata* Buddhas, such as Amitabha, Medicine Buddha, and Vairochana, and there are many senior *bodhisattvas* in the pantheon as well. All of this makes for a Buddhism that's radically different from what Shakyamuni began.

Along with those changes came another reformation. The *bodhisattva* known as Nagarjuna unveiled in India an esoteric practice, which was later transmitted to Afghanistan and eventually made its way to Xinjiang province, from which it spread to the interior of China. It was in the Tang Dynasty that this happened, so the practice has been known as Tang Esoteric Buddhism. The people of China have different values and concepts than most nations, owing to the legacy of Confucianism. Esoteric Buddhism involves the practice of men and women in Tantric union—something not acceptable to society at the time. And so it was eradicated during the Buddhist purges in the Tang Dynasty's Hui Chang era, and vanished from the interior of China. There is still a school of Esoteric Buddhism in Japan, however, known as Shingon, but its founder, who learned the practice in China, never underwent ritual anointment. Yet Esoteric Buddhism holds that anyone who learns its *dharma* without first undergoing anointment is stealing its teachings, and won't be recognized as a legitimate heir to the transmission. Another branch originated in India and passed through Nepal before being transmitted to Tibet. It's referred to as Tibetan Tantric Buddhism, and has been passed down to this day. This is just to give you a very basic sketch of how Buddhism as we know it came to be. Other Buddhist disciplines have come about along the way, such as Zen Buddhism, which Bodhidharma founded, Pure Land Buddhism, and Flower Garland Buddhism. In each case it was begun by an individual who came to a certain understanding of something that the Buddha once taught, so all of these count as reformed Buddhism. Each of the dozen or so Buddhist denominations that exist has assumed a religious form, and should be considered religious Buddhism.

The new religions that came into being this century are by and large false, as are many that were begun around the world in recent centuries. A divine being who comes to save people will necessarily have a heavenly kingdom of his own, and this has been the case for each Buddha that has come offering deliverance, from Shakyamuni to other well-known ones such as Amitabha and Vairochana. In this Milky Way galaxy alone there are more than a hundred paradises such as these, and our Falun Dafa has a corresponding paradise known as the Falun Paradise.

Then where would the followers of false religions go to, if they were in fact saved? These religions haven't the ability to save people in the first place, as it turns out, since what they teach is not the Way. Of course, when religions like these first began it wasn't necessarily the founder's intent to play the devil's part and undermine true faiths. Rather, the person may have experienced some level of enlightenment and had his powers freed, and gained insights, though incomplete, into reality. Yet his spiritual attainment would have been quite limited, in fact, and he would be far from sufficiently divine to save people. He would merely have gained insight into certain facets of reality and have come to see some of the problems with this world. So he would counsel people to do good, and at least initially would not have been in opposition to established religions. Later, however, people would come to place faith in figures like this and venerate them, since people would find their teachings compelling. Their faith in the person would increase over time, such that eventually they came to place faith in *him* instead of a true religion. His desire for worldly influence would grow and lead him to adopt some spiritual title or other, with which he would establish his own, new faith. I can tell you that in all such cases it amounts to heresy. Even if those faiths don't overtly harm people, they are still deviant beliefs since they lead people away from the true faiths. The true faiths offer salvation, whereas the false cannot. And over time the latter do underhanded things. Many of these have spread to China in recent times, such as the so-called "Quan Yin Method." So be on guard, by all means. Reportedly one country in East Asia has over two thousand practices like these, and in Southeast Asia as well as the West there are all sorts of beliefs. In one country they have what is blatantly black magic. All of these are the devil's doing in these latter days. The term "latter days" isn't meant to apply to the circumstances of just one religion, but to the decline experienced by a great many realms spanning from high to low. It refers to the decline of the Way in true religions as well as the fact that humanity has lost its innate moral compass and the self-restraint that would normally come with it.

Staying True to One Practice

We say that you have to stay true to one practice. Regardless of which discipline you decide to do, you shouldn't mix other things into your practice and foul it up. For example, some laypersons practice what's taught in Buddhism right alongside our Falun Dafa. But doing so will ultimately cause them to gain nothing for their efforts; nobody will bestow anything upon them. Though both practices count as Buddhist, there is a problem with your thinking as well as the issue of not staying true to one practice. You have just one body to work with, so which of the two's energy is your body supposed to develop? What kind of transformation would your energy go through? And where are you trying to go? The discipline that you practice will take you to its domain. Practicing Pure Land Buddhism leads to Buddha Amitabha's Paradise of Ultimate Bliss, for example, just as following Medicine Buddha leads to the Lapis Lazuli Paradise. What we're discussing is a common religious tenet, referred to as "only one way."

With spiritual practice, all that's involved in developing higher energy proceeds according to your specific discipline's designs. So those who dabble in different practices, and haven't figured out where they are headed, will end up with nothing to show for their efforts. Just as energy practices and religious practice shouldn't be mixed, neither should two spiritual disciplines, two different energy practices, or even two religions. Even different denominations within the same religion shouldn't be combined. You have to settle upon one. If you practice Pure Land, then it's Pure Land and nothing else; and the same goes for if you choose Tantric Buddhism or Zen, for example. Those who dabble in multiple practices will attain little. So even religious devotional practices should be exclusive and avoid the mixing in of other doctrines or practices. Those faiths are a means of developing higher energy, too, and qualify as spiritual practice just the same, so how they form energy follows the designs specific to their own practices. The means by which higher energy comes about in other dimensions is extremely intricate, profound, and mysterious, and not something to be trifled with as when you freely mix foreign things into your practice.

When some people who are lay Buddhists hear that this is a Buddhist practice, they try to drag learners to a temple for conversion. If anyone here is doing that, you should *not* be. You would be violating our practice as well as the ordinances of Buddhism, disrupting our learners, and causing them to get nothing out of it. All of which are problems. Spiritual practice is a serious matter, and one must stay true to a single practice. Though the part of our practice that the general public* engages in isn't religious, we do share in the same goals as religions have, for we all seek to experience awakening and be spiritually perfected.

The Buddha stated that in the latter days it would be hard even for temple monks to gain salvation, much less lay Buddhists, who would no longer be watched over by higher beings. You might have formally become a student of some teacher, but if that individual isn't doing genuine spiritual practice, then he will be no different from an adherent himself; spiritual progress isn't possible without working on the mind. The ceremonies of conversion are human affairs, and couldn't possibly be all it takes for you to become, for instance, Buddhist, and enjoy the Buddha's care and protection. That's not how it works. And neither will praying and bowing to a statue so fervently that your body aches, nor lighting scores of devotional candles, change anything. What you have to do is really work on your heart and mind with all due sincerity. In the latter days the universe has changed dramatically, and even many places of worship are in a troubled state. Those with special powers (monastics included) have observed this. At present I am the only one anywhere publicly teaching what could actually be called the Way. Never before has anyone done what I am doing, let alone been as welcoming as this, and in these latter days. An opportunity like this is normally very, if not extremely, rare. But your deliverance from this world rests in your own hands, and comes down to whether you have what it takes for spiritual practice. What I teach covers an enormous scope of the universe.

My point isn't that you have to learn Falun Dafa, but to convey a principle. Namely, that in spiritual practice you need to stay true to one practice. Otherwise it simply won't work out. So naturally, if you aren't interested in our spiritual practice, we won't try to coerce you in any way; the teaching is meant for those who are sincere about practicing. So you must commit to one practice and not even mix in concepts from other ones. Nor should you incorporate any techniques related to the mind. Our Falun Dafa doesn't make use of those, and they are not something I teach. This point really has to be heeded. There are basically no mental techniques used in our discipline. This is consistent with the Buddhist belief in "emptiness" and the Daoist idea of "nothingness."

On one occasion I allowed my mind to be linked with the minds of four or five enlightened ones in extremely high realms. Their level of attainment was so great that nonpractitioners would think I was exaggerating were I to describe it. They wanted to read my mind. Others have no way of doing that, given how many years I practiced for; their powers have no way to breach my space. Nobody is able to know me or what I am thinking. Yet in this case, I consented to their wish to know my thoughts, and linked my mind with theirs for a period of time. But once the connection was made I found it hard to take. That's because regardless of my level of attainment, I am part of this mortal world and acting with a purpose—to save people—and my mind is on that. Whereas their minds were so still it was unsettling. Were it just one being who was that still, it wouldn't have been that significant, but there were four or five sitting over there, with stillness like a pool of standing water, and I couldn't sense anything from them. Those few days my mind really felt uneasy; the sensation that was lingering would be hard to describe. That kind of complete emptiness, free of all intention, is beyond what most people could imagine or ever experience.

In advanced practice, the mind is not in any way consciously directed. You were at the beginning stage when you started, as a regular person, and so foundational work was needed. The foundational work, however, has been done for you. Normally by the time more advanced stages are reached, all of the mechanisms related to one's body or energy will have become fully automated, and our practice is a good example of this: you will keep developing higher energy, independent of the exercises, as long as you work on your character. Our exercises merely serve to strengthen the automated mechanisms, while the meditation, which is motionless, brings us to a state of complete inaction. While you might see Daoist practices teaching an array of physical regimens, mental exercises, and ways to guide energy with the mind, all of those,

I can tell you, are dispensed with as soon as adherents progress past the stage of more basic *chi*; visualizations aren't used past that point. Yet some of our practitioners have a hard time moving on from the breathing methods and ways of using the mind that they're familiar with from previous energy exercises or practices. I am offering them university level instruction, so to speak, only to have them ask about elementary things like "guiding energy" and "directing awareness." Those have become the norm for them. True energy exercises for spiritual development are different from what they imagine.

Supernormal Powers and Spiritual Power

There are many who don't have a good command of spiritual terminology, and they get certain terms mixed up. One example is how people confuse the term "supernormal powers" with "spiritual power." The higher energy that comes from working on your character is attuned to the qualities of the universe, and it is derived from virtue. This energy is crucial because it determines your level of spiritual attainment, as well as your spiritual prowess and divine standing. Supernormal powers are something that comes about in the course of practice, and we call them "powers" for short. The higher energy that I just mentioned, which determines your level of attainment, is what's referred to as your "spiritual power." The higher your level of attainment, the greater this will be, and the more potent your powers.

When supernormal or psychic powers appear they are

but a byproduct of the spiritual journey. Experiencing them doesn't say anything about your progress or degree of achievement, nor your spiritual power; they are simply more available to some people than others. Nor should these powers be treated as the main goal of practice; they are not something to be had by effort. They can only be developed through sincere spiritual practice. But they still shouldn't be a motivating goal. If they are, you should ask yourself why. Do you plan to use them around people? They are forbidden from being used like that, and the more you want them, the less likely they will come about. That's because you would be wanting them, and that would be an attachment. And attachments are precisely what spiritual practice aims to do away with.

Plenty of people have reached great spiritual heights without having any powers come to them. Their masters sealed off their powers for fear that they wouldn't exercise self-restraint and would misuse them; their masters prevented them from using their powers along the way. This has been the case for many individuals. Your powers are governed by your thoughts, and so, were the situation otherwise, you could very well lose control over them while asleep in a dream, and awake the next morning to discover that everything around you was laid to waste. Which of course mustn't happen. Since our practice is done in the secular world, whatever great powers someone has generally won't be available to him. The vast majority will be sealed off. But this isn't a hard and fast rule. Many individuals who make solid spiritual progress are allowed to experience some of their powers, since they have good self-control. These are people who would firmly refuse to show them off, if people wanted them to. They have self-control.

Reverse Practice and
the Borrowing of Energy

There are people who have never done an energy practice or have maybe just learned a few techniques at a *tai-chi* or *chi-gong* class, for health reasons rather than spiritual growth, and yet overnight they unexpectedly get energy. I want to explore together how this kind of energy comes about. There are several means.

One way is what's called reverse practice. This happens when someone who is older wishes to do spiritual practice, yet hasn't enough time left to begin the journey from scratch. When *chi-gong* was in its heyday in China not long ago, there were older folks who wanted to practice it, like everyone else. They knew that it could not only lead to self-improvement, but also benefit others. So they were motivated to practice it and better themselves. But remember that when the surge of interest in these practices took place, the teachers involved were only serving to popularize them; none were offering true instruction of a more advanced sort. To this very day I remain the only person to be truly, publicly instructing in a higher practice. At that time the people who experienced reverse practice were over fifty. They were somewhat older but had excellent innate foundations, and what their bodies carried was excellent. They were almost good enough to be selected as apprentices or successors to a master. But these individuals were getting on in years, and it would have been really hard for them to practice. Simply finding a qualified teacher who would instruct them would have been difficult. Yet their wish to practice shined from their hearts like gold, and would echo throughout the universe. It would mean that their divine nature, to use a religious term for it, had shone through.

A person's life, as seen from higher realms, is not meant to be lived as a human being. His or her life was produced in a dimension in the universe, and so it was naturally attuned to the universe's qualities of *zhen, shan, ren* and was originally good and kind. But as beings form relationships with one another and as their numbers increase, certain ones among the group turn selfish or bad. At that point they can no longer remain in the higher, heavenly realm where they began, and must drop to a lower one. If they become bad yet again in the lower realm, they must drop again, with the process repeating until finally they drop to this mortal world. Lives are supposed to be annihilated upon descending to this plane of existence. Yet higher beings decided, out of mercy, to give man one last chance by placing him in the most trying of settings. And that was how this dimension came to be.

In other dimensions people do not have bodies like those here, and they can float in the air and enlarge or shrink. In this dimension, by contrast, people are saddled with the physical bodies that we now have. With this kind of body, cold or heat will be unpleasant, and it's difficult when you are tired or hungry. Pain is inevitable. There are the miseries that come with illness, and you are subject to the cycle of being born, aging, becoming infirm, and then dying. All of which is meant to pay off your karma, through suffering. You are being given one more chance to go back, and that is why you are in this beguiling place. After dropping here, you are furnished with eyes as you now have, which prevent you from seeing other dimensions or seeing the material world for what it is.

Those who make it back, however, will find that the worst of their suffering here was in fact the most valuable. Practicing by relying on faith while in this confusing place is extremely trying, yet it is also what makes a swift return to heaven possible. But if instead you become still worse here, then your soul will be extinguished. So the point of human existence, as higher beings see it, is not to be human but to recover our original purity and go back to our heavenly home. The average person doesn't realize this, however, for this secular world is all he knows, and what tends to occupy his mind is figuring out how to get ahead and live the good life. But the better off he is, the more selfish and greedy he may become, in which case he strays only further from the qualities of the universe and heads for destruction.

That is the view of things as seen from higher realms. What you think of as *progress* might in reality be heading *backward*. People think that they are progressing forward, with science advancing to new frontiers, when in fact things are merely unfolding according to cosmic patterns. Even few Chinese know why the Daoist figure known as Master Zhang Guo rode his donkey sitting backwards. He decided to ride it backwards upon realizing that forward progress was actually a regression. And this is why higher beings consider it so precious when a person has the wish to do spiritual practice, and will freely help him. And similarly, I will do all that I can to help the learners sitting here today who decide on practicing. But I can't help you, and it won't work out, if you are just like the average person who comes in order to get healed, or for other motives. The reason is, in that case you just want to be a regular person, and regular people are meant to experience the cycle of being born, aging, becoming ill, and dying. It is how it should be, and there are deeper workings behind these things that shouldn't be disrupted. Previously, true spiritual practice may not have been a part of your life. But now that you have decided to take it up, the life ahead of you needs to be redesigned, and so we have grounds for rebalancing your body.

So when a person wants to do spiritual practice, higher beings see that intent and consider it simply precious. But [in recent times] it hasn't been possible for these higher beings to support people by finding a teacher in this world to instruct them. What's more, the people I've been describing would have been over fifty and getting on in years. Higher beings cannot come and teach people directly; to reveal themselves and teach the Way and exercises would amount to divulging higher secrets, and their divine standing would be lowered for doing that. Human beings fell into this maze on account of having done wrong, and so they must rely on faith and discernment as they practice here. And for this reason, higher beings cannot teach them. Were a divine being to appear in full glory and teach the Way and exercises, even those who are guilty of unpardonable evil would come to learn, and everyone would believe. Faith and discernment would no longer be involved. That would be a problem, since everyone fell into this maze of their own doing and was supposed to be destroyed—only they have been given a chance to work their way back out. Some will manage to work their way back out, while some won't, and will continue to reincarnate until, eventually, they are destroyed.

The spiritual journey must always be one's own. What could those higher beings do to help, then, if a person wanted to practice? They figured out an approach. As I mentioned, there was a surge of interest in energy practices at the time, which resulted from cosmic changes. So, in keeping with these cosmic tides, the higher beings supplied energy to such a person on the merits of his character. They would attach to his body a type of soft tubing that would act like a water faucet; energy would come forth whenever he turned it on. He would find that energy would come to him if he wished to project it, and wouldn't if he did not. This then is what's meant by "reverse" practice; i.e., the person works towards spiritual perfection in reverse, from what would normally be a higher stage of practice, towards a more foundational one.

Usually a person will progress in practice from a basic stage towards more advanced ones, all the way until his powers become available to him and he achieves spiritual perfection. But in cases of reverse practice, the person is older and there isn't enough time for him to follow the standard progression from basic to advanced; quicker progress could be had by starting directly from the advanced stage. This phenomenon was a product of the times. The person would have to have excellent character, as this would determine how much energy he was given. But what, then, was the purpose of all this? For one thing, it was to support cosmic developments then occurring. Also, the person experiencing it would get to face ordeals while doing good deeds [with his newfound powers]. Since he would be dealing with worldly folk, he might have to interact with all sorts of people. For example, there might be some who misunderstand his healing of them. Though he removes many bad things from their bodies while treating them and cures them of their ailments, that might not be apparent at first. So they might be unhappy about it or might not show him any gratitude. And they might even accuse him of swindling them. Trying scenarios such as these would thus serve to temper the practitioner's mind. So the second purpose of giving him energy was to enable practice and make it possible for him to grow spiritually. And while doing good works he could develop his powers and increase his energy. Not everyone experiencing this would realize it, however. But as I said, the Way couldn't be taught to them and it was up to them to realize what was taking place. It was a question of discernment. And so nothing could be done to help those who were failing to realize what was happening.

When energy came to them, some individuals would suddenly feel unbearably hot as they slept one night, and would have to peel off their blankets. After rising the next morning they would find that they felt static electricity from whatever they touched. Realizing that they now had energy, they might use it to help someone in pain, such as by rubbing the ailing area with their hands, and it would seem to do the job. And they would know that this energy would be at their disposal going forward. So they would act like masters and start an energy healing practice, declaring themselves experts and making a business of it. At first, being good people, they would turn down the money or gifts offered to them for their healings. But the corrupting influence of this world would prove too much for them over time, and they would end up polluted by it. This owed to the fact that those who did reverse practice hadn't gone through the process of working sincerely on their character, and it was hard for them to handle things well. They would gradually go from accepting small tokens of appreciation to accepting larger gifts, to at some point even taking offense at lesser gifts. And they might eventually reject gifts altogether, demanding money instead. And they would take issue if the money offered wasn't enough. They would grow full of themselves from all the praise that they heard, and no longer be respectful of true teachers. Criticism from anyone would upset them. Their attachments to worldly things like status and wealth would grow, and they would think that they outshined everyone else and were something special. They mistakenly believed that they were given energy so that they could become masters and strike it rich, when in fact, it was to make spiritual development possible for them. But as they became increasingly worldly by wanting status and wealth, their character only worsened.

Remember that your energy will only be as great as your character. Not much energy can be provided to someone whose character has sunk, for it is given on the merit of character, and the two are proportionate. The stronger someone's worldly desires are, the lower he sinks in this mundane world, and his energy will drop in kind. Energy will no longer be given if he eventually bottoms out, and he will be left without a trace of it. This has been the case for many in recent years, with a large number being women over fifty. A typical case would involve an older woman who does an energy practice but hasn't ever received true instruction; at most she would have learned a few exercises for health at a class. But then out of the blue, energy comes to her one day. Her character isn't solid, though, and she begins to crave status and wealth, and ends up falling, with nothing to show for her efforts—not even energy. Many who experienced reverse practice have fallen like this, and just a scant few remain who have energy. Their failing was that they didn't realize that the energy given to them was for the purpose of spiritual development, and they mistook it as a means to worldly ends and to a distinguished career as a master, enjoying wealth and renown. But in reality it was meant as a means for spiritual practice.

Another phenomenon involves people borrowing energy. In this case age isn't a factor, but for it to happen the individual involved must be of especially noble character. Typically the person will know that there is something spiritual about energy practice, and they are drawn to it by this. But despite their interest, where would they even begin to look for a good teacher? And even the reputable teachers who *were* around a few years ago would have only been offering instruction meant for health and wellness. There was nobody teaching the kind of practice that leads to higher spiritual realms; no one was doing so.

There is something I want to discuss while on the topic of borrowing energy. Human beings have not only a true soul (a conscious mind), but also a secondary soul (a subconscious mind). An individual might have anywhere from one to as many as five of these secondary souls. Their gender isn't necessarily the same as that of the person, as they might be either male or female, and it differs from person to person. And in fact, the true soul isn't necessarily the same gender as the physical body, either. We have observed that there are now an unusually large number of men with female souls, and women with male souls. This is consistent with the Daoist belief that *yin* forces are dominant in these times, due to a cosmic reversal of *yin* and *yang*.

One's secondary soul usually comes from a higher plane than the true soul, with some having come from realms of exceptional height. Secondary souls should never be confused with possessing entities. These souls are born with you at the same time from the womb, and have the same name as you, as they are physically part of you. Normally it is the true soul that decides what you think about or do. The main task of the secondary soul is to prevent the true soul from doing wrong. Yet when the true soul is headstrong about something, the secondary soul is powerless to help. The secondary soul isn't misled by the secular world, while the true soul easily falls for it.

Some secondary souls hail from realms quite high, and it's possible they are on the verge of attaining a divine standing. The secondary soul might wish to engage in spiritual practice, but it is powerless to do so if the true soul doesn't want to. What used to happen during this time when interest in energy practices in China was at its height, was that the true soul of a certain individual might one day wish to do spiritual practice. The thought was simple and pure, of course, and not tainted by desires for worldly things. The secondary soul would be delighted by this, for it had long wanted to do spiritual practice but hadn't any say, and now this person wanted to as well. But where would this person find a true guide? The secondary soul would be quite resourceful and take leave of the body to seek out the higher beings that it knew from a previous life; it might be possible for it to leave the body since it could be a soul that had come from realms quite high. Upon visiting the higher beings, it would convey its wish to practice and ask to borrow energy. Beings such as these would see that the person was quite good, and naturally be happy to help since it was for purposes of spiritual practice. So this would be how the secondary souls borrowed energy. Often the energy would be a dispersed type that was delivered to the individual via a tube-like conduit. In other cases what was borrowed would come in finished form, and it would typically bring with it supernormal powers.

That being the case, the person might gain powers along with energy, and experience something like what I described earlier, where he's unbearably hot while sleeping at night and awakes the next day with energy. He would feel static electricity from whatever he touched and find that he could do healings for people. He would know that energy had come to him, though not where from. He would just have a sense that it came from somewhere in the universe, but without knowing exactly how. His secondary soul wouldn't tell him, since it was the one engaging in practice, rather than the true soul. All that the individual would know is that energy had come to him.

Age usually wouldn't be a factor in deciding who could borrow energy. The borrowers in recent years have tended to be younger, with people in their twenties, thirties, and forties experiencing it as well as older folks. Younger people find it harder to handle themselves well, however. They might be good people under normal circumstances, and take worldly things lightly when they're nobody special. But after a taste of success they are apt to fall prey to the lure of things like status and wealth, and start becoming ambitious about life, and want to throw their hat in the ring and fight for their piece of the pie. So it's quite possible that they would regard their powers and newfound abilities as a means of achieving selfish, worldly ends. That's a problem, though. Those powers aren't to be used in that way, and doing so will come at the cost of energy. So these individuals would end up devoid of any energy. Even more of this group have fallen; not one is left now, from what I've seen.

In both scenarios I just described, the individuals involved had excellent character initially. Their energy wasn't the result of practicing, but rather, was provided by higher beings. So naturally the energy was good.

Entity Attachment

Many of you may have heard from various religious traditions about animal spirits such as those of foxes, weasels, hedgehogs, or snakes attaching to human bodies, and wonder what it's about. People claim that energy practices can develop psychic powers, but that's not how it works; what people are taking to be psychic powers are actually innate human abilities. It's merely that as the world progresses, people are increasingly fixating on the tangible things of this physical dimension and growing more dependent on modern technology. This has led to a steady decline of our innate abilities to the point we are at now, where they are disappearing altogether.

To gain psychic powers you have to first recover your original state of purity through disciplined spiritual practice. Animals, on the other hand, haven't the complicated thinking that man does. The qualities of the universe flow through them, as a result, and so their innate powers are available to them. Some people claim that snakes or other animals know how to practice or that foxes know how to amass energy. But that's not the case; they too begin with no knowledge of it. It's merely that their innate powers are available to them. That said, it is possible for animals to gain energy or even psychic powers with the right conditions, the right setting, and enough time.

In this manner animals can come to have certain abilities, which have previously been referred to as psychic energy or special powers. To ordinary people, animals like these might seem formidable and easily able to dominate man. But I would say they're nothing of the sort. They pale in comparison with a true practitioner. It would take barely your little finger to crush them, even if they have practiced nearly a thousand years. So while we do believe that animals have certain innate powers and can gain abilities, there remains a law in this universe that animals *may not* practice, let alone succeed at it. That's why in ancient texts you might read of disasters large and small wiping out animals every several centuries. If at some point an animal does manage to develop energy, it might be eliminated by a thunderbolt or the like. They are forbidden to practice since they don't have human nature and cannot practice as man does. They lack the qualities that human beings have and would surely become fiends if they were to practice and succeed at it. So they aren't allowed to and would incur divine wrath if they did. And they are aware of this. But the world has declined terribly, as I've indicated, and there are people who do all manner of evil. I think you would have to agree that humanity is in peril.

But the pendulum always swings back eventually. We have found that each time in prehistory when civilization was cyclically destroyed, it occurred when people's moral values had been terribly corrupted. The dimension in which we now exist is in imminent danger, as are many others; the same is true for other dimensions at this plane. Animals want to quickly flee and climb to higher planes since they think that this would bring them safety. But it's not that simple, since a human body is necessary for spiritual progress. So this is one reason why some spiritual practitioners have fallen prey to entity attachment.

Some people might wonder why no higher beings or powerful masters have put a stop to this. It's because the way this universe works is that nobody is going to stop you if you've decided upon something. Here we simply teach you how to go about the practice correctly and explain the teachings in depth, while leaving it up to you what to make of them. You decide for yourself whether you want to learn the practice. As it's said, "the master teaches the trade, but the apprentice's skill reflects his own efforts." Nobody will force you or coerce you to practice, for it is always your own personal decision. This means that nobody will try to dissuade you once you have decided upon a certain course, or try to change what you want or hope to gain. Others can only try to encourage you to do what's best.

When some people do an energy practice, the benefits of it are all in fact reaped by attached entities. Then how common is this on a national scale, and how did those entities get on people in the first place? It's so common that the number is alarming; many people would be scared away from these practices if I were to give figures. This begs the question of how the problem came about, then—something as serious as spirit entities disrupting the world. It turns out that it's something people have brought upon themselves. Demons lurk everywhere now, due to people's depravity. Those entities on the bodies of false teachers are a telling example, and those teachers in fact spread these when they teach. Yet never in history were animal spirits allowed to attach to human bodies. Any that tried to would be killed; no one who saw it would let it slide. But in today's world people pray to them, ask for them, and even worship them. Now while you might be thinking that you've never done anything like that knowingly, you may have wanted to get extrasensory powers. The divinities who oversee the authentic spiritual traditions would never grant you such powers, since your yearning is a worldly attachment that should go. Only animals or demons from other realms would grant them to you. Those entities will come to you when you try to gain special powers, for it's as good as inviting them.

You'd be surprised by how many people start practicing for the wrong reasons. In spiritual practice one needs to strive to be virtuous, do good works, and act with kindness at all times and in all places. Yet despite all the people doing energy practices out in the parks or at home, few are thinking in that way. In some cases, I don't even know what they are doing. They will be swaying all about as they practice, and even complaining about things like how neglectful their daughter-in-law is or how bad their mother-in-law is. And some people go on about anything and everything, from issues at work to national affairs, even getting angry about the things that aren't agreeable to them. But could that count as practicing? Another example might be someone who practices by holding a stance so long that his legs start to tremble, yet his mind isn't at peace. He might be thinking about how expensive things are getting nowadays, and be worrying about whether his workplace can make the payroll, which gets him thinking about supernormal powers and how he could become a healer with them and get wealthy. And he will only get more anxious about it when he sees others gaining powers, and then try all the harder to get powers like higher vision or the ability to heal. Think about just how far that is from the qualities that underlie the universe—*zhen, shan, ren*. It's completely counter to them. You could say that his practice has turned evil. But he wouldn't be aware of this. And if his mind goes further down that road, the thoughts that he emits will grow only worse. But this is someone who hasn't learned the Way or the importance of being virtuous. So he mistakenly thinks that powers will come to him by his own efforts in practicing, and that he can get whatever he wants through effort.

It is only because the person's thoughts aren't wholesome that he attracts bad things. Animal spirits can see when someone wants to gain renown, wealth, or powers from practicing. They'll be delighted by this, since the person's physical makeup might be pretty good and his body might have great things in it. And they will see that his thoughts are awful, since he seeks paranormal powers. But they won't be scared off even if he in fact has a master. They know that the more someone wants those powers, the more determined his master will be *not* to grant them; particularly the master of a true practice, who would see it as an attachment to be broken. So the person's strong attachments will only make it less likely that he's granted special powers. But if he doesn't come to realize it, he will keep at it and his thinking will grow only worse. Ultimately his master will have no choice but to sadly abandon him, since he seems hopeless. Some individuals who don't have a master might have one in passing, who keeps an eye on them for a bit. This is common, given how many higher beings are present in other worlds. He will observe the person a bit after spotting him. But after only a day or so of following and observing the person, it will be apparent that he hasn't got what it takes, and the master will depart. The next day the same scenario might play out with another master, only to have him, too, discover that this person isn't suitable, and so he departs as well.

An animal will know that the person's master, be it his own or one-in-passing, won't grant him what he wants. Animals can't see the realms of higher beings, and so they aren't afraid of those beings and exploit one of the laws of the universe, namely, that normally nobody should try to stop someone from going after what he wants. So animals figure there is nothing wrong with giving the person what he wants, and they do just that. At first an animal won't have the nerve to latch on. What it does instead is to give the person some energy as a test-run. So one day, unexpectedly, the person really does get energy like he'd hoped for and can even use it for healing. But that was just the opening act, so to speak. The animal will see that it's going over well and that the person is receptive, and decide to get on his body under the guise of providing more energy, more directly. It will see that this person wants to have his inner eye opened, and it's happy to give him everything. And so it affixes itself to his body.

So the person's inner eye gets opened, just as he longed for, and what's more, he gains the ability to project energy, along with other, lesser powers. He's delighted by all of this and thinks that he has finally achieved what he has been practicing for. But the truth is, none of it has resulted from his efforts practicing. And nor has his inner eye actually been opened, even if it seems that he can see into people's bodies and discover what ails them. Rather, it's that the animal is manipulating his brain. What the animal does is to convey what *it* sees with its own eyes to the person's brain, which leads him to believe that his inner eye has opened. And he's sure to try to project energy. But what happens is that when he extends his hand to send out energy, the animal extends a paw out from behind his body; or perhaps, in some cases, it's a snake that has attached to the person, which sticks out its forked tongue from its little reptilian head toward the person's ailment or tumor, and licks at it. Many cases of entity attachment fall into this category, where it's something the person brings upon himself.

So, as a result of his longing for worldly things, the person now has extrasensory powers, can do healings, and see with his inner eye, all to his great delight. The animal might see that he yearns for money and fulfill his wish. It's incredibly easy to manipulate the minds of ordinary people. And so the animal might direct droves of people to come see the person for energy healing. Goodness, he'll be giving treatments there while the animal is off directing the media to give him publicity. It can make ordinary people do things like that. And if those who come to him for treatments don't pay him enough, the animal can make them have a headache or do whatever it takes to coax more money out of them. So status and wealth both come to him; not only does he get a windfall, but also a dose of fame as some kind of master. The people this applies to aren't typically attentive to their character, and make outlandish claims, as if they were second only to God. They might go so far as to say they're the Queen Mother of Heaven or Jade Emperor in the flesh, or even a Buddha. They never went through the process of earnestly working on their character, and so they want to get psychic powers with their practice. And this is how they end up with an animal spirit on them.

Some of you might be thinking that it's not a big issue, given all the prestige and income that would come from it. And no small number of people are thinking that way.

But I can tell you that the animal has its own agenda, and it won't give you something for nothing. The way the universe works is that everything comes at a cost. Something is in it for the animal, as I just touched on, which is a chance to obtain the limited bit of essence that your body has. This can then be used to develop a human form; they seek to take the essence of people's bodies. But your body has just that limited bit of essence, and your spiritual progress is dependent upon it. If you let an animal take it away you might as well forget about practicing, for you wouldn't have what it takes; the material needed simply wouldn't be there. Progress just wouldn't be possible. Now, some people might dismiss this concern since they're not interested in spiritual practice to begin with and just have their sights set on money. But I think you'll want to reconsider it after I explain a few things. Here's why. Your limbs might be lame after the animal leaves your body, even if it doesn't stay on you long. And that could be a lifelong condition, since it might have taken too much of your essence. Worse yet, if it leaves your body later than this, you could become a vegetable and be bedridden for the rest of your life, hanging by a thread. So even if you did get rich or famous, could you enjoy it? It's a frightening prospect.

What I described is a significant problem among people who do energy practices today, and there are many cases of this. Those entities not only possess the body but kill off the person's soul; they burrow into the Niwan Palace and stay there. So while the person might seem to be human, he is not. It's a telling reflection of the state of the world. There are people who won't be convinced if you see them doing wrong and point it out, for humanity's moral fabric has changed. They think that the endless pursuit of wealth is perfectly justified, and will trample on and hurt others and stop at nothing for it. But those spirit entities, which want to take from your body, won't let you enjoy such wealth for free—everything comes at a cost. So these problems are of people's own making; they stem from people's thoughts not being right or virtuous.

Now let's see how this applies to Falun Dafa. You won't experience any of the problems we just discussed while doing our practice, as long as you can keep your thoughts in check, since good is a far greater force than evil. But if you can't keep your thoughts pure, and you have other intentions mixed in, then you are asking for trouble. Some people just can't let go of what they formerly practiced. We teach that you have to commit to one practice, as any legitimate discipline will tell you. You shouldn't think so highly of teachers of practices who have been published. I can tell you that in some cases their books are plagued by the same sorts of things that their practices are, such as snakes, foxes, and weasels. If you read those books, the animals will leap out from behind the words at you. As I've indicated, charlatans outnumber the true masters many times over, and you can't tell them apart. It's vital that you realize this. My point here isn't that you have to practice Falun Dafa. It's fine for you to do whatever practice you'd like. But there used to be a saying: better to go a thousand years without learning a true doctrine than spend one day practicing a false one. It's advice you definitely want to heed. With real practice of the true Way, you don't want to mix anything in—not even mental techniques. Some people's *falun* have become deformed. If you probe why, they will say that they didn't practice anything else, and wonder what happened. But the fact is, when they do our exercises they add things in with their minds from their former practices. And naturally that's going to bring foreign things in. I'll just say this much on the topic of entity attachment.

Cosmic Tongues

There is a phenomenon that's sometimes referred to as speaking in "cosmic tongues." It happens when a person is spontaneously able to speak a kind of confusing babble, which even he or she can't understand. Someone with telepathic abilities might have a general sense for it, but won't be able to make out the specifics of what's being said. And some people can speak multiple languages. Some who do this think it's a special power or gift, and take pride in it. But it's not the kind of power or gift that a practitioner would have, and it doesn't indicate spiritual achievement. So what is it, then? It is a case of one's mind having been taken over by an entity from another dimension. And yet people may think it's a great thing, be pleased to experience it, and be happy about it. Yet the happier they are, the tighter that entity's grip on them becomes. I think you would have to agree it's not befitting a practitioner to let something like that control you. And besides, those entities come from awfully low realms. Since we are people engaged in true spiritual practice, we don't want to invite that kind of trouble.

Man is the most precious life form and the highest of all creatures. So it's terribly inappropriate to let those entities take over you. How sad that people would relinquish control over their own bodies! Some of those entities attach to a person's body, while some don't but instead keep a short distance and manage to direct you or control you all the same. These entities grant the ability to speak their languages to people who want it, and these individuals then find that they can speak a sort of gibberish. This ability can also be spread from one person to another. Maybe an onlooker wants to learn to do it, so he plucks up his courage, opens his mouth, and finds that he too can speak it. But in reality, what happens is that those things come in swarms, and if someone wants to speak in tongues, one of them will get on him and make it happen.

So why has this phenomenon come about? It's similar to what I described earlier; i.e., that those entities want to go to higher realms, but since there is no suffering in their dimension, they have no way to practice or elevate. So they came up with the approach of trying to do good things for people. But they didn't know how to go about it, though they did know that the energy they emit could have a soothing effect on the sick and temporarily alleviate pain, even if it couldn't effect a cure; and they saw that they could accomplish this by using people's mouths to emit their energy. So this is what it boils down to. People have referred to it as a "divine language" or "Buddha's language." But that's blasphemous and downright absurd.

You should know that divine beings speak only with great discretion. If they spoke in this dimension they might trigger earthquakes in the world. It would be terrible, with such a thundering sound. So while some people may claim that they saw with their inner eye that a higher being spoke to them, that's not what happened, in fact. And the same holds true in cases where people believe that my spiritual bodies spoke to them. What happens is that the thoughts they project are accompanied by stereo sound, and so to you it seems as if they have spoken. They are capable of speaking in their dimensions, but if people in our world were to hear them directly, it would be unintelligible. This owes to differences in space-time between the two dimensions: a two-hour block of time in this dimension might be a year in the large dimensions where they are. Time is slower in our world than over there.

Yet there is a saying that "a day in the heavens amounts to a thousand years on earth." The saying refers to independent worlds where there is no such thing as space or time; namely, the worlds where divine ones reside, such as the Paradise of Ultimate Bliss, the Lapis Lazuli Paradise, the Falun Paradise, and the Lotus Paradise. The time in the large dimensions I mentioned, by contrast, is faster than ours here. If you have the ability to receive and hear what a being there says, as when your celestial ear has opened [and you have clairaudience], you will be able to hear those divinities speaking. But you won't be able to make out what they say. Whatever you hear would sound like the twitter of birds or a turntable playing at a high speed. You wouldn't be able to make out a single word. Of course, there *are* people who can hear music or speech from another dimension. But for that to be possible they must have a power that serves as a vehicle and fixes the discrepancy in time, and only then, when it's transmitted to their ears, can they hear with clarity. So that is what's at work. "Cosmic tongues" are most definitely not some kind of divine speech, contrary to what's been claimed.

When two divine beings meet, they need only smile to one another to convey whatever they intend. They may use a type of silent telepathy that takes the form of stereo sound in the ears of the receiver. With but a smile they can exchange their thoughts. However, they don't rely on one method alone, and sometimes use other means. You may know that the lamas of Tibetan Esoteric Buddhism hold *mudras* in high regard. They will tell you, if asked, that *mudras* are the supreme yoga. If you probe further you will find that they don't know more beyond that. *Mudras* are hand movements that are actually a language of the divine. Divine ones use larger *mudras* in the presence of a larger audience, and they are both exquisite and diverse; in the presence of a smaller group they use smaller *mudras*, which are also pleasing to the eye and widely varying. *Mudras* are very sophisticated and rich, since they are a language after all. All of this used to be a guarded secret, but now I've disclosed it. Tibetan *mudras* represent just a few of the many that exist, having been drawn from them and systematized for use in Esoteric practice. They just amount to a language that's been adopted for purposes of practice, and there are only a few, limited forms associated with this. Actual *mudras* are quite elaborate.

What I Do for Learners

When some people meet me they grab hold of my hand and shake it, and just don't want to let go. And others, upon seeing this, want to shake my hand in a normal way. I know what thoughts are behind it in each case. For some learners it's simply that they are happy to be able to shake hands with their teacher, but for others it's about getting energy, and that is why they hold fast to my hand and won't let go. But let me remind you that true practice is about you. We are not here to heal you or build up your health, so we aren't about to give you energies or do healings. We don't engage in those things. Any diseases that you have will be eliminated by me right here, while those who learn the practice at our exercise sites, or by studying the book on their own, will have theirs handled by my spiritual bodies. It's humorous, isn't it, to think that people could get higher energy just by touching my hand?

Higher energy comes only through working on your character. It won't increase if you don't sincerely work on yourself, for the quality of your character is the limiting factor. Beings in higher realms can see that higher energy develops when you remove your attachments and their material, and that atop your head a measuring stick materializes. The stick exists in the same way as your energy column, and its height will determine that of your energy. It signifies how much of it you have cultivated and it reflects your quality of character. It's not something that anyone can boost for you. Even if just a tiny bit were added, it wouldn't hold and would have to fall off. I could have you instantly reach the stage of practice known as "three flowers gathered at the crown," but the energy involved would fall off as soon as you left here. It wouldn't be yours since you hadn't cultivated it, and so it couldn't remain there. Nobody could put energy there for you since your character hadn't reached that stage. It must be the fruits of your own spiritual efforts, of your own refinement of the mind. Spiritual progress is only possible if you work solidly on developing higher energy, constantly improve, and attune yourself to the qualities of the universe. And this is why I'm reluctant to accommodate autograph seekers. If I did, they would show off by telling others about it, and hope to get protection from the energy that the autographs have. But isn't that again an attachment? You have to do your part in spiritual practice, so there's no point in hoping for protective energies. Some-one who is well advanced in practice would hardly concern himself with such things. They don't amount to much and are only relevant to people who are into energy practices for health purposes.

The higher form of energy that you develop through spiritual practice is, on a deep, subatomic plane, composed of particles in your image. Once your practice has gone beyond the human realm, it will be a divine body you are developing. Your energy will then have the image of a divine being, and this being will sit atop a lotus flower and be exceptionally beautiful. And every tiny particle will be like this. The energy that animals have, by contrast, is always in the image of things like small foxes or snakes, and even their tiny particles at a deep, subatomic plane are like that. Another thing is that some people drink teas that supposedly have "psychic energies" mixed in, without giving thought to what kind of energy is involved. Most ordinary people are happy to just postpone and suppress their health problems, as long as they can get temporary relief. That's only to be expected. But however much harm they might be doing to their bodies, it's none of our business, still. I am only disclosing these things to you because you are practitioners. You shouldn't be dabbling in psychic energies or going in for those things anymore. You should want no part in them. Some teachers of energy practices claim that they can transmit psychic energies to people around the country. But I don't know what you could expect to get out of that. I can share that it won't do much for you, and even if there is something positive to it, it's just for health purposes. As people engaged in spiritual practice, we have to depend on our own efforts to develop energy; any psychic energies supposedly sent to you wouldn't do anything for your spiritual growth. They only offer health benefits for regular people. It's critical that you keep your thinking straight. Nobody can do spiritual practice on your behalf. Progress can only come from your own, sincere efforts.

You'd probably like to know what I do give you, then. Many among us here have never practiced before and have various ailments, as you might gather. There are also many who have done energy practices before, even for years, but who still linger at the basic stage of *chi* energy and who haven't any higher energy. And of course there may be some among you who do healings, but don't realize what's involved. When I discussed the problem of entity attachment, I took off all such things from your bodies, regardless of what they were, inside or out. They are gone now from the bodies of all of you who are sincere in practicing Dafa. And similarly, I will cleanse the bodies of anyone who becomes sincere in the practice after learning it on their own. Your surroundings at home need to be cleaned up as well. You should get rid of any shrines to the spirits of what may have in fact been foxes or weasels; those spirits have now been cleaned out and are gone. We can do all of what I've described and make things as easy as possible for you because you have the desire to practice. But this only holds true for those who are sincere about it. Some people have no real interest in spiritual practice, of course, and even at this point still haven't come around. So we can't look after them. We can only take care of those who are sincere about the practice.

There are also people who at one time were told, or had sensed, that entities were attached to their bodies. I removed those for them, yet they still worry that the problem persists, that those things are still there. But this counts as an attachment, and it's called *doubt*. And if they go on like this they might just bring those entities back again. So they should stop having doubts, and know that I eradicated those things for them during my classes. All of those things were removed.

Early stages of Daoist practice require certain foundations to be laid, which include forming a cosmic orbit and energy center along with other things. What we do here is to place in you a *falun*, energy mechanisms, and a wide array of things needed for spiritual development—thousands upon thousands. All of these must be given to you, and they are planted in you like seeds. Once your ailments are purged for you, all that should be done for you will be done, and all that should be given to you will be given in full. Only then will true spiritual achievement be possible for you in our practice. Were we to do anything less, and not provide much, the practice would only serve health purposes. And actually, anyone who isn't serious about character would probably be better off just doing regular physical exercises.

We take responsibility for true practitioners. All that I've described will be done for you as long as you are sincere about spiritual development, even if you are doing our practice on your own. As I've said, we need to take all of you as students and guide you in earnest. Along with this, it's a must that you learn the Way of higher realms thoroughly and know how to practice it. I will instruct you in our full program of exercises, all five, right from the start, and you will find that you can master them all. Eventually you might well attain spiritual heights beyond what you could imagine, and even a divine standing will be possible. As long as you keep at the practice you will find that the teachings always offer the guidance you need at different stages, since there are many dimensions to what I teach.

Now that you practice, the course of your life will be changed. My spiritual bodies will rework things for you. Let me explain. There are some people who only have limited time left to live, though they wouldn't realize it; serious illness might strike in half a year or a year, and could go on for years; or it could be that a stroke will occur or some condition comes on, which leaves them immobile. But practice wouldn't be possible if that were the life ahead of you. So we have to clear those things out for you and ensure that they don't take place. But there's one thing: this can only be done for those who are sincere about practice. It would be wrong for me to freely do such things for regular, worldly people. There are reasons for the ordeals of life that people are subject to, and they can't be rashly undone.

We regard those who engage in spiritual discipline as the most valuable of all people, so their lives can be altered—but theirs alone. Here's how it works. If a teacher has great spiritual power, i.e., if the strength of his energy is great, then he can dissolve karma for you. A teacher whose energy is great can dissolve much of it, while one whose isn't can only dissolve a small amount. To give you a sense for it, let's say that we gather together the various forms of karma that await you in your life, and dissolve a portion of it—say, a half. But if even just a half were to remain it would be too much for you, as it would still be larger than a mountain. Then how is it dealt with? Many people stand to benefit from your gaining enlightenment someday, and so they will be given a portion of the karma to bear for you. It normally doesn't amount to anything for them, since the karma will be distributed among so many other entities, as well—from the many supernatural beings that you will have developed within your body, to the many other selves that you have, not to mention your true and secondary souls. This means that there will be relatively little left to bear when you go through ordeals. Little as it may be, though, it *is* still sizeable, and you still wouldn't be able to bear it all at once. The solution, then, is to divide the karma up into many, many portions and distribute them throughout different stages of your practice so that you may perfect your character and develop your energy as you work through them.

It should be said that spiritual practice is not easy. It's a very serious matter, as I see it. It is greater than anything of the mundane world and more challenging than anything known. It goes beyond this world, doesn't it? And so the demands it places on you are greater than anything people know. This is partly because every person's soul is immortal. So your soul is apt to have done wrongful things to people in previous incarnations. You might have killed people, become indebted, been abusive, or hurt people. Those whom you wronged will see clearly, in other dimensions, the progress you make as you practice here. If you were just practicing to heal your body, they wouldn't think anything of it, since they would know that you were just deferring the payback on your debts, which would only be worse later on. And so they wouldn't mind if you didn't pay up for the time being.

But if you take up *spiritual* practice, they won't stand for it. They will think, "You're trying to do spiritual practice and leave here, but once you have higher energy I won't be able to get you anymore, I won't be able to touch you." So they won't go for it, and will try to block your practice and do anything and everything to get in your way. They will plague you in all kinds of ways, and may even try to kill you. Of course, they won't be able to do that and behead you, for example, right there as you meditate, since that would be out of place in this world. So it might happen that you are hit by a car when you go out, that you fall off a roof, or meet with some other form of danger—any of which would be quite perilous. True spiritual practice isn't as easy as you might have imagined; progress doesn't happen just by wishing for it. So you might face imminent, mortal danger once you really begin the spiritual journey. A large number of teachers won't even attempt to bring their students to higher stages of practice, for this very reason. They haven't the means to protect them.

Many past teachers could only mentor one student at a time, for that was all that they could protect. Most wouldn't attempt to take on and protect as many as we have. But as I have indicated, I can do this due to the countless spiritual bodies I have, each of which is endowed with the same great powers of the Way that I have, and they can exercise these with the force of the Way. Also, there is more to what we are doing today than meets the eye; I didn't undertake this on an impulse. I can share with you that there are many higher beings focusing their attention on this, for this is now, in the latter days, the last time we shall impart a true Way. So with something as great as what we're doing, it's imperative that we not veer from the right course. Nobody will dare to rashly do anything to you as long as your practice stays on track. And besides, you have the protection of my spiritual bodies. So no harm will come to you.

Accounts do have to be settled, though, so it's possible some dangerous things will take place on your spiritual journey. But those events won't be frightening to you nor result in any serious harm coming to you. I can give some examples. There was one person who was taking our class in Beijing. She was crossing the street on her bike when a car suddenly rammed into her while rounding a corner. This learner was a woman over fifty. The car hit her out of nowhere, and it was a terrible collision. Her head hit the roof of the car hard, with a loud bang. The impact was so sudden and hard that she was still astride her bike when her head hit the car, yet she didn't feel any pain. And not only that, but there wasn't any blood or even swelling. The driver was scared out of his wits, though. He sprang from the car and said, "Are you hurt? Let's get you to the emergency room." She responded by telling him that she was "just fine." It goes without saying that this was someone of excellent character. She wasn't about to give the driver a hard time. Though she was fine, as she indicated, the collision had left a big dent in the car.

Events like that are meant to take your life, but you won't be at risk. To give another example, the last time we gave a class at Jilin University, there was a learner who had just left the campus and walked his bike through the front gate. When he was crossing the street, two cars came at him from out of nowhere and were about to sandwich him. Even at that instant, though, he wasn't the least bit scared. And that's common for our practitioners in these kinds of episodes. As it turned out, the cars came to a halt just before hitting him, and he was fine.

Another incident happened in Beijing. Nightfall comes early in the winter there and people retire for sleep somewhat early; the streets are usually deserted and still. Someone who was learning the practice was biking home swiftly, and the only thing ahead of him on the road was a jeep. The jeep was driving along when suddenly it hit the brakes. Our student didn't notice it, and kept pedaling with his head down. But the jeep abruptly went into reverse, and was backing up at a fast speed and going to crash into him. The colliding of the two forces was meant to take his life. But just as they were about to collide, out of nowhere there came a power that pulled the student's bike back more than half a yard, and the jeep came to a halt just as it touched his wheel. Maybe the driver realized that someone was behind him. This student wasn't scared when it happened. And that's true for all the others who have gone through things like these; at most they might have felt frightened after the fact. In this case, our student was merely surprised and his first thought was that he should thank whoever pulled him back. He turned around to thank them, only to discover that the street was quiet, without a soul in sight. Then it dawned on him that it was actually his teacher who had protected him!

There was another incident, this time in the city of Changchun. A building was going up near the home of someone who was learning the practice. Buildings are built really high nowadays, and the scaffolding used during the construction phase consists of steel poles two inches wide and four yards long. This practitioner hadn't gone far from home when a steel pole fell vertically from the scaffolding of one such building, and was coming down right straight toward his head. The passersby froze with fear when they saw it. But the next instant, our student was asking who had patted him, as he thought that someone had patted him on the head. He turned around and noticed a large *falun* spinning overhead. Only then did he realize that a pole had fallen and just grazed his head, barely missing him. It fell with enough force that it stuck into the ground, straight up. You can just imagine what would have happened if it had struck him with all that force—it would have been like skewering fruit on a stick. It could have been disastrous.

There have been countless incidents like these, but no danger has ever really materialized. Yet you won't necessarily go through anything like that, personally. Only a very few of us will. But either way, I can assure you that practitioners of ours won't be in any true danger. There are some people, however, who act without regard to character, unlike what the teachings set forth. They only do the exercises and don't work on their minds, in which case they can't be considered practitioners.

So you now know what I give you as your teacher. My spiritual bodies will constantly protect you until the day comes when you can protect yourself, at which point you will be about to surpass the mundane world in your practice and gain enlightenment. You have to see yourself as a true practitioner, though, for that to ever be possible. If you are sincere in the practice you will never be like the person who once walked down the street waving my book, shouting about having "Master Li's protection" and not being afraid of traffic. Doing that was harmful to Dafa, and someone like that won't be protected.

The Field That Our Energy Has

A field forms around us when we do our exercises. As for what it is, exactly, people have given various descriptions, from its being a *chi* field, to a magnetic field, to an electric field. But none have been very fitting, for the field around us consists of extremely diverse types of matter. Virtually every kind of matter that makes up the universe's dimensions is found in the kind of higher energy that we develop. So it's more fitting to call it an *energy field*, and that's how we usually refer to it.

Let's talk about what exactly this field does. As you know, we are practicing a true Way that embraces compassion and that's perfectly attuned to the universe's qualities of *zhen, shan, ren*. And so, many of you know or have experienced that you don't have any bad thoughts while attending our class; and those who have a history of smoking won't even think of doing so. It feels very serene and pleasant in this space. And that is what the energy of practitioners of a true Way is like and how it feels in their presence. By the end of this class the vast majority of you will have really, truly developed higher energy, since I am giving you what's needed for authentic practice, while you, on your part, are working on your character in light of our teachings. And as you continue to do so, and keep at the practice, your energy will grow only more powerful.

We subscribe to the belief in saving all living things, and not just achieving our own liberation. And so the *falun* benefits you as it turns inward, and others as it turns outward. When it turns outward it disperses energy, to the benefit of others. So whoever is within the range of your energy field will benefit, and might find it noticeably pleasant. And you might have this effect on people wherever you are, be it out on the street, at the workplace, or at home. You might be unwittingly rebalancing the bodies of whoever is in your presence, since it has the power to correct anything not right. And that includes the ailments of the body, since the human body is meant to be free of such things; illness is not the normal state of the body. Similarly, your field could have the power to alter any improper thoughts that might be going through the mind of someone immoral who is in your presence. Or it might cause someone who was about to use foul language to change his or her mind suddenly and not do so. But this is only possible with the field of energy that comes from doing true spiritual practice. You should now be able to understand an old Buddhist saying that goes, "Bathed in divine light, conduct and thought become right."

How to Introduce the Practice to Others

Many people think highly of the practice after attending our classes, and want to share it with their family and friends. That's fine to do. You can share it with anyone. But there is one thing I need to explain. There's no way to put a price on all that we have done for you. It is done solely on grounds of practicing, and wouldn't be possible otherwise. This means that when you share the practice with others, you shouldn't try to gain from it personally. So you can't collect fees the way we do for our classes. Fees are necessary for us to cover the costs of printing books and materials, as well as for all the travel involved when teaching this practice. The fees that we have are the lowest in the country, yet we offer more than anyone else does, as you know, since we are truly guiding people to greater spiritual heights. We have the following two rules for you, as students of Falun Dafa, for when you introduce the practice to people.

The first rule is that you must not charge a fee. All that we give you is to save you and prepare you for spiritual practice—not to benefit you in worldly ways. If you charge a fee, my spiritual bodies will recall everything that was given to you, and you will cease to be a practitioner of Falun Dafa. You wouldn't be teaching people Falun Dafa in that case. You should introduce it to people without any thought of gaining from it personally. It should be a voluntary gesture in the service of others. Our students everywhere have taken this approach, and our volunteers in each locale have set a good example with this. Everyone who is interested is welcome to come and learn the practice, and we will always help them free of charge.

The second rule is that you mustn't confuse Dafa proper with your own experiences or interpretations of it. For example, when you introduce the practice to someone you should simply explain Falun Dafa on its own terms, and not in terms of what you may have seen with your inner eye or come to know through special powers. Those limited insights you have gained at your current stage of practice really don't amount to much, and cannot begin to compare to the actual teachings in profundity. So it's crucial that you be careful about this when you introduce the practice from now on. By doing so we will be able to preserve the integrity of Falun Dafa's teachings.

It's also not permitted for you to teach the practice the way I do, addressing large audiences like when I give a teaching, for the Way is not something you yourself can teach. That is because what's being taught is deep and far-reaching, and has many dimensions to it. You are still working your way through the various stages of practice, however, and will find that you keep making progress and arriving at new insights, with new rewards in store for you, as you keep listening to the recordings of our teachings. And that's even more the case with reading the book. There are many layers to what I teach, and it's not something you could instruct in. Nor should you use my words as your own, as that would amount to plagiarizing my teachings. What you should do is to say precisely what I have said and indicate that it's what I have said or written. And that's really the only way to go. The reason is, when you say it this way it will carry the power of Dafa. But if, instead, you tell people your own ideas as if they were Falun Dafa proper, then you are not in fact sharing our practice with them, and it amounts to undermining it. Your own ideas and opinions are not Dafa's teachings, and haven't the power to save people or do much of anything. None of you can teach the Way as I have.

You can introduce the practice to newcomers by playing the audio or video recordings for them at the practice site or wherever you offer instruction, and afterwards have a volunteer teach them the exercises. You can also have group discussions where you learn from each other and share your insights together. Those are the formats we use. Another thing is, you should refrain from calling any learner (or student) who introduces Falun Dafa to people things like "teacher" or "master." There is only one teacher of this practice. Everyone else is a practitioner, regardless of how early on they may have begun the practice.

Some of you might be concerned that you won't be able to give people a *falun* when you introduce the practice to them, or bring their bodies into balance, as I do. But there's no need to worry. Each of you is accompanied by one or more of my spiritual bodies, as I have indicated, and they are the ones who handle these things. People will get a *falun* right then and there, while you instruct them, if it's in their destiny. And if it's not destined just yet, they may still come to have one, though gradually, as they do the practice and my spiritual bodies bring their bodies back into balance. It's also possible for other people [who don't come in person] to obtain all that they should, I can assure you. It's possible as long as they really regard themselves as practitioners and manage to learn the teachings and exercises, even if on their own—whether it be from reading the books, watching the videos, or listening to the audio recordings that we have.

Healings are another thing that we don't allow you to do. Anyone learning Falun Dafa is strictly prohibited from giving people treatments. We are teaching you how to progress to higher realms, and we don't want you to form new attachments or harm your body. Joining our group exercise sessions is better than anything similar you could do, and you will find, if you practice at one, that it does more for your health than any therapy or form of treatment ever could. My spiritual bodies sit in a circle there, and above the practice site is a shield, with a massive *falun* on it, and a gigantic, spiritual body watching over the site from above the shield. This isn't like most sites where regular people gather to do exercises, but a place for spiritual refinement. Many among us with extrasensory powers have seen that wherever we gather to practice Falun Dafa the spot is enveloped by a shield of red light, and all within is bathed in this light.

My spiritual bodies [that accompany you] can directly bestow a *falun* upon people, but you shouldn't get attached to the idea. When you teach newcomers our exercises they might sense that they have received a *falun* and tell you about it in excitement. And you might think that it was your own doing, when it wasn't. I'm sharing this with you to discourage you from letting this attachment form. The work is done by my spiritual bodies. You should now have a good sense for how practitioners of Falun Dafa are to share the practice.

Whoever tampers with the exercises of Falun Dafa is violating our practice and our discipline. An example would be the person who turned the instructions for our exercises into little rhymes. That was completely out of line. Any true means of spiritual practice will have been passed down from before recorded history and date back to a remote past. And it will have given rise to countless divine beings. Normally nobody would dare to alter something of this nature. Only in these latter days would something like that happen. Never at any point in the past would something like that occur. So you need to be careful about this.

THE
FOURTH TALK

Costs and Rewards

COSTS AND REWARDS are often discussed in connection with leading the religious life as well as by people more broadly. How we look at these is different from how most people do. The "rewards" that people usually hope to experience for their efforts consist of worldly things, like living a more prosperous and pleasant life. For we who practice, however, the rewards that we look to enjoy are of a completely different nature, and would be something regular people could never experience, even if they wanted to—unless they took up spiritual practice.

We aspire to give of ourselves on a scale far greater than people normally would think of. People usually consider themselves to be giving when they perform acts of charity, give aid to those in need, or perhaps help the homeless. Those are one facet of being a giving person, of course, and do involve making sacrifices. But they only mean that you are less attached to money or material things. We aspire to much greater sacrifices than just those, as significant as they may be. As part of our spiritual refinement we strive to give up a wide range of attachments, from self-promotion to jealousy, from competitiveness to being excitable. We want to let go of each and every possible thing that we might be holding on to. So the "costs" of leading a spiritual existence are for us far broader than what people might normally imagine, as it entails forgoing all attachments and wants common to this world.

This might seem worrisome to some of you, as it sounds like we're taking vows of poverty just as monks and nuns do, but even less feasible, since we are supposed to do this while living and practicing as part of this world. But in our practice, for all of us who are still part of this world, we strive to lead lives that are as normal as possible while going about our spiritual practice. And so you aren't asked to give up anything in a material sense. You can enjoy a high-power position or be extremely wealthy as long as you aren't attached to it, as that is what's key for us.

Our practice aims squarely at your attachments. What's key is to try to worry little about your own self-interest and the disputes that might arise with other people. The spiritual practice done in monastic settings or the wilderness is meant to cut one off from the world and forcibly break one's attachments to it; you are denied material comforts and made to let them go. Doing spiritual practice *in* the world, by contrast, entails a different approach. It demands that you find a way to care little for material things while still leading a regular life. This is hard to do, of course, but it is the crux of our practice. So what "costs" are entailed in our practice aren't what people might normally think of. And it's worth noting that the acts of charity and goodwill that people engage in [might not be as meaningful as they seem], since nowadays some of the beggars out there are pros, and may have even more money than you. We should expand our vision and have bigger goals, and not get hung up on the smaller things. In spiritual practice you should confidently set your sights on the things that matter. Ultimately you will find that spiritual practice is really only at the "cost" of bad things.

People tend to believe that the things they want are good, when in fact, from a higher perspective these might be seen as self-serving or shortsighted. The world's religions have taught that wealth and influence, however great, last only a few decades and don't go with you to the next life. What makes the higher energy we get from practice so precious, by contrast, is that it accumulates and is stored on your soul, and it *does* go with you across lifetimes. And what's more, it has the potential to earn you divine standing, and so it's not something easily come by. All that you will be sacrificing are undesirable things, and yet by doing so you will be able to regain the purity you once had. The "rewards" for our efforts are great, thus, and include not only the elevation of your soul, but the chance to one day achieve spiritual perfection and truly become divine. What's solved is the fundamental problem of existence. Of course, it's not realistic to think that you could give up all worldly longings and meet the benchmark for a true practitioner overnight. A process has to be allowed for. But you shouldn't take this as license to approach practice in a casual and leisurely way. You need to be strict with yourself even if we allow for gradual progress. Nobody becomes divine overnight. It takes a process, and with time you will get there.

Our spiritual efforts, in fact, only "cost" us something we don't want anyway: karma. It's something that goes hand in hand with attachments. For example, when someone has all sorts of unhealthy attachments he will act selfishly and be driven to do wrongful things. And for his actions his only reward will be the black material known as karma. So karma is directly connected with attachments. If you want to free yourself of this undesirable thing, you will first have to change your ways.

Reworking Your Karma

Black matter and white matter can be changed into and replaced by one another. Getting into a dispute with another party is one thing that triggers this process. Doing good works will earn you white matter, virtue, while wrongful acts meanwhile will get you black matter, karma. Karma can also be passed on. It doesn't just come from earlier in your life, as people may imagine, but is accrued across multiple lifetimes. There has long been a belief that the soul is immortal. This would mean, then, that one's soul likely became indebted to others, took advantage of others, or did other forms of wrong such as taking life during its previous incarnations—and any of those acts would result in karma. Karma is something that accumulates in other dimensions and always goes with you, like virtue. There is another possible source for these, which is from within the family line, or from one's ancestors. The older generation used to make comments about accumulating virtue or blessings, and how someone's ancestors did so, or about someone "losing" or "squandering" these. What they said was remarkably accurate. Most people nowadays wouldn't take such comments to heart. Kids these days really wouldn't take you seriously if you tried to tell them they are lacking or short on virtue. But those comments were actually quite profound, for how "virtuous" someone is isn't simply about him or her having noble thinking or exemplary moral conduct, as people take it to be. Rather, it also has a physical reality, and both types of matter that I've been describing accompany our bodies.

I have been asked whether black matter prevents you from progressing to advanced stages of practice. You could say so, for having too much of it will affect one's ability to believe. That's because it will form into a field that envelops the body and encases the person, cutting him off from the qualities of the universe, *zhen, shan, ren*. He is apt to have little faith as a result. And so he will regard talk of spiritual or energy practices as naive, and won't believe any of it; he may even find it humorous. That's often the case, at least. But this doesn't mean that spiritual practice will be impossible for him, or that he won't achieve much, should he try it. We hold that anything is possible through Dafa, so anyone can practice if they have the heart for it. As it's been said: a master can teach the trade, but it is up to the apprentice to do the actual work entailed for progress. Anyone who is willing to patiently endure, put in what it takes, and suffer a little will find that spiritual practice is doable. There will be nothing you can't overcome if you are deeply committed, and I can say that your karma will not be an issue.

Those who have more of the black matter usually need to put in more effort than those with more white matter, since the latter is by nature in sync with the universe's qualities of *zhen, shan, ren*. So someone with more white matter will get higher energy simply by elevating his thought and character; it can happen just by handling interpersonal disputes well, for example. Those with more virtue have greater faith, are able to take hardship, to endure physically, and discipline the will; and they will still increase their energy even if they suffer more physically than psychologically. The same can't be said for those with more of the black matter, however. They have to first go through a process whereby that material is reworked into white matter, and the experience is agonizing. So it's usually the case that people with weaker faith have to endure more, since it bespeaks of having more karma. And so spiritual practice is much harder for them.

Let's look at a concrete example of how this plays out in someone's practice. Buddhist meditation requires the legs to stay in the lotus position for a long time, and they start to feel like pins and needles as the length of time increases. It grates on the mind and is terribly trying. It's trying for both mind and body, and pleasant in neither regard. Some people can't bear the pain that the legs experience, and uncross them rather than persevere through it; some hold out a bit longer but still end up uncrossing them. But doing so renders their efforts for naught. It doesn't do any good to stretch out the legs and shake out the pain before continuing on. That's because the pain that the legs experience comes from black matter assailing them, in our observation. That black matter is karma, and suffering has the power to eliminate it and convert it into virtue. When pain arises in the legs it means that karma is being dissolved, and greater pain reflects greater pushback from the karma. So the pain felt in the legs is not without rhyme or reason. The pain experienced in meditation usually comes in bursts. A rush of pain might come and be especially hard to take, but after it passes, things settle down again, only for the pain to ensue again afterwards. That's often how it goes.

Because karma is eliminated piece by piece, the legs will feel better after a piece is dissolved and feel pain again when another piece comes up. The black matter doesn't just break down and disappear after it's eliminated. The conservation of matter holds true here, too, and so karma that's dissolved is converted straight into white matter, i.e., virtue. This conversion is possible because the person suffered, put in the effort, and endured the pain. We hold that virtue comes to those who bear pain, endure adversity, and do good works; and that's why the above happens during meditation. Some people uncross their legs and straighten them out as soon as pain appears, and shake it out before crossing them again. But that achieves nothing. And the same holds true when people are doing an exercise where they need to hold their arms up, but put them down due to fatigue. What's a little pain? Spiritual achievement takes much more than simply holding your arms up. So this is some of what happens when meditative exercises are part of one's practice.

That's not the main approach our practice takes, though it does play a certain part in it. In ours, most typically, the majority of your karma is reworked via interpersonal things that grate on your mind. When people you don't get along with really irritate you, it can be even more trying than physical pain. I would say physical pain is much easier to bear, as you can simply tough it out. It's much harder to take it when someone is scheming against you.

To illustrate it, suppose someone who is learning our practice arrives at work and overhears two people speaking badly of him. What they have to say is really unpleasant, and his anger starts to flare. But as we have taught, a practitioner should refrain from fighting back and always hold himself to high standards. So he remembers that I've taught that practitioners are different from others and should take the high road, and he avoids getting into a dispute with his co-workers. But often tensions like these won't count or achieve what they are meant to, or help you to improve, if they don't actually bother you. For that reason this practitioner isn't able to get it off his mind, it proves irritating, and it may really provoke him. And so he can't resist looking over his shoulder to catch a glimpse of those two colleagues speaking badly of him. But he won't be able to take it when he sees the looks on their faces, and his anger will surge. He might even get into an argument with them right then and there if his anger gets the best of him. It is the mind that's hardest to control when you aren't getting along with someone. While it would be nice and easy to work through it with meditation, that's not always possible.

This means that you will meet with all kinds of ordeals going forward in your practice. But just think, could spiritual progress be possible without them? Your character wouldn't develop if everyone got along well with you, nobody quarreled with you for selfish reasons, and worldly attachments never preyed upon you. You have to truly temper yourself through real, lived experience if you are to grow and progress. Some people don't understand why they have so many challenges after taking up the practice, and the challenges are surprisingly ordinary. But that's because you do your practice in the world. You won't experience anything radical like suddenly getting yanked up into the sky, feet first, and being tormented there. It won't be anything out of the ordinary. Your challenges will always take the form of normal events, such as being provoked, angered, mistreated, or being insulted for no apparent reason. All of which is to see how you respond.

You encounter those things on account of your karmic debts, though we have reduced the debts for you greatly. The few that do remain are allotted to different stages of your practice and will take the form of ordeals. These are meant to develop your character, strengthen your will, and break the attachments you have. They are ordeals fashioned just for you, and we make use of them to perfect your character. And we can help you to overcome them. All of them can be overcome as long as you elevate your mind. You should be able to pull through unless you are not determined to. So, going forward, don't think that the issues you experience with people are by chance. They're not, even if they come out of the blue. They are meant to perfect your character. You will manage to handle them well as long as you act as a practitioner.

Naturally, you won't be forewarned when challenges or tensions are coming your way. Little spiritual growth would be possible if everything were disclosed to you, and those events wouldn't serve their purpose. They will usually come unexpectedly so as to test your character and help you to grow; and by doing so your character will be revealed for what it is. So tensions with others don't happen by chance. Challenging situations will unfold throughout the course of your practice and facilitate the reworking of your karma. They are far more trying than suffering physical pain, contrary to what people imagine. It's not realistic to think that higher energy could be developed just by putting in long hours meditating or exercising, or standing in some special position until the arms and legs ache. That only serves to transform your innate body. You still need strengthening from energy of a higher plane; merely doing exercises doesn't foster spiritual growth. The key to real spiritual progress is to train your will. If physical strain was all it took, you would expect that China's farmers would all be great saints, given the strains that they endure. Whatever you might put your body through, it wouldn't match their efforts, working the earth day after day under the scorching sun, tired and spent. So it's not that simple. Mastering the mind is the real key to spiritual attainment, as I see it, and is what truly makes progress possible.

We should try to keep compassionate and pleasant while karma is being reworked. By doing so, your judgment won't be clouded by the situation at hand and lead you to mishandle things, as might normally happen for people. And you will be able to handle anything unforeseen that comes along. If your heart is always very kind and compassionate, you will usually have breathing room and space to think when situations come up unexpectedly. By contrast, if you are always a contentious person and getting into disagreements with people, then I think it's inevitable that you will fall into an argument when issues come up. So as I see it, the tensions you experience are meant to change your body's black matter into white matter, virtue.

With humanity having reached this point, virtually everyone is born with karma rolled over from previous lifetimes, and the amount on each person's body is sizeable. So, often the way it works is that while your karma is being dealt with and reworked, your energy and character will be developing in tandem. So if you find that someone is testing your character, it could be a reflection of that process at work. If you persevere through it, your karma will be reduced, your character will grow, and your energy will increase. They go together. People in the past were very virtuous and had noble character, and persevering through even just minor ordeals could result in their gaining higher energy. But people aren't like that today. They tend to lose their enthusiasm for spiritual practice as soon as the going gets tough, and then they have only less belief in it, which makes things even harder.

The altercations or mistreatment that you encounter as you practice might be either of two scenarios. One is that you mistreated the other person during a past life. Perhaps the situation preys on your mind, and you can't believe someone would treat you as they are. Well, then you shouldn't have treated them that way in the past. You might say that you didn't know better back then and that this lifetime has nothing to do with that one. But you can't write it off like that. Another thing is, karma is surely being reworked with any altercation you get into, so we should be magnanimous and not handle it like most people would. This should hold true at the office or wherever you work, and even if you run your own business. And the interactions you have with the general public are no different. You can't avoid having some sort of interaction with the world. If nothing else, you have dealings with your neighbors.

You will experience a range of difficult encounters while interacting with others as part of society. For those of us who practice *in* the world, it doesn't matter how rich or powerful you may be, or whether you are self-employed and work alone, or have a business to run, or do any type of business: the key is to deal fairly and act with integrity. The various trades and professions in this world are meant to exist. Your heart is what counts, not your occupation. People have long had a perception that most businessmen are dishonest, but that's not a very insightful take on it. I would say that the problem lies with people's hearts. You will do business fairly if you have a good heart, and if you make more money than others it will be a reflection of your efforts; you would have worked for the money that you got. Getting paid for doing honest work follows from the laws of costs and rewards. You can be a good person in any strata of society. Each class has its own, unique interpersonal challenges, and this includes the upper class. But there are always proper ways to handle them. You can be a good person whatever your strata of society, and have few wants and attachments. Spiritual progress is possible in any segment of society, and you can always show yourself to be a good person.

The interpersonal things that people now experience in China are quite abnormal, be it at the state-owned enterprises or elsewhere. It's not something you see in other countries or that would have happened in the past. People get into heated disputes while trying to get ahead, and scheme against each other even for petty things. The thoughts people have and the tactics they resort to are terrible. It's hard to be a good person there. For example, you might arrive at work one day and notice that things don't feel right. Later you find out that someone spoke terribly of you and complained about you to your supervisor, making you look awful. And you find that your co-workers are looking at you strangely. The average person wouldn't be able to take the humiliation. He would try to get back at whoever caused this, and rally people to his side. Responding like that might win you the respect of worldly people, but it's beneath a practitioner. When you retaliate like an ordinary person, you become one, or worse—if you're more worked up than people normally would be.

Then how should we handle situations like these? When we get into a disagreement we should first of all stay calm and not act like others. Of course, it's fine to try to explain things with good intent; there's nothing wrong with trying to clear things up. But if you do it with too much attachment it won't work out. When we experience these trying situations we shouldn't respond in kind. If you stoop to the other person's level, then you are no different from them. And not only shouldn't you respond like them, neither should you feel hatred or resentment. And I sincerely mean that. Any bitterness towards another person means that anger got the best of you. And in that case you have failed to live up to the standard of *ren*, and even less so *shan*. Yet we practice *zhen*, *shan*, and *ren*. So you mustn't act as the other party does, and really mustn't become angry—even if they made you look so bad that you can't hold your head up high. And rather than being angry at the other party, you should thank them in your heart, and genuinely so. Worldly people might think that responding this way makes you a self-deluded fool. But I can assure you that that's not the case.

So it only follows that you should hold yourself to high standards, since you are a practitioner. You can't just do things as others do. Greater treasures await those who engage in spiritual practice, and so you have to live by higher principles. Yet when you act like the person who you're experiencing problems with, you are the same as him or her. I've said that you should feel thankful towards that person rather than bitter. To understand why, just consider what you are going to get out of it. The laws of this universe hold that nothing can be gained without some cost being entailed; everything comes at a price. The other person may have caused you to look bad and get a raw deal, and so he gained from it in a worldly sense. But the worse he made you look and the bigger the ruckus he caused, the more you had to endure, and so he will lose that much more virtue for it—all of which is passed on to you. And while enduring it all, it's possible it won't even get to you or weigh on you.

The laws of the universe also hold that the karma of someone who suffers greatly will be reworked. In the scenario just described, you were the one who took abuse, and so your karma will be converted into virtue equaling what you endured. And virtue is of course something practitioners want. So there's a second benefit, in that your karma was reduced through it. Also, it would be hard to perfect your character without going through situations like the one that person created. We couldn't expect our energy to increase if everyone got along well and just meditated away as one happy family. It was in fact due to the situation that the person created that you had an occasion to work on your character and grow. And assuming you did, then that's a third benefit. And since you are a practitioner, your energy is going to grow whenever your character does. That makes it a four-for-one deal. What's not to feel thankful for, then? You really should feel thankful towards that person, and I mean it.

Of course, the other person's intention was bad or else he wouldn't have given you virtue. But he did provide you with an opportunity to strengthen your character, and for us that should be the heart of spiritual practice. That's because spiritual growth is only possible by whittling away your karma and having it turn into virtue, and all of this happens while working on your character. So they go hand in hand. Those in higher realms look at the happenings in this world quite differently from the average person. Things will look radically different to you if you view them from a higher plane. What seems "right" to us here in the secular world might be seen otherwise. More often than not, only what is seen as right from higher planes turns out to really be so.

I have explained the workings of the universe to you in depth in hopes that, with them clear to you, you will sincerely apply yourself to spiritual practice. Some of you might, being still in this world, find the immediate lure of worldly things too great to resist. The secular world holds too much sway over some people and they don't aspire to higher standards. Of course, there's nothing wrong with looking up to heroes and role models if someone just wants to be a good person in the normal sense. But those can only serve as an example to non-practitioners. Successful spiritual practice all comes down to how much heart you put into it and your own discernment. There's no template to follow. You are fortunate in that Falun Dafa has been explained to you, whereas, before, something like this was never openly taught, even to those who sought spiritual growth. So with the knowledge you have, you can now put Falun Dafa into practice in your life, and I believe you will do well. How it goes and how far you progress is all up to you.

Of course, the reworking of your karma won't always take place in the ways I just described; there are other possibilities as well. It could take place out in the world as well as on the domestic front. You might run into challenges as you are walking down the street or in another public setting. You will be made to give up all of the worldly attachments that you hold onto. Any and all attachments you have must be ground down, and it will take place through any of a number of scenarios where you will be made to stumble or do poorly, and from these come to new spiritual insights. This is how you will make it through and succeed.

Here's an example of a fairly typical scenario. We have many people who find that their spouses get really upset when they do our exercises. No sooner do you start to practice than your spouse launches into a fit. Yet when you do other things he doesn't mind. He might not be happy if you take up too much time playing table games, but it's nothing like how angry he gets when you exercise. Your practice does nothing to bother or inconvenience him, and it should be seen as a good thing since you are taking care of your body. But as soon as you practice he erupts. In some cases it has reached the point where couples have even considered divorce. Yet few practitioners have given much thought as to why this happens. Your spouse will have no explanation if you ask him to explain his anger after one of these episodes. He really won't be able to, and will agree that he shouldn't get so upset and allow his anger to flare like that. So what's really going on, then? Your karma needs to be reworked for you as you go about your practice. Yet for that to happen, there have to be costs involved. But take heart in knowing that whatever costs are entailed, you will be better off for it.

Let's look at another possible scenario, where your wife gives you a hard time as soon as you walk in the door. If you can manage to patiently endure that kind of situation, you will make progress in your practice that day. But it might prove too much for you, even if you're normally on good terms as a couple since you know how central virtue is. Her outburst might feel like an affront to you, and be just too much, and so you get into an argument with her. But that would, in effect, offset the progress you might have made in your practice that day. The episode happened because karma was right there at that moment and she was helping you to remove it. You didn't go for it, however, and instead succumbed to fighting. So it wasn't removed. There are many instances like this. A lot of you have experienced similar things without giving them much thought. But just consider that she always gives you a hard time about your practice—something good—and yet is okay with whatever else you might do. The reality is that she's unknowingly helping you to remove karma. That doesn't mean she is just fighting with you outwardly, though, while still feeling good toward you inside. Her anger truly comes from within. You can be sure that whoever your karma is distributed to will feel upset about it.

Perfecting Your Character

Many people have let their thoughts get the best of them, and this has caused a lot of problems and led to their spiritual progress stagnating. There are some individuals who, for example, are naturally endowed with quite good character (*xin-xing*), and their inner eye might suddenly open to a higher realm after they start practicing. They develop higher energy rapidly since their innate foundations are good and their character is excellent. But eventually, when the progress of their energy catches up with that of their character, the tensions and interpersonal things that they experience will have to be intensified if their energy is to develop further. So these practitioners, who are spiritually well-endowed, are apt to find that their practice goes well at first and energy comes to them readily, only to then, unexpectedly, and much to their confusion, find themselves plagued with troubles. Everything seems to suddenly go wrong, from others treating them badly to upset supervisors and tense situations at home. Issues spring up everywhere, and it doesn't seem to make sense. But the initial smooth sailing they had was due in fact to their having quickly reached a certain level of attainment, thanks to their good innate foundations. Yet that would be nowhere near the kind of attainment it takes for a practitioner to achieve spiritual perfection. Further progress is still needed. So the bar has to be raised. And only when that new, higher bar is cleared will they progress beyond where they had reached with the initial smooth sailing, which owed to their good endowment.

There are also people who hold off on starting spiritual practice on grounds that they want to first build up some savings and make sure their family is financially secure and worry-free. But that sounds like wishful thinking to me. For one, you don't have the power to change another person's life or fate, ultimately, even if they are your closest of kin. Could you really change a person's destiny? And secondly, if you really were to have no worries on the home front and be free of all troubles, what would your spiritual practice consist of? It's hard to grow spiritually if your life is full of comfort and ease. So it's not how you may have imagined it, with conventional thinking.

In spiritual practice you have to go through ordeals, and they serve to test whether you can become free of your emotions and desires and the sway they hold over you. Being attached to those things will impede your progress. There are reasons behind everything. What makes people human? It is the presence of emotion, as people simply live for it. There is love for family members, romantic love, love towards parents, emotions associated with relationships, and the affection that goes with friendship. People act for the sake of emotional bonds, and emotion follows you everywhere you go. Everything human about this world stems from emotion, from likes to dislikes, from joys to sorrows, love to hate. And so you will have problems in spiritual practice if you don't manage to free yourself of it. Those who do, will be free of human sentiments and unflappable. In its place will arise compassion, something far more noble. Of course, you're not likely to end emotion overnight; spiritual development is a long journey of gradually stripping away attachments. But you have to be strict with yourself.

Tense situations with others will come up unexpectedly for those of us who practice. How can you be prepared, then? If you can always be compassionate and calm, you will handle the issues that arise in your life well since you will have a buffer, in a sense. Things will work out well if you are always compassionate and good to others, thoughtful towards people, and handle whatever situations you get into with people by first pausing to consider how well your actions will go over with the other party and whether anyone will be hurt by them. You should hold yourself to high standards and raise the bar still further as you practice.

There are people who always seem to lack faith. For example, they might see visions of a higher being that they worship, and pray to it, but when they do so they mix in all sorts of complaints about their unanswered prayers, as they think that this being hasn't done much for them or made life easier. But that higher being won't respond to their wishes, of course, since the ordeals in their lives were in fact planned by him and meant to develop their character; things like interpersonal strife can do a lot to perfect one's character, after all. And so divine beings typically won't help as people wish. There is no way to perfect your character or increase your energy if a higher being answers your worldly prayers; it would defeat the whole purpose of the ordeal. Our human lives are not ends in themselves, but are for returning to heaven, as divine ones see it. They hold that the more adversity you experience, the better, since you can pay off your karmic debts more quickly that way. Some people just don't catch on, however. When their prayers go unanswered, they might start to complain to their god about receiving no assistance despite all of their worship. And some get so worked up that they even smash their religious images and curse their god from then on. Their character declines with all of this and any higher energy they had disappears. And they will only feel more resentful toward their god when they realize that they have nothing now, thinking that he is ruining their lives. They use human logic and criteria to judge a higher being's character and things of a higher order, which isn't appropriate. So it's a common failing for people to view the difficulties in their lives as unfair, and many have fallen as a result.

Many well-known teachers of energy practices have fallen in recent years. The true masters, however, retired from the public eye after fulfilling their historic missions. Only those who lost their way in the world, whose character has declined and who have lost the higher energy they had, have remained active. Some of the figures who are still publicly active and who have enjoyed some degree of fame have had their secondary souls led away by their teachers, and their energy went with them. Their teachers had seen that they had fallen for worldly things like fame and fortune, and that they wouldn't be able to free themselves. Cases like these are common and not out of the ordinary.

In our discipline it's rare to see people fall like that, and what instances there are, aren't that noteworthy. But the positive changes that people's characters undergo with our practice *are* noteworthy. We once had a student in Shandong province who worked at a textile mill and who taught Falun Dafa to her co-workers after she had learned it. The attitude of the entire factory changed for the better as a result. It used to be that employees would hide small towels in their clothing and take them home. After this woman had learned our practice, though, not only did she stop taking things, but she even decided to return the items she had taken before. Others at the factory stopped taking things as well when they saw the change in her, and some even returned what they had taken. This happened throughout the factory.

In another city the coordinators from our practice site went to a factory to see how things were going for everyone who was learning Falun Dafa there. The factory's manager personally came out to receive them, and told them, "Since learning Falun Dafa these workers have been putting in extra hours and working conscientiously and with a lot of heart. They don't quibble over the work they're assigned to do, and aren't just thinking about themselves. Just by being like that they've changed the morale of the whole factory, and our profits have grown. Your practice is fantastic. I want to attend your classes the next time your teacher is in town." While the main goal of Falun Dafa is spiritual progress, and not, in fact, to bring about changes like those, it can nevertheless do a great deal to foster civility and moral living in society. If each and every person were to self-reflect and give thought to how they should act, I would say the world would become a more stable place and people would become moral again.

Another case involved a woman in her fifties who was on her way to my class in the city of Taiyuan, together with her husband. As they were crossing the street a large car sped by and snagged the woman's clothes with its side-view mirror. It dragged her over ten yards before she hit the ground, hard. The car went another twenty-some yards before coming to a halt. The driver got out of his car and lectured her for being careless, which is typical nowadays; people often react to mishaps by trying to shift the blame, even if they are at fault. A passenger who was with him told him to see if she was hurt and needed medical attention. The man came to his senses and quickly asked if she was okay, and offered to take her to the hospital. Our student slowly got to her feet and replied, "It's nothing. You can head on your way." She brushed herself off and continued on to our class with her husband.

They shared the story with me after they arrived. It made me happy, since it clearly meant that she had grown in character. She told me that she wouldn't have handled the incident so well if it weren't for learning Falun Dafa. Just consider how well she did. This was a woman in her fifties who was retired and without benefits or an income at a time when prices are so high, and she had just been dragged a long way by a car and thrown to the ground. If she were an ordinary person she might have responded by just staying there on the ground and telling the driver that she was injured in multiple places.

And she might have readily accepted the offer of going to the hospital, and stayed there as long as she liked. But she is a practitioner, and didn't do that. We believe that one thought can determine the outcome of things, for better or for worse. If she were just an ordinary woman at that age, could she possibly have gone unscathed? And yet she wasn't even scuffed up. One thought made all the difference. If she had lain there on the ground instead, moaning in pain, pleading for help and thinking that she had sustained this or that injury, then maybe she *would have* suffered a broken bone or been paralyzed. And she might have been hospitalized and bedridden for the rest of her life—a fate that no amount of financial compensation would offset. The crowd that had gathered around after the accident was puzzled that she didn't try to get money out of the driver. People's values are a mess nowadays. The driver hadn't meant to hit her, even if he was wrong for speeding. It was an accident after all. But with the way people are today, even witnesses to an accident will get worked up if you don't try to get money out of the driver. Many people have lost their moral compass, and won't listen to you if you tell them they are doing something wrong. And with the change in moral standards that has taken place, some people put profit before all else, and will do anything for money. Some people now even live by the motto, "Every man for himself."

There was once someone who was learning our practice in Beijing who took his son for a stroll after dinner down the Qianmen pedestrian street. They spotted a stand that was offering a draw for a prize. His child wanted to join in the fun and give it a try. The father told him to go ahead if he'd like, and gave him a dollar to do so. He drew a ticket, and lo and behold he'd won a second-tier prize—a deluxe children's bike. It was awarded to him on the spot, much to his delight. But then it dawned on the father, "I'm a practitioner. I really shouldn't have tried to get this. I'll probably lose quite a bit of virtue if I take it, since it's not something I've earned." So he told his child, "We should just buy one ourselves if we want one." The kid was upset, and responded, "I kept asking for one and you didn't buy one. Now I win one and you won't let me have it." He cried his eyes out, leaving his father no choice but to take the bike home. After returning home, the more the father thought about it the more it didn't feel right. So he decided to simply give money to the people who were holding the drawing. But then it occurred to him that the drawing would be over by now, and the individuals would just divide up the money he gave them and pocket it. In the end he decided to donate the money to his own workplace.

The father was lucky in that many of his colleagues were learning Falun Dafa and management had a good understanding of them. Normally, at your typical workplace, people would think there was something wrong with you if you didn't want to keep the bike that you won and were planning on donating an equivalent sum of money to your workplace since you're a practitioner; even your boss would think you were mad. And rumors might start up about how something went wrong in your practice or made you lose your mind. As I indicated, people's values have become fouled up. In the 1950s or 1960s what the father did wouldn't have seemed like a big deal. Gestures like that were common back then and anything but a cause for concern.

We believe that however badly people's values may change, the underlying qualities of the universe—*zhen, shan, ren*—will never change. The criteria that people use to judge things have become all confused, and so those who people deem to be good or bad aren't necessarily so. Only those who embody the qualities of the universe are good people. And these qualities are the sole measure of one's person; these are what are recognized throughout the universe. While humanity may seem to have made great strides, people's morals have declined significantly, and the social fabric of the world is changing for the worse; many people now put profit before all else. But the universe doesn't change in keeping with humankind. So as someone with spiritual aspirations, you can't rely on the standards that other people have. You can't do things on the grounds that everyone thinks they're right. What the average person considers good or bad isn't necessarily correct. People's values are so fouled up now that they won't even listen to you if you point out to them that they are doing something wrong. So as practitioners you have to view things in light of the qualities of the universe if you are to really tell right from wrong.

Ritual Anointment

In certain religious or spiritual communities there is a practice known as ritual anointment (*guan-ding*). It is a religious rite that was originally used in Tantric Buddhist practice. Its objective is to ensure that the adherent remains loyal to the discipline, and it is a way of formally recognizing him as a disciple. What's strange is that this religious rite is no longer just seen in Tantric Buddhism, but also in *chi-gong* and Daoist practice. I've indicated that deceit is involved whenever someone is publicly teaching what they claim to be Tantric Buddhist methods. I say that because Chinese Tantrism disappeared from the face of China over a thousand years ago, and it's simply non-existent now. And Tibetan Tantrism never fully came to China, due to the language barrier. Also, being esoteric practices, their adherents are supposed to engage in secretive practice off in a monastic setting and receive veiled instruction at the hands of a master, who guides them in secret practice. It is never supposed to be taught without those conditions first being met.

Many people travel to Tibet in search of a master to teach them Tibetan Tantrism and such practices, hoping to become a high-profile, well-to-do master of an energy practice down the road. But consider that an authentic Tibetan lama who is the keeper of a true teaching will have great powers and be able to make out what is on the learner's mind. He will easily see what the person is up to. He will know that the person's incentive for learning is to become a master for worldly ends, which would defile their practice. But as you might figure, they aren't about to let someone just come along and defile a serious spiritual discipline like theirs, let alone someone whose motives are surely impure. So, little will be taught to this sort of person, much less the heart of the teachings. At most he might learn something superficial somewhere, with all the temples and monasteries that are out there. It's likely he will fall prey to entity attachment if his heart is impure and he seeks to become a master for the wrong reasons. And while those entities or animals might have energy to offer him, it's surely not from Tibetan Tantrism. Those who go to Tibet sincerely in search of the *dharma* are apt to settle down there and never leave; those are the true ones.

It's strange that there are now many Daoist practices doing anointment with energy. Daoist practices make use of the body's energy channels, so it doesn't make sense for them to do that. Anointment has become especially popular in Guangdong province, from what I learned during my travels in southern China when I was there to teach. There are a dozen or so practices in the region that have made a real mess of things doing anointment. The idea is that you supposedly become their disciple through anointment, and shouldn't learn any other practices after that—lest you be punished for it. And they do that. But isn't that cunning and evil? What they offer is just for healing and wellness, and people are drawn to it simply by the prospect of good health. What business have they punishing their followers for disloyalty, then? The many who take this approach are really doing people a disservice, since they aren't about to guide anyone to spiritual perfection.

So anointment is now seen in Daoist practice, though it doesn't belong there. The Daoist *chi-gong* master who makes the biggest deal about anointment has an energy column that's merely two or three stories tall, from what I observed. It's really a pity to see the energy of a famous master having fallen so fast. Many have lined up for anointment from him. Yet his energy was limited from the outset and quickly consumed. And after that, he couldn't possibly have had any energy left for doing anointment. So he's been conning people. True anointment, as seen from other dimensions, transforms the bones from head to toe such that they resemble white jade. It involves the use of *gong*—a high-energy matter—to purify the body, and it is poured through the whole body from head to toe. So it's not something that the master I've been describing could do. And it's not for religious purposes that he does anointment, if you are wondering. Rather, it's to have you belong to him after learning his practice, since then you will have to attend his classes and study with him. The motive is to get your money. He wouldn't make money if nobody was learning his practice.

Committed practitioners of Falun Dafa will have anointment done for them many times by their master, just as happens in other Buddhist disciplines—even though you may not sense it. Those with paranormal powers or who are especially sensitive may be able to. The anointment might take place while you are sleeping or at another time, and what happens is that a warm current suddenly flows through your entire body, from head to toe. The objective isn't to heighten your energy, since that must come from your own efforts. Rather, it is a means of blessing whereby your body is purified and cleansed one step further. The procedure needs to happen multiple times, for at each stage of practice you need assistance cleansing your body. We don't practice any rites of anointment, since, as I've indicated, you just need to focus on practicing and your teacher will take care of the rest.

Yet there are people who still wish to pay homage to me. I want to talk about this in light of what was just said, as this applies to many people. This era of history is different from that of older, bygone times, and so you don't need to kneel down or prostrate yourself before me to count as my student. Those rites don't feature in our practice. It's funny that many people now think that they can get energy just by outward acts of religious devotion and becoming a bit more pious. True spiritual progress is the product of one's own efforts, and prayerful wishes do little. There is no need for religious acts of devotion such as offering incense and paying homage. Higher beings will smile upon you if they see you sincerely engaging in disciplined spiritual practice. But they will be displeased with you if you engage in wrongful acts, however much you might worship them. I think the idea should be clear. Genuine spiritual practice is up to you, and there is little point in paying respects to your teacher if afterwards you turn around and do whatever you please. So religious rites really have no place in our practice. And ironically, you might even hurt my reputation if you do those things.

We have given all of you so much. I will consider you my student and guide you as long as you strive to put the teachings into practice and are strict with yourself about following the Great Way. I will do this as long as you practice Falun Dafa. If you don't practice it, however, there is nothing we can do and there is no point in formally seeking to be named a student. Those who just do the exercises aren't my students even if they were among the first to attend our classes. You have to do sincere spiritual practice and work on your character as we've taught, if you are to gain a healthy body and really progress to higher stages. So rites like anointment don't have a place in our practice. You will be one of us as long as you do the practice. My spiritual bodies are all-powerful and all-knowing, and know even your thoughts. But they will not look after you if you aren't someone who practices. For those of you who do practice, however, help will be provided straight through to the finish.

The adherents of some practices have never met their teachers but are told to bow facing a certain direction and pay hundreds of dollars and then they can be counted as students. But isn't that misleading? And these people go in for it quite willingly, and get protective of the practice and its teacher afterwards, even telling people that they can no longer study other practices. It strikes me as quite absurd. I also wonder what, if anything, is achieved when some teachers do what they refer to as "touching the crown of the head."

Any energy practice that promotes itself as being "Tantric Buddhist," or even just part of religious Buddhism more generally, is false. Bear in mind that the methods and disciplines of practice found in authentic Buddhism date back thousands of years. Any alterations people might now make to them change them into something else. The disciplines of spiritual practice are for the solemn purpose of achieving divinity, and are incredibly profound and intricate. Even just a slight alteration will foul things up. The process of converting matter into higher energy is extraordinarily complex, so what a person can sense of it really isn't reliable and should never inform how he goes about practicing. The religious rites that Buddhist monks engage in are a means of practice, in fact, and any changes made will turn their practice into something else. Every true practice has a higher divinity presiding over it, and each such practice will have produced many divine ones of its own via its methods of spiritual discipline; nobody would be so bold as to rashly alter the methods involved. Then what business would the teacher of some lesser energy practice, who lacks spiritual might, have altering a religious tradition's means to divinity? And besides, supposing he did really alter it and make his own practice, then it could no longer be considered part of that religion, and he would have no business borrowing its name under false pretenses. So you should be able to make out inauthentic practices in cases like these.

The Mystery of the Mandorla*

In ancient Chinese religious texts like *Principles of Mind-Body Practice*, the Daoist Canon, and various alchemical manuals, one comes across references to "positioning" something known as a mandorla, or how this mandorla "presides over an aperture." Many spiritual teachers have a hard time explaining what's meant, since most of them, at their stage of practice, cannot perceive these things and aren't allowed to. Someone needs to have reached at least the stage of wisdom vision in his spiritual development to see them, and this is why most run-of-the-mill instructors can't—they haven't reached that point. There have long been religious discussions about what the mandorla is, where the "one aperture" is located, and how it's positioned. The ancient texts don't shed much light on these questions, however, and are apt to be confusing; they only discuss the phenomena in the abstract and don't say much of substance, despite all that's been written on the topic. This was done intentionally so as to keep outsiders from learning the heart of the teachings.

I would like to offer you a bit of advice, on the grounds that you are students of Falun Dafa: stay away from the mess of books about energy practice that are now out there. I don't mean the ancient texts that I was just speaking about, but the deceptive energy-related books that are now being written. You shouldn't even flip through them. The entities carried by those books will attach themselves to your body as soon as you find even just one line of the text agreeable to you. Many of the books were written at the direction of possessing spirits that seized upon the writer's attachments to status and money. Deceptive books on energy practice are

181

everywhere these days. Many people just aren't being responsible, and write at the command of evil spirits or whatever attaches itself to them. And generally speaking, it is best not to read even classical works like the ones I was mentioning a moment ago, for there's the matter of committing to one discipline and not disordering your energy.

Someone high up in the Chi-Gong Association of China shared something with me that had me laughing hard. He spoke about a man in Beijing who was always taking *chi-gong* classes and who thought he had learned all there was to know about it after a while. What gave the man that impression was that everything taught in the various classes was equally basic; everyone was teaching more or less the same things. This led him to believe, as do false masters, that there was nothing more to *chi-gong* than that. And so he decided to write his own book on *chi-gong*. But just consider the absurdity of it: someone who didn't even practice *chi-gong* was going to write a book about it. Yet that's typical of *chi-gong* books nowadays, as plagiarizing is common. He got stuck in the writing process when he got to the topic of the mandorla. Few really understand what it is, after all; even just a handful of genuine spiritual masters are clear on it. So this person inquired with a master who wasn't legitimate, not realizing it, though, since he didn't understand *chi-gong* that well. This false master was worried that he would be exposed as an impostor if he couldn't answer the man's questions. So he went so far as to make up some nonsense, and said that the one aperture of the mandorla is located at the tip of the male excretory organ. As ridiculous as it may sound, it's no laughing matter, as his book has since been published. This suggests just how absurd *chi-gong* books have become. Reading those things won't do you any good and can only bring harm.

Let's explore what's meant by "positioning the mandorla." As a person goes about spiritual practice in the human realm, he will, when he has passed the middle stage and is practicing at an advanced stage, begin to develop an angelic body within. The angelic body is different from what are known as cherubs. Cherubs are small and rascally, and joyfully spring about and play. In contrast, the angelic body does not move, and simply sits in place, motionless, atop a lotus flower with its legs folded meditatively and its hands conjoined in the *mudra* of *jie-yin*;* the only exception is when one's soul moves in to control it. The angelic body is born from one's energy center and can be seen in an invisible, micro realm while smaller than even the point of a needle.

There is something else I should explain. There is just one true energy center (*dan-tian*) in the body, and it is located at the lower abdominal area. It is inside the body and spans from above the perineum to the lower abdomen. Many higher energies, powers, and other abilities as well as spiritual bodies, the angelic body, and cherubs—an enormous array of supernatural beings—are born from this center.

In the past there were a handful of spiritual practitioners who fostered the idea that there are upper, middle, and lower energy centers in the body. But the idea isn't accurate, even if it allegedly has a doctrinal basis and was passed down by masters for generations. Bear in mind that there was certainly nonsense in ancient times. Having an ancient pedigree doesn't necessarily make something accurate; lesser, folk practices have always circulated among the public, but they don't amount to spiritual practice or anything significant. When people claim that there are upper, middle, and lower energy centers, what they mean to say is that wherever an energy cluster can be made counts as an energy center. But it's folly to think that. An energy cluster can be generated at any location in the body if a person just concentrates his mind on that spot for long enough. Anyone who doubts it can verify this for themselves by focusing their mind on their arm and fixing their attention there, and after some amount of time an energy cluster will indeed form there. This fact has led some observers to claim that energy centers are found throughout the whole body. But that's even more of a stretch. They are under the impression that wherever an energy cluster forms is an energy center. While it is an energy cluster, it's not an energy *center*. It would be okay to say that clusters of energy can be made anywhere, or that there are upper, middle, and lower energy clusters. But the center that can truly give rise to countless powers has only one site, and it is at the lower abdomen. So what people have said about upper, middle, and lower energy centers is wrong. The truth is simply that an energy cluster will form wherever the mind focuses for a sustained amount of time.

The angelic body comes into being in the energy center at the lower abdomen, and gradually grows larger in size. When it has grown to be the size of a ping-pong ball, the contours of its body can be made out, with the nose and eyes having been formed. And while it is this size, a small, round bubble will come into being beside its body. The bubble will grow from then on in parallel with the angelic body. When the body has grown to a height of just over five inches (thirteen centimeters) tall, the first petal of a lotus flower will appear. Once the body has reached six-and-a-half to eight inches (seventeen to twenty centimeters) in height, all the petals of the flower will have basically come into shape, forming one tier of a lotus flower, and it will be upon this that the angelic body sits, golden and radiant, and simply beautiful. It is an incorruptible Divine body, and has been traditionally referred to as a "Buddha Body" by Buddhists and as an "Immortal Infant" by Daoists.

In our discipline both this and the body you were born with are developed and needed; this means that your innate body also needs to undergo transformation along the way. But as you might imagine, a divine body isn't something that may be revealed in the secular world. Some people may be able to reveal the form of theirs if they go to great lengths; they might be able to display a glowing figure that's visible to the naked eye. The body of *this* dimension, however, will look no different from any other, despite its transformation. The difference won't be perceptible to people, though this is a body that can travel between dimensions. When the angelic body has grown to be between five and six-and-a-half inches tall, the bubble will have grown to the same size and be translucent like an inflated balloon. The angelic body will sit still in meditation, motionless. At this point the bubble will take leave of the body's energy center. It is fully developed now and conditions are ripe for it to ascend inside the body. The process of ascension is an extremely slow one, but its daily movement can be perceived. Slowly but surely it moves upward, ascending. You can sense its existence if you pay close attention.

After the bubble has ascended to the spot where the Middle of the Chest acupoint is, it will stay there for a period of time. It does so because the most essential things of a person's body are there, and much more (the heart is also located there), and the bubble needs to form a system of these within it. The most essential things need to be supplied into the bubble for its enrichment. Then, after some time, it continues to ascend. Things will feel constricted when it passes through your neck, as if your blood vessels were constricted or swollen, and it feels awful. But after just a day or two the condition will pass. When the bubble has arrived at the crown of the head, we refer to it as "reaching the Niwan Palace." Though we put it that way, it's actually as large as your head, and your whole head will feel swollen. Since the Niwan Palace is a critical location for a human being's life, the bubble will again need to form some essential things within itself while there. Afterwards it squeezes outward through the passageway of the inner eye, and the sensation is hard to bear. That area will feel swollen to the point that it aches, and the temples will feel swollen as well, while the regular eyes will feel sunken. Things will carry on like this until the bubble has squeezed out, at which point it promptly hangs at the position of the forehead. And this is in fact what "positioning" the mandorla refers to—its presiding over that spot.

A person who does Buddhist or Daoist practice and has an open inner eye won't be able to see out of it at this point in time, which expedites the formation of things inside the mandorla. At the front as well as back there will be a set of doors, both of which are closed now; it will resemble the two doors on either side of the passage at Tiananmen Square, in Beijing. The doors will remain closed except for in extremely special circumstances. This enables the formation and enrichment of the mandorla to happen as swiftly as possible. So those who can normally see through the inner eye won't be able to at this point, as it's prohibited. As for why the mandorla is hung at this position, it's because the many channels of the body converge at this point, and at this time all the channels must traverse through the mandorla for one loop before going on; each channel must travel the mandorla so as to help lay certain groundwork inside it, so that ultimately a system of interconnecting elements is formed. The human body is a microcosm, so the mandorla will ultimately develop into a miniature world in which is found all that is essential to the human body. But what has formed thus far, at this stage, are merely facilities that aren't yet fully operational.

In practices known as the Mystical Ways, the mandorla stays open, by contrast. When it's ejected out, it will be in the form of a straight tube, and only gradually become round again. And the doors on both sides of it remain open. Since the Mystical Ways are neither Buddhist nor Daoist, their adherents aren't watched over by the many masters who protect followers of the other two systems. Buddhist and Daoist practitioners can go for a time without seeing through their inner eyes and still be safe, whereas practitioners of the Mystical Ways can't, and need to be able to see with them in order to protect themselves. However, when they view things through their inner eyes in this scenario, it's as if they are looking through the optical tube of a telescope. [Whatever the practice,] in the month or so that follows, after a few things that are needed and that work together are formed there, the mandorla starts its return. It begins by coming back inside the head, which is referred to as a "shifting" of the mandorla.

As the mandorla goes back into the body, there will again be an unpleasant sense of pressure. Afterwards it will squeeze out of the body again, this time through the acupoint at the nape of the neck called the Jade Pillow. The sensation as it squeezes out will be hard to bear, and it will feel as if the head were being split open. But the tension will dissolve promptly after the whole mandorla comes out. It then hangs there in a deep dimension after exiting the body. It won't be in your way when you lie down to sleep, however, as it will be present on your body of another, much deeper, dimension. But one thing you may sense when the mandorla is first being positioned is that something is before your eyes. Though these things are happening in another dimension, your vision in this world might seem hazy, as if something were blocking your view, and it won't be too pleasant. The Jade Pillow acupoint is a key one and a major juncture, and so a few things will also be formed there that will work together, at the back of the head. The mandorla will then start to go back in again. The phrase I referred to earlier about the mandorla presiding over an aperture isn't really about one aperture alone, since the mandorla needs to change its position several times. Once back inside the body, it returns to the Niwan Palace and begins to descend, proceeding straight down to the acupoint between the kidneys, known as the Life Gate. And here it is ejected out again.

The Life Gate is a crucial and central "aperture," as Daoists call it, or "juncture," as we put it. But more than just a major juncture, it is actually like an iron gate—like countless layers of them, in fact. We know that there are many layers to the body, with the cells of the flesh being one layer, and the molecules within them another. There is a gate at every plane, from atoms to protons, electrons, and so on, down to infinitely small particles. And so an enormous array of powers and magical skills are locked up by the gates of each layer. Other practices take the approach of forming an energy cluster that is eventually exploded, and when that happens, the first spot to be blasted open is the Life Gate; this is necessary in order to free up one's powers. Here the mandorla forms a system of things once again, and then re-enters the body. It then returns to the lower abdomen, which is referred to as the mandorla "returning to its seat."

When the mandorla does this, it doesn't in fact go back to its original spot. By this time the angelic body will have grown quite large, and the bubble will cover and enwrap it, and grow in tandem with it. In Daoist practice the angelic body is generally allowed to take leave of one's body when it has reached the size of a six- to seven-year-old. This is known as the "birth of the Immortal Infant." This happens when a person's soul takes charge of the angelic body and uses it to leave the physical body. His or her physical body will stay put, motionless, when the soul leaves it. In Buddhist practices like ours, however, the angelic body will usually be out of danger when it has grown to the same size as the person. And at that point the angelic body is normally allowed to take leave of one's body, and can separate from it and go out. By this time the angelic body will have grown to be the same size as the practitioner, and the bubble—which is the mandorla—that envelops him or her will be large and have surpassed the size of the person's physical body. This is only natural, given the angelic body's size.

You may have observed that the statues and images of divine beings seen in temples or other religious settings, and especially the paintings, often depict these beings surrounded by a circle or oval behind them. A large number of images are like that, and it's always the case with the paintings in ancient temples. Nobody can offer a good explanation why. But I can disclose to you that it is the mandorla. So in the process I was just describing, the mandorla, at this point of maturity, should now be called otherwise. It should be called a "paradise," even if it isn't one in the fullest sense of the term yet. It merely has the facilities needed, so to speak. It's like a factory that has the equipment it needs but which can't produce anything owing to a lack of energy and materials. A few years back a number of spiritual figures were stating that their energy had surpassed that of various divinities. Those who heard them thought it was a stretch. But what they said wasn't an exaggeration by any means, as your energy does need to be developed to a great height while you are still in this world.

It's hard to fathom that they could have surpassed divine beings in achievement. But we shouldn't understand remarks like theirs so superficially. Yes, their energy did reach very high since it was sure to be that way once they had progressed to an advanced stage and the point of enlightenment, and of having all of their powers accessible to them. But right at the point when that would occur, eighty percent of their energy would be snapped off and taken down together with their measure of character. The energy would then be used to enrich their very own paradises, which I was just referring to. As we know, the energy and the height of character that a practitioner achieves are extremely precious, as they were developed through countless trials and tribulations over his lifetime. Eighty percent of this precious, higher energy will be used to enrich his paradise. And that is why one day, when his spiritual journey has come to a successful close, he will only have to extend his hand to have whatever he wants, and it will instantly manifest; and whatever he wills to be done, shall be done. His spiritual authority will mean that all of these are possible for him in his paradise. And all shall be the rewards of his spiritual labors.

The energy of a being who is divine like this can be transformed into anything at his command. And so he is free to consume or enjoy whatever he would like, and whatever he wishes for shall be, since these are the fruits of his practice. They come with his Divine status; anything less than this status would mean that his practice was ultimately not a success. At this time, what was formerly the mandorla can now be rightfully called his own "paradise," or "world," and he will achieve spiritual perfection and attain enlightenment with the twenty percent of his energy that's left. Though only twenty percent remains, no part of his body will be locked at this point in time—if he even has a body, that is. And if he does, it will have been fully remade with high-energy matter by now. His powers will be revealed in all their glory and be unrivaled in their might. They will no longer be held back, as they previously were, despite all of the progress he had been making while practicing in this world.

THE
FIFTH TALK

The Falun's Design

THE FALUN IS THE SYMBOL of our Falun Dafa. People with special powers can see that the *falun* rotates, such as those on *falun* pins. Our practice is guided by the cosmic qualities of *zhen, shan, ren*. The scope of our practice is simply enormous, since it is based on the laws governing the changing universe. The *falun* as illustrated at the front of our book is, in a sense, a microcosm of the universe. Buddhist thought conceptualizes the universe as a group of worlds that exist in ten directions. There are the four sides and a total of eight directions.* Some people might have seen that there is a column of energy both atop and beneath the *falun*. So counting these two additional directions of above and below, we have a total of ten directions upon which are built worlds—the worlds that make up the universe. This is the Buddhist concept of the universe, in simple terms.

This universe has innumerable galaxies, of course, one of which is the Milky Way. The universe as a whole is in motion, as are all the galaxies within it. And this is why the *tai-chi* symbols and smaller *srivatsa* 卐 symbols inside the *falun* design rotate, as do the larger *srivatsa* 卐 in the center and the design as a whole. So in a certain sense, [the larger *srivatsa* 卐] represents the Milky Way galaxy; and this Buddhist symbol is at the center since ours is a Buddhist practice. That's how to look at the face of it. Yet, in other dimensions everything has extraordinarily diverse and intricate forms of existence, and the process by which any given thing comes into being is similarly complex. So the *falun* design is a miniature representation of the universe. In all other dimensions it has forms of existence as well, along with processes through which it evolves, and so I consider it a world.

When the *falun* turns clockwise it automatically draws in energy from the universe, and when it turns counterclockwise it sends out energy. One feature of the *falun* is that it benefits the person it resides in when rotating inward (clockwise), and benefits those around him when rotating outward (counterclockwise). People have asked why there are *tai-chi* symbols in it when ours is a Buddhist practice and *tai-chi* are something Daoist. The reason these are included is that what we practice is immense, and equivalent to working with the entire universe. Just consider what would happen if either of the two major systems of practice in the universe—the Buddhist and Daoist—were excluded from the *falun*: it wouldn't amount to a complete universe or be appropriate to call it that. So we include something Daoist. People have asked why Christianity, Confucianism, and other faiths aren't represented in the *falun*, while the Daoist system is. What I can disclose to you is that Confucian practice is considered Daoist when it reaches a really advanced stage; and many Western religions are considered Buddhist, and part of its system, at advanced stages. There are just two systems that are major.

You might be curious why there are *tai-chi* with red and blue in them as well as red and black, when usually the *tai-chi* is thought of as consisting of black and white matter, or the energies of *yin* and *yang*. But the latter is a rudimentary understanding of it, since the *tai-chi* displays itself in different ways across dimensions, and at the highest planes it manifests in the colors that we are using here. Daoist practice as we know it does in fact have a *tai-chi* made of red and black. Let me illustrate the idea that's at work here. Some of us whose inner eyes are open have found that what appears in this dimension to be red is green in another dimension next to ours. And what appears as golden yellow here may, in another dimension, appear to be purple. So there is variation in the colors that people see, and this owes to the fact that colors differ across dimensions. The *tai-chi* with red and blue in it belongs to the Great Way of the Prior Heavenly Realm, which includes the Mystical Ways. The small *srivatsas* 卍 on the four sides are Buddhist, and, like the one in the center, belong to the Buddhist system. The *falun* is vivid with these colors, and so we have made this design Falun Dafa's symbol.

The *falun* that some of you see via your inner eye won't necessarily be of the same color as our symbol. The color of the background may change, though the design will not. And when your inner eye perceives the turning *falun* that I place at your lower abdomen, the background color might be red, purple, green, or perhaps transparent. The color regularly changes among red, orange, yellow, green, blue, indigo, and violet. So you might see a different color from the one that our symbol has. Neither the colors nor the layout of the *srivatsa*s 卍 and *tai-chi* will change, however. We liked the look of the *falun* symbol with the background color that you now see, and so we settled on it. There are many things that people with higher powers can see in the *falun* beyond this dimension.

Some people comment that the *srivatsa* 卍 calls to mind Hitler's emblem. But that shouldn't be a concern, as the symbol isn't by nature connected with any particular group of people. Another concern I've heard is that if it were tilted to the side, it would be the same as Hitler's. But that's a non-issue since ours spins, and in two directions. The symbol came to be widely known in the world some twenty-five hundred years ago, during the time of the Buddha. By contrast, it has only been a matter of decades since Hitler and World War II, and what's more, he usurped it. Also, his was black, unlike ours, and was used standing on end, with the tip pointing upward. We'll leave the discussion of the *falun* at that. Note that I'm limiting my remarks to just its outermost form.

You might be wondering what the *srivatsa* 卍 represents in the Buddhist system. Regular people think of it as symbolizing fortune and happiness, but that's a rather worldly take on it. I can disclose to you that the *srivatsa* 卍 indicates the level of a Buddha's attainment; only beings who have achieved the divine status of a Buddha have it. Lesser divinities such as *bodhisattvas* and *arhats* don't, except for the Four Great Bodhisattvas. We have seen that these eminent *bodhisattvas* have far surpassed the attainments of a typical Buddha, and are even higher than *tathagata* Buddhas. There are countless Buddhas who have surpassed the level of *tathagata*, which has but one *srivatsa* 卍. Those who achieve a level of attainment above *tathagata* have more *srivatsas* 卍. A Buddha whose status is twice as high as *tathagata* will have two *srivatsas* 卍, while those still higher may have three, four, or five, and so on. They might be so many as to cover the body, including the head, shoulders, and even knees. And when no room is left they will even appear on places like the palms of the hands, the pads of the fingers, the arches of the feet, or the pads of the toes. The number of *srivatsas* 卍 will keep increasing in proportion to one's level of attainment, without end. So the *srivatsa* 卍 represents a divine status, with the number increasing proportionally to one's rank.

The Mystical Ways

Alongside the Buddhist and Daoist practices there is another type known as the Mystical Ways (*chi-men*)—or "Mystical Practices," to use their own term for it. It's usually held, and has been since ancient times in China, that the Buddhist and Daoist approaches to spiritual practice are orthodox, or "proper." The Mystical Ways, by contrast, have never been made public and their existence is known to few. At most, people may have come across them in fictional works.

This might lead some to wonder whether the Mystical Ways really do exist, when in fact, they do. During my own journey of spiritual practice—in the later years, to be specific—I encountered three accomplished members of the Mystical Ways who transmitted to me the best parts of their disciplines; what they imparted was exceptionally unique and good. And because what they have is so unique, the things gained from their practice are quite peculiar. Most people wouldn't be able to make sense of them. Mystical Ways have been described as neither Buddhist nor Daoist, since their practice doesn't fall into either category. And that led to their being labeled as "alternative" or "unorthodox," while they prefer to call themselves Mystical Ways. While it might seem derogatory to call them alternative or unorthodox, it definitely doesn't mean that people are opposed to them. People aren't saying they are evil. Those terms don't imply anything nefarious. Historically in China both Buddhist and Daoist practices have been called true, or central, spiritual disciplines, and so when practices such as the Mystical ones are misunderstood, they end up getting called alternative—as opposed to being completely proper or mainstream. And as for the "unorthodox" label, it was just meant to suggest "a clumsy approach." It often had this sense in classical Chinese. So hopefully this sheds some light on the label.

There is nothing malevolent about the Mystical Ways, as they are morally strict and align their practice with the qualities of the universe. They don't violate the features or norms of the universe, nor do anything wrong. So their practices shouldn't be thought of as deviant. And Buddhist and Daoist practices shouldn't be considered virtuous on account of the universe's qualities aligning with them, but rather, vice versa: they are virtuous because they align their practice with the qualities of the universe. The Mystical Ways certainly aren't evil if they do the same, and deserve to be called virtuous as well. What is good or evil, or virtuous or wicked, must be measured against the qualities of the universe. The Mystical Ways are virtuous and true practices in that they abide by these. The only difference is that they require different things of their adherents than do Buddhist or Daoist practices. They don't offer their teachings to many students, and prefer to keep the scale of instruction small. Daoist practices are similar in that they will only pass on the true teachings to one student, even if many are trained. Buddhist practices, by contrast, believe in benefiting all lives and welcome whoever is willing and able to practice.

The Mystical Ways pass their teachings down to just one recipient; over a long stretch of time only one person is selected for the transmission. And for this reason what they do has never been revealed to regular people. When *chi-gong* was in its heyday a few years back, I observed that, naturally enough, a few people from these practices came out to teach. But their attempts to teach the public were repeatedly unsuccessful, for there were certain things that their masters strictly forbade them from divulging. When teaching to the general public, one cannot pick and choose students, and those who come to learn will include people of both good and poor character. People with all sorts of preconceived notions will come, and so it's not possible to be selective. For this reason the Mystical Ways aren't suitable for a wider audience. Their unique approaches would likely put students at risk if they were taught publicly.

If Buddhists aspire to become enlightened and Daoists to become perfected beings, what about those in the Mystical Ways? They will become boundless immortals who are not tied to any one specific domain in the universe, as would happen with a heavenly paradise. As you may know, the Buddha, Shakyamuni, presides over the Saha Paradise, Buddha Amitabha over the Paradise of Ultimate Bliss, and Medicine Buddha over the Lapis Lazuli Paradise, with each divine figure like these having a paradise of his or her own. Each great divinity has a heavenly kingdom of his or her own making, where many followers reside. Successful adherents of the Mystical Ways, by contrast, have no set domain in the universe and will be boundless immortals with no specific post in heaven.

Practicing an Evil Way

Practicing an evil way can assume any of several different forms. Some individuals practice evil means exclusively, and what they practice goes back for generations. What motivates them to do so is the lure of worldly things such as status, material gain, and wealth. Of course, these are people of poor character and they will not be developing higher energy. What they will get, however, is karma. One feature of karma is that if enough of it is amassed, it forms into a type of energy; yet this type of energy is nothing to speak of, and no match for the energy of practitioners. But it will be able to exercise power over regular people, since it is a form of energy and can strengthen the powers of the body if its density grows high. This is why people have passed these practices down through the ages. Adherents claim that they can develop energy by doing bad deeds and verbally abusing people. But they can't. What they are doing is increasing the density of their black matter, or karma, through wrongful things. So they can, in effect, strengthen and develop the lesser powers of the body by way of karma, but those powers don't amount to much. So they're mistaken in thinking that they can develop true energy by doing wrongful things.

While it's been said that "evil is more powerful than good," that is a harmful secular view. The Devil's powers will never surpass those of the Way. Some background is in order. The universe known to man is but one small universe among countless ones, and we just call it "the universe" for simplicity's sake. Each time this universe has passed through a great number of ages, a cataclysm of cosmic proportions has visited it and destroyed everything in its wake, including planets and all life. The motion of the universe follows a set pattern, and in this current cycle more than just humanity has turned bad. Many lives have now observed that it has been a long time since the last explosion occurred in this dimension of the universe. Astronomers today can't observe the last explosion because what's seen with the most powerful telescopes today are events that are one hundred and fifty thousand light years removed. Not until an equal number of light years are spanned will the changes currently happening in the universe be visible here.

The entire universe has undergone immense changes as of now. Past changes of this scale have always spelled complete destruction for all life throughout the universe. In each instance, all of the universe's traits and material elements were to be obliterated by explosion, with nothing remaining and lives across the board perishing. However, in each instance the explosion has not been total. So whenever divine ones of an extraordinarily high realm have constructed the universe anew, there have always been certain beings that were present in the universe already, as a vestige from the past. Yet the new universe that the divine ones were remaking would be done according to their own traits and criteria, which were different from those of the past.

The beings that didn't perish in these explosions would bring with them into the new universe the traits and ways of operating that they knew from the last. However, the newly formed universe would be governed by the traits and laws of the new universe. And so the beings that carried over from before would serve as evil that hindered the operations of the new universe. Such beings are not outright evil, however, since it's simply that they embody the traits of the previous universe. They have been known as dark forces. They don't pose a threat to regular people and certainly wouldn't harm them; the issue is simply that they hold fast to the old ways of doing things. This is something that ordinary people were previously forbidden to know. I would say that those entities are nothing really, and pale in comparison to the many divine beings in the heavens far above, beyond the *tathagata* level. Aging, sickness, and death are also kinds of dark beings, though they exist in order to uphold the nature of the universe.

Buddhist teachings on the transmigration of souls mention what are called *asura*. *Asura* are really just creatures of another dimension that don't have the innate nature man does. They are exceedingly low in level and powerless in the eyes of the greater divine beings, but to ordinary people would seem terrifying. They carry a certain amount of energy and consider humans to be beasts, and so they delight in feeding upon them. In recent years some have come out to teach energy practices. But they are nothing, and don't even have a human appearance. They look frightening. When a person learns their things he inevitably crosses over to where they are and becomes one of them. When some people do energy practices their thoughts aren't right, and those entities might, if the thoughts agree with them, come over to teach these individuals. But as it's said, "Good is a far greater force than evil." No one will tamper with you unless you have bad motives. But if you do harbor bad intentions they will come to assist you, and you may end up heading toward the dark side.

Another phenomenon is what's known as unknowingly practicing evil, and it refers to instances of people practicing in an evil manner without realizing it. This is something extremely common and far too widespread. It relates to what I said the other day about many people having inappropriate thoughts in mind while practicing. You might see someone who by all appearances is practicing hard, holding some special posture, arms and legs shaking from fatigue, but his mind might be elsewhere. That person might be anxiously thinking about needing to make some purchase or other before prices go up, for example. Or he might be worried about getting passed over for housing, which his company is allotting, due to the person in charge having personal grievances with him. And he will only get more worked up as he dwells on it further, thinking it'll surely go wrong, and he might even start calculating how to challenge the person on it. The mind could go anywhere, from family matters to national concerns, with some things even triggering anger.

Virtue has to be a priority with any energy practice. If you aren't having good thoughts as you practice, at least you shouldn't have bad thoughts. Having no thoughts at all is best, because certain foundations have to be laid in the beginning stages of practice and will play a critical role later on, and one's mind does exert a certain effect. If you are mixing things into your energy as you practice, could what you're developing be good? Wouldn't it be dark? Yet few people are free of this problem. Most never stop to consider why they don't enjoy good health even after practicing at length. In other cases people might not be thinking bad thoughts as they practice, but they are always wanting to gain psychic powers or other things as they practice, with strong longings and inappropriate mindsets. That in fact amounts to practicing evil unknowingly. But they won't want to hear it if you point it out since they are convinced that all's well since they learned from some master or other. But he might have told them the importance of being virtuous, which they didn't take to heart. So, little good will come of their practice if they are always adding in bad thoughts. It would amount to practicing evil unknowingly. This is something quite common.

Tantric Union Practices

There are methods of Tantric practice that are referred to as "union practices." You may have seen Tibetan Buddhist statues or paintings depicting a male and female figure conjoining as a means of practice. In some cases the male figure has the look of a Buddha and will be embracing a woman who is unclothed; in others the figures are transformations of Buddhas, such as warrior deities with oxen or horse heads, which are similarly embracing an unclothed female figure. If we're to make sense of this we have to delve into a few things first. Centuries ago in the ancient past, humanity's moral values were more or less the same throughout the world; the conservative values seen in China weren't simply the result of Confucian influence. This suggests that the practices of Tantric union didn't in fact originate here on this earth, but came from another planet. The method can indeed serve as a component of spiritual practice, however. When the method was transmitted to China at one time, people weren't receptive to it on account of its having men and women conjoined in practice, as well as its having secretive components. And so it was abolished by the emperor during the Hui Chang era of the Tang Dynasty. It was forbidden from being taught in the interior of China. At that time it was referred to as Tang Esoterica. But it has been passed down ever since in the unique setting of Tibet. Then how does it serve a spiritual purpose, you might be wondering? Tantric union practices strive to achieve a balance of *yin* and *yang* by gathering *yin* to supplement *yang* and vice versa, through mutual supplementation and refinement.

As you might know, both Buddhist and Daoist thought hold that the human body innately has both *yin* and *yang*; this is especially apparent in the Daoist concept of *yin-yang*. And it is the presence of both *yin* and *yang* in the body that makes it possible for you to develop higher powers, an angelic body, cherubs, spiritual bodies, and other supernatural beings. *Yin* and *yang* are what make these possible with spiritual practice; this holds true for the male as well as the female body. These supernatural beings can be generated in the energy center of either gender's body. So the Buddhist and Daoist views on *yin* and *yang* in the body make plenty of sense. Daoist practice often regards the upper half of the body as *yang* and lower as *yin*; some regard the back of the body as *yang* and front as *yin*; and others regard the left side of the body as *yang* and right as *yin*. So this is where the Chinese saying about "man left, woman right" comes from, and there is merit to it. Because the human body naturally has both *yin* and *yang*, the body can, through the interplay of *yin* and *yang*, achieve a state of *yin-yang* balance and generate an abundance of supernatural beings.

This tells us, then, that we can progress to great spiritual heights without adopting Tantric union practices. What's more, using them runs the risk of falling prey to evil and lapsing into a dark practice, if it's not handled well. These practices are normally used by a monk or lama only at a very advanced stage of Esoteric Buddhist practice, and so he will be spiritually accomplished; and he will be guided through the practice by a master. And because this individual's mind will be virtuous, he will be solid and able to handle it well, and not succumb to evil. By contrast, someone who is not very spiritually developed has no business using it, as he would surely fall prey to evil. His character wouldn't suffice. He would still have worldly, covetous thoughts along with sexual desire, and that would be the plane on which he dwelled. So it would be sure to turn out evil. This is why I believe it's devious to teach such things to those who are still not very far along in their practice.

A number of teachers of energy practices have been teaching Tantric union in recent years. And oddly, it's seen in Daoist practice too; and this isn't just a recent development, but goes back many centuries to the Tang Dynasty. Yet it makes no sense for Daoist practice to go in for Tantric union. The Daoist theory of *tai-chi* holds that the body is a microcosm of the universe and naturally endowed with both *yin* and *yang*. Any true spiritual teaching that has been authentically transmitted will have been passed down from a distant age. Any casual alteration or anything that's arbitrarily introduced into it will compromise its practice and make the goal of spiritual perfection no longer attainable. So under no circumstance should you do Tantric union practices if they aren't part of the discipline you follow. Doing so would take you astray and lead to problems. This very much applies to anyone who does Falun Dafa. We don't have Tantric union practices or anything like them. So now you know our take on this.

Practice for Both Mind and Body

Practice for both mind and body is something I've touched upon. It occurs when the spiritual practice that you do works on both your mind as well as your physical body, such that your body changes from its core. With this process your cells will be gradually replaced by high-energy matter, and the aging process slowed. Your body will show signs of changing and reverting to a more youthful state, incrementally, until in the end the material of your body will have been replaced entirely by high-energy matter, and your body will no longer consist of the same material it once did. It will be the kind of body I was describing earlier, which has transcended and been freed of the five elements. It will be a body that is truly immortal.

The practice done in Buddhist monastic settings deals solely with the mind and doesn't make use of physical techniques or work on the body. Instead, the focal point is an approach taught by the Buddha, called *nirvana*. His practice was profound, in fact, and he was fully capable of transforming his innate body into high-energy matter and taking it with him after death. But as an example to others, he opted instead to enter into *nirvana*, wherein the body is left here. He decided upon this approach in order to help people abandon attachments to the utmost extent, giving up everything—including even their own bodies, ultimately. All attachments were to go. So he opted for *nirvana* in order to help his followers become as detached as possible, and so successive generations of monks have gone the same route. With *nirvana*, the monk's physical body is cast off with his passing while his soul ascends and carries forth his energy.

In Daoist practice the emphasis is on developing the body. They are selective about students and don't try to save all lives, so those whom they deal with are excellent and outstanding persons, and can be taught magical skills and how to spiritually transform the body. In Buddhist practice, by contrast, those approaches generally can't be taught. This is especially so for religious Buddhism. Not all Buddhist practices shun such methods, though. There are a number of profound, great Buddhist practices that do use them. Our discipline is one example. In Falun Dafa the innate body and angelic body, which are two different things, are both desirable. The latter is also a physical body, one composed of high-energy matter, though it's not something that can be freely revealed in this dimension. It's necessary to have an innate body, as we do, if you are to maintain a normal human appearance in this dimension. So you will still look about the same as a regular person after your innate body has changed, since your body's molecular configuration will be the same; it's only that your cells will have been replaced by high-energy matter. But your body will be different from a regular person's, as yours will be able to cross over into other dimensions.

By doing a practice for both mind and body, you will gain a youthful appearance and look much younger than your years. I was once approached by a practitioner who asked me to guess her age. I would have thought she was in her forties, when it turned out she was almost seventy. With no wrinkles, a glowing complexion, and a rosiness to her skin, she hardly looked like someone approaching seventy. Changes like that are likely to happen when you practice Falun Dafa. If I'm allowed to tease a little, I'd say that young women will naturally achieve the beautiful skin tone they're always after, provided they sincerely do mind-body practice—and without needing to go to the lengths they once did. I'll leave it at that. People used to consider me young since it was mostly older people who made up China's workforce. Things are better now, with more younger professionals out there. And I'm not young anymore myself, in fact. I am now forty-three and quickly approaching fifty.

Spiritual Bodies

Have you ever wondered why it is that some religious images seem to radiate energy? Few people can explain it. Some offer that it stems from monks having chanted scriptures before these images, or in other words, from their having engaged in spiritual practice facing them. But when a monk or anyone else practices, the energy that's emitted is dispersed rather than directed at one spot. There should be even and equal amounts of energy over the floor, ceiling, and walls of the place of worship. So it doesn't explain why only the images give off such strong energy. Much less does it shed light on why many religious statues found deep in the mountains, in certain caves, or carved into natural edifices exude energy. Many interpretations have been offered as to why this is, yet none have hit the mark. The real reason for the energy on those statues is the presence of a divine being's spiritual body (*fa-shen*). The statues have energy because a spiritual body is present.

We can begin to understand how spiritual bodies come into being if we stop and consider that well-known divinities [who have these], such as the Buddha or Guan Yin, must have once upon a time been regular practitioners themselves. They would have formed them, as people do, when their spiritual development reached a certain height beyond the human realm. Spiritual bodies are generated in the body's energy center and are formed from the Way as well as from higher energy. They materialize in other dimensions. A spiritual body is endowed with the original person's considerable powers, yet its consciousness or thoughts will be dictated by the person's main body. That said, a spiritual body is in fact a complete, independent, fully bona fide life in its own right, and so it can do anything on its own. Its actions will be consistent with, and even identical to, whatever the person's conscious mind would want done. The spiritual bodies will do things however the person himself would if he were to do them. So this is what we refer to as a spiritual body. Whatever I wish to have done—such as mending the bodies of sincere practitioners—will be carried out by my spiritual bodies. Bodies like these have to materialize in other dimensions since they aren't equipped with a regular human body. These supernatural beings are not fixed and unchanging, but can expand and contract. In some instances one of them might become so large that not even all of its head is visible, while at other times it might become so small as to be tinier than a cell.

The Blessing of Sacred Images

A religious statue fresh out of the factory is merely a piece of art. And so sacred images are often formally blessed in order to invite the spiritual body of the divine one they represent to reside on them. And thereafter the statues can serve as tangible representations of that being for people to worship. The spiritual body will provide sincere believers who worship these statues with protection and look after them as they go about their practice. This is what the blessing of images is meant to accomplish. But the ritual that's involved will only achieve its intent if the person doing it has virtuous thoughts; if divine ones of higher planes are involved; or if it's done by someone who is spiritually accomplished and has the powers for it.

In Buddhist temples it's commonly held that Buddha statues will have no power if they don't first go through this kind of procedure, which is referred to as "image consecration" in Asia. There are few monks still alive today in temples who have a mastery of the Buddhist teachings. In the wake of China's Cultural Revolution and its destruction, junior monks who were never fully initiated into the teachings have since become abbots. Much of what was once transmitted has been lost. If you ask them what consecration is for, they will say that the statue has power afterwards, but they can't really explain what that means in concrete terms. So they are merely holding a ceremony in that case, and what they call consecration only amounts to placing a small piece of paper with scripture on it inside of a statue, sealing it up with paper, and then chanting to it. But does it serve the purpose that consecration is meant to? It depends on how they do the chanting.

The Buddha taught about "right mindfulness" and that recitation of scriptures must be done with a focused mind, free of distraction, and only then will one's words have resonance in the paradise connected to one's practice. And that's what it takes to summon a divine being. Unless one of his or her spiritual bodies engages the image, the objective of consecration won't be met.

It happens that some monastics or religious figures may be preoccupied as they recite scripture at a consecration ceremony, thinking about how much they will be paid for it afterwards. Or they might be mulling over how someone has wronged them, since now there's even infighting in monastic settings. There is no denying that these things are happening now, in these latter days. My point here isn't to criticize religions, but to say that certain religious settings simply aren't pure in this age. And as you might imagine, a consecration ceremony won't achieve its purpose if the minds of those involved are preoccupied with worldly and inappropriate thoughts, and these are what they're projecting; the ceremony will fail to summon a divine being. But that said, there are still some monasteries and religious settings that are good, even if they are rare.

In one city I observed a Buddhist monk doing a consecration procedure whose hands were as dark as coal. He would stuff a scripture into the hollow interior of the statue, seal it up, mutter a few words, and then pronounce the consecration complete. He would then grab the next statue, mutter for a moment or two, and make forty more dollars for another consecration. And monks now even treat it as a kind of enterprise, gaining wealth by consecrating images. But I could tell at a glance that the procedure hadn't achieved what it should have, as the monk involved really didn't have the powers needed. Yet monks are now going in for such things. I have seen other surprising things as well. At one Buddhist temple I observed a man who looked like a lay follower. He claimed that he was doing consecration for the Buddha statue there. He had a mirror in hand and was angling it to reflect the sun's light upon the body of the image. And he claimed that by doing so, he was performing a consecration.* So it has reached the point of absurdity. Yet things like this are quite widespread, with Buddhism being what it is today.

There is a giant bronze Buddha statue installed on Lantau Island, in Hong Kong, that was made in Nanjing city. It's an enormous statue. At the time of its inauguration a large number of monks assembled from around the world to partake in its consecration. Someone there was holding up a mirror angled toward the sun, trying to reflect its light onto the statue's face, thinking that this would consecrate it. To see something like that transpire at such a sacred gathering, on such a solemn occasion, was really tragic. But the Buddha did say that it would be hard for even monks to ensure their own salvation in the latter days, let alone save others. Things are in turmoil now, with many monks interpreting the scriptures in light of their own, limited perspectives, and with non-Buddhist scriptures having made their way into the temples. It should be noted, of course, that there *are* monks who are sincere about spiritual practice and quite good. So consecration is ultimately about inviting a divine being's spiritual body to reside on a religious image, and when that happens it is successful.

A religious statue that hasn't been successfully consecrated or blessed should not be worshipped, as doing so can have serious consequences. Recent scientific research can help us to understand why. Researchers have found that a person's thoughts, or the ideas in his brain, can generate something material. And we do find thoughts to have material form when we look upon them from higher planes, though the form we're referring to shouldn't be mistaken for the "brain waves" that research has uncovered; rather, this material assumes the form of a complete human brain. Normally, any brain-shaped material that a regular person emanates while thinking will dissipate before long, since his or her thoughts don't have energy behind them. But the material will last much longer in the case of practitioners, owing to their energy. So bringing this back to the topic of religious statues, we shouldn't expect them to have the faculty of thought at the time of their production. A statue won't if it hasn't gone through the procedure of consecration, and been through a successful one, at that—even if it took place in a religious setting. And if the procedure was done by a false master or someone involved in the dark arts, then it's worse [than nothing being done at all], and dangerous, since a fox or a weasel might get on the statue.

This means that significant danger is posed by venerating unconsecrated images. I'll give you a sense for just how dangerous it is. I have indicated that humanity has been declining in every regard in recent times, and everything about this world as well as the universe has been declining in turn. People are reaping what they have sown. True, virtuous teachings or practices are hard to find. Obstacles of every sort await those who try to find them. And even simply praying to one's god might go wrong, since people have no idea whether what's on the statue or icon they're praying to is the entity they intend. So things are really complicated now. I can explain why, for anyone in doubt. Things go downhill quickly when people start praying to an unconsecrated statue, since few today do so for the salvation of their souls. Most pray in hopes of lessening the adversity in their lives or making out better financially. But there is no scriptural basis for prayers and longings like those.

When someone seeks financial help and bows before an image of the Buddha, his god, or a holy being, and prays for monetary support, lo and behold, a complete thought forms and issues forth. And it will land right on the statue, since it was directed toward it. The form of the statue in other dimensions can expand or shrink. So after the person's thought rests on the statue, the statue will come to have a brain and the ability to think, though not yet a body. The prayers from others that follow provide it with a certain amount of energy. And if it is practitioners doing this, the danger is all the greater, for the statue will receive their energy right from the outset, and it will form into a tangible body in another dimension. That body will reside in another realm and know the workings of the universe to some extent. And so it will have the power to do things that help people, and it can develop some amount of energy. But whatever it does for people comes with conditions attached, or at a price. It moves about freely in another dimension and can readily control ordinary people. But its appearance will be identical to the statue from which it arose. So although you might have a vision of what appears to be a holy being, and it might look just like the image you prayed to, it would be a false entity and the product of worship or prayers. The minds of false entities like these will be terrible and think only of money. Yet they won't attempt to do anything gravely wrong, since they were born in another dimension, have the faculty of thought, and know to some extent how the laws of the universe work. They will, however, venture to do bad things of a lesser degree. And sometimes they will help people, for if they didn't make such gestures they would be purely evil and be slain. But just consider what kind of "help" they offer. Suppose someone prays before a sacred image, asking for an ailing family member to be healed. Very well, then—that bad entity will lend a hand. It will have you put money into the donation tray beside it, since money is what's on its mind. And the more money you offer, the faster it will make your family member recover. From another dimension it can impact an ordinary person using the energy that it has. The stakes are even greater if someone with higher energy prays to that entity. Of course, it should go without saying that someone dedicated to spiritual practice has no business praying to get things, let alone asking for money. And yet some do. Even just praying for your family's well-being is considered an emotional attachment to them. As much as you might want to positively influence someone's life, you have to understand that everyone has his or her own fate. If you pray to a false entity and ask for financial blessings, it will respond by helping you. It is all too eager to see you asking for more money. It can take more from you in exchange, in that case. And it's a fair trade. So it will let you have some of the money that people put into the donation tray, since there is plenty there. It might play out as your stumbling upon a wallet or handbag as you walk down the street, or getting a bonus at work. It will try all avenues to get you money. But it comes at a cost. Nothing is to be had for free, after all. And so it will snatch a portion of your energy cluster, if that's what your practice generates, or your energy, since it lacks these and wants them.

These false entities can be quite dangerous. Many who are involved in spiritual practice and whose inner eyes have been opened believe that they have seen higher beings. Some have claimed that groups of them have come to their temples, with one named something-or-other leading the groups. And they described how they were visited frequently by them, with one group coming one day and then another the next, and so on. So what was going on? These belong to the category I've been describing. They were not true holy beings, but false ones. A considerable number fall into this category.

What I've described is all the more dangerous if it unfolds in a religious community, as that entity will take charge of the monks who venerate it. And it would have grounds for doing so, since they would clearly be praying to it. And so it would watch over them and direct their practice. But where would these monks go even if they *did* manage to complete their spiritual journey under it? No deities above would welcome them, since they would have been under this lower entity's guidance and would belong to it. So the monks' efforts would be for naught. It is terribly hard now for people to gain true divine standing through spiritual practice. The phenomenon I just described is quite common. While many people have thought that they saw a divine light or presence in well-known mountains and river valleys, the majority of it came from these false entities, since they have energy and can cause apparitions. True divine beings, by contrast, would not reveal themselves so readily.

At one time there were fewer of these false entities, whereas now there are many. Any wrongful acts that they commit will result in their being slain by those above. But they may manage to elude the retribution by taking refuge on a religious image. Higher divinities won't generally intervene in the affairs of the world without good reason. The higher a being's realm, the less likely it is to disrupt the affairs of the secular world, and it will try to avoid any intrusions altogether. So they generally wouldn't do anything radical like destroying the statue that harbors such an entity with a lightning bolt, and so it's ignored. And those entities know to flee when their execution is imminent. This means that there is no telling whether the apparition that someone sees is real.

This might raise for many of you the question of what to do with any religious statues or images that might be in your homes. A number of you may have thought of asking me for help. I want to help anyone learning our practice, so you can handle it as follows. While holding my book (since it contains my photo) or a photo of me, hold the statue or image and form the *mudra* known as greater lotus. Then, just as if I were really present, you can simply request that I bless or consecrate it for you, and it will be done in a matter of seconds. But I should add that this only works for our practitioners. Trying to do this on behalf of your friends or family won't work, for I only look after our practitioners. Some people claim that you can ward off evil for friends or family by placing my picture in their homes, but I am not going to do so for non-practitioners. Your doing that is about the most disrespectful thing you could do to your teacher.

Having talked about false apparitions, there is something else to address. Many people in ancient China did spiritual practice deep in the mountains or woods, though it seems that few still do. But that's not the case. Rather, it's that they keep from being seen by regular people; their numbers haven't dwindled at all. They have higher powers at their disposal that can keep them veiled. It's not that they are no longer around. They are still there. There are thousands in the world today, with China having relatively more. Their population is greater in the famous mountains and valleys there, and they can be found on some of the higher peaks as well. They use their powers to seal up the entrances to their caves so that no one can see them. Their practice is rather slow and their methods somewhat inefficient, since they haven't understood the keys to spiritual development. By contrast, we focus directly on the mind and base our practice on the highest qualities, or way, of the universe. So our energy naturally develops quite fast. The methods of spiritual practice can be thought of as having a pyramid-like shape, with only the center axis being the main avenue. Those practicing on the side paths, or in lesser ways, might have all of their powers released even though their character isn't necessarily that elevated or their spiritual progress that advanced. But such approaches are far inferior to the main path of true practice.

The teachers of the lesser ways also pass down their teachings and have disciples. There are limits to how far one can progress in those disciplines or to what extent they can change one's character, so the spiritual development of their followers is necessarily limited. The further from the main path that a lesser, worldly practice is, the more elaborate its theories will be and the more complicated its methods, since it hasn't understood the keys to spiritual progress. They haven't grasped that the mind is what matters most in spiritual practice, and instead believe that progress can be made just by enduring hardships. So it takes them years of prolonged practice, even hundreds or thousands, to gain even just a little bit of higher energy. But the fruits of their practice are not in fact the result of hardships. Rather, they stem from the wearing away of attachments over all those strenuous years, similar to how the passions of youth naturally fade with age and the passing of one's dreams. So while followers of lesser paths may find that they can develop higher energy via meditation, concentration, and hardship as they make strides in their practice, what they don't realize is that it comes from *the removal of their attachments*. And this is something that's happening only slowly, by wearing them out over the course of many long and grueling years.

Our practice has a well-defined focus. It really makes your attachments evident and sees to it that they are removed. This accelerates your spiritual development. While traveling I have often run into people like I was describing, who have practiced for many years. They would tell me that nobody has realized that they are there, and that they wouldn't intervene in or try to disrupt what I'm doing. They could be considered relatively good.

There have been bad ones as well, however, and these we have had to deal with. One example stems from when I went to Guizhou province to teach the practice for the first time. Someone approached me right in the middle of my class, stating that he was the student of someone who studies under such-and-such master, and that this master had practiced for a great many years and wanted to see me. I looked and saw that this person carried awful *yin* energy, which gave him a sallow complexion. I declined his request by saying that I didn't have time to meet with the master. This made the master upset, and so he started to meddle with me, making trouble day after day. I don't have any interest in contesting with others, and there was no need to. So whenever he sent bad things my way I would simply clear them out and go back to giving my teaching.

Back a few centuries ago, during the Ming Dynasty, there was a person who became possessed by a snake during his time practicing. He eventually passed away without succeeding at his practice. At that point the snake took over his body and assumed a human form. And this "master" who wanted to see me was none other than that snake-in-human-form. As he was still the same creature essentially, he changed back into a large snake and began meddling with me. It really went too far, so I clasped it in my hand and used an extremely powerful type of energy, called "dissolving energy," to dissolve the lower part of its body and reduce it to water. After that its upper body slithered back home.

One day, the female volunteer who ran the Falun Dafa center in Guizhou was also sought out by someone whose teacher studied with that snake, claiming that their master wished to see her. And so she went. Everything was pitch black when she entered the cave where their master resided. She could only make out a silhouette sitting inside, with green light emanating from a pair of eyes. The cave would light up when the eyes opened and go dark when they closed. The shadowy figure said in a local dialect, "Li Hongzhi will be returning. Next time none of us will do those things that we did. That was wrong. Li Hongzhi has come to save people." His student's follower interjected, "Grandmaster, are you able to stand? What's happened to your legs?" He responded, "I can no longer stand because my legs were injured." He was asked what had happened to them, and so he recounted how he had made trouble for us and the consequences that followed. But then the following year, in 1993 at the Asian Health Expo in Beijing, he again started trouble with me. At that point I destroyed the snake completely since it was always doing evil and trying to disrupt my teaching of Dafa. After I did so, people from the same discipline, old and young alike, male as well as female, wanted to take action against me. I then said a few words to them that startled and frightened them. They abandoned their plans for revenge upon learning what had happened. Some of them were no different from worldly, ordinary people, even after having practiced for so long. So this is just to share a few incidents while on the topic of consecration.

Occult Healing

Occult healing is something that many spiritual teachers instruct their students in, since they regard it as a spiritual art. But it shouldn't be seen as part of spiritual practice. It is more akin to a kind of secret trick, incantation, or technique that's passed on. The forms it assumes, such as making talismans, burning incense, burning paper effigies, or chanting spells, do have the ability to heal, and its approach to healing is rather unique. Consider how a boil on the face might be treated, for example. A practitioner of these arts will dip a brush in cinnabar ink and draw a circle on the ground, which he then makes an "X" inside of. The person with the boil will be asked to stand in the middle of the circle while the practitioner begins to chant a spell. Then he dips the brush in the cinnabar ink again, and this time draws a circle on the person's face. He chants a spell while drawing, and keeps going like this until he finally makes a dot on the boil. At that point he will be finished chanting, and will declare that the boil is healed. When the person touches his face to check, he will indeed find that it has shrunk and no longer hurts. So it worked. Minor ailments can be treated, though not major ones. Another example might be a treatment for an aching arm. The occult practitioner will begin chanting a spell and ask that the person extend her arm. He will then blow a puff of air into the Union Valley acupoint of the hand that's extended, and have it exit the person's body via the same point of her other hand. She will feel a breeze go through her, and then find that her arm is no longer sore to the touch like it was before. Other methods include burning paper effigies, making talismans, and putting up protective charms.

The lesser Daoist practices of the secular world don't teach about the spiritual development of the body. They just concern themselves with things like fortune-telling, *feng-shui*, warding off evil, and healing. Occult healing is common to them. While occult techniques can heal, the methods used are not by any means good. But I am not going to spell out exactly how it is that they heal. Followers of Falun Dafa shouldn't use those techniques, for the energy involved is both low and bad. In ancient China healing methods were categorized into different divisions, such as bone setting, acupuncture, massage, naprapathy, acupressure, energy healing, herbal medicine, and so on, with many categories. Each method of healing was referred to as a "division." The occult healing that we've discussed here was categorized as the thirteenth division, and so its full designation was "occult healing, the thirteenth division." Occult healing doesn't belong in our spiritual practice.

Its powers don't come from the energy born of spiritual practice, but rather, by way of magical arts.

THE
SIXTH TALK

The Fear of Practice Going Wrong

THERE IS A MISCONCEPTION in China that has affected many people, both spiritual and otherwise: that energy practice can go wrong and lead you to the dark side, or madness. Some have hyped it up enough to scare people away from practicing, as it sounds frightening. But I can tell you that the problem simply doesn't exist.

I should start by saying that many people involved in energy practices *have* brought entity attachment upon themselves, due to their bad intentions. A person like this isn't in control of his mind, and yet he might attribute his abnormal state to "powerful energy." But what has happened is that his body has been taken over by a foreign entity, and so he isn't himself when he practices, and may stagger about, yelling and screaming. People get scared away when they see someone acting like that. And yet many individuals attribute their abnormal states to having strong energy. But they could hardly have real energy if that's what they are doing. The altered states that they experience are lower ones, and at best have only physical benefits. And they are dangerous. If someone gets used to being that way, with his conscious mind never in control, it's possible that his body will be controlled by his subconscious, by foreign energies or signals, by entities that attach to him, or other things. And they might even prompt him to do dangerous things. These episodes really do a disservice to energy practices more broadly. Problems like these stem from the person's having had impure intentions and being driven by attachments to show off. It is not that these practices make people crazy. There may be people who have somehow assumed the title of this-or-that "master" and who buy into the idea, but the fact is that doing an energy practice will *not* make anyone crazy. People who have that idea often get it from fictional stories, like martial arts movies or books. You won't find it anywhere in classical works or religious texts, if you feel compelled to check. And it is not something that will ever happen to you.

There are actually several phenomena that tend to confuse people, and what I've been describing is one type. A person could go off track and bring on entity attachment, or seek to show off by using a supposedly higher "energy state," and both of these involve impure states of mind. Some people even focus on getting psychic powers as they practice, or do practices that aren't legitimate, and become accustomed to letting their minds go whenever they exercise. They lose all self-awareness and turn their bodies over to other beings or forces, like their subconscious or foreign energies or signals, which make them act in bizarre ways. They might leap out of a window or jump into a lake if those things tell them to.

They relinquish their will to live and turn their bodies over to others. This isn't the fault of the practices these people are doing, however; it's that they have strayed from them. They started off by doing those things willfully, and eventually it turned into a bigger problem. Many people mistake being in a trance-like state for being a way of practice, when in reality it's not, and it is going to have serious consequences. So any problems that follow shouldn't be blamed on the practice itself, but on the attachments and intentions that got mixed into it.

There is another scenario that confuses people. It's when energy gets stuck or can't pass through some place, such as the top of the head, and it frightens the person. This is more likely to happen in Daoist practice, where the human body is seen as a micro universe and a student will work on getting energy to move through its "gateways." He may encounter energy stagnation issues, such as having his energy pool at a gateway if it fails to advance through it. This can happen at other places in the body, too, not only the head; it's just that the top of the head is the most sensitive spot in the body. So, if energy ascends to the top of the head and is ready to gush down, yet the person can't break through the gateway, his head will feel heavy or bloated, as if it were wrapped in a thick blanket of energy, or he may experience other similar things. But the basic kind of energy involved, called *chi*, doesn't have any real effect on things or cause real issues for people; and it certainly won't make them ill. So it's a problem when people who don't understand what is really happening make irresponsible and mystical-sounding remarks about it that confuse people. People then start believing that they might go crazy or get into trouble if energy gets stuck at the top of the head, and it scares them.

If energy does get stuck there, it's only a temporary condition. It might persist for as long as half a year in some instances, however. In that case the person can seek out a true instructor to help guide the energy down. But anyone who can't advance through a gateway or whose energy won't descend should examine their character for the cause and consider whether they've stalled at a certain stage for too long and not done the inner, spiritual work that they should. They will find that the energy comes down swiftly after they have made the necessary progress. If you are focusing on changing your body's energy, rather than your character, sweeping changes aren't going to happen; you have to make spiritual progress first. Energy that really isn't moving as it should will not result in much of a problem. The problems that do occur are usually the product of a person's own psychological factors, plus fear, which sets in if someone hears misleading claims about the problems in store for him. And once the person is frightened, it's an attachment—fear—which has to be dealt with, then. And so the greater the person's fear, the more it will seem that he has some condition. He simply must be made to break the attachment, learn a lesson, and grow from it spiritually by letting go of his fears.

Nor will the spiritual work that's in store for you, as a practitioner, be easy. Many forms of higher energy will develop in your body, and all of them will be powerful things that move to and fro inside you and which might feel unpleasant. The main reason it feels that way is that you always worry your body has some condition or other. The reality is, powerful things have come about inside of you; what your body has developed are energies, powers, and many supernatural beings. If any of them move about, your body may have a sensation of itchiness, pain, or something unpleasant, as the peripheral nerves are sensitive; a whole range of phenomena are possible. These are good things, though, and you will experience them up until your body has been remade with high-energy matter. But if you always regard yourself as an ordinary person and mistake such things for health issues, you are going to have a hard time practicing. If you still take yourself to be an ordinary person when you meet with challenges in your practice, then your character has dropped to the human level, at least in those instances.

A true practitioner will look at things from a higher plane, rather than through a human lens. By believing that you are sick you might just make yourself sick. That's because when you take it to be sickness your thoughts are no higher than this world. Neither energy practice nor true spiritual practice will result in health problems, and particularly not the type I was describing, where energy gets stuck somewhere. It's known that illness is actually seventy percent psychological and thirty percent physical. When a person's health takes a turn for the worse, it's usually that he is first worn down mentally, stressed out, and having trouble coping. I'll give an illustration. There was once a person who was tied down to a bed. His arm was lifted and he was told that he was going to be made to bleed. Next he was blindfolded. His wrist was then scratched (without drawing any blood), and a water faucet was turned on so that he heard a dripping sound. He mistook it for blood dripping, and in no time he was dead. Yet he didn't lose a drop of blood; it was the tap water that was dripping. His mind was what caused his death. You might just bring yourself health problems by often thinking that you have them. That's because your thoughts have sunk to the same starting point as the average person, who, naturally, does experience illness.

If a practitioner always thinks he is ill, he is in fact asking for it—asking to be ill. And then that illness can push its way in. A practitioner's plane of thought should be high. You shouldn't always worry that something ails you, for your fear is an attachment and will bring you trouble just the same as other attachments. In spiritual practice you must eliminate karma, and that is painful. A higher energy like *gong* is most definitely *not* something gained through comfort and ease. Without suffering, there would be no way to break your attachments. Let me share a story from Buddhism. There once was a person who went through a great deal of spiritual effort and was on the verge of becoming a holy being (*arhat*), with divine standing. So it was hard not to be happy— he was about to depart the three realms and gain eternal life, after all! But joy is an attachment, and it meant he was excitable. A holy being should be completely detached, however, and not stirred by anything. So he fell and his efforts were in vain. He had to start all over again and work his way back up. After enormous efforts he made it back to his previous stage of achievement. Yet this time he was worried, and had to tell himself not to get excited or he would fall again. And with that fear, he fell again. For that too was an attachment.

Another scenario that confuses people comes about when someone who is mentally ill does an energy or spiritual practice. And there are those who want me to cure this for them. But it is not a disease, as I see it, and I haven't the time to remedy it. It's not a disease in the sense that the mentally ill are not afflicted with a virus; their bodies haven't had pathological changes, as when ulcers form. So it's not a disease, in my view.

Being mentally ill is simply a matter of a person's conscious mind being very weak. So weak, in fact, that the person isn't in command of his own body. It's as if his spirit has no wish to take charge of his body, and so the person is never mentally present or very "with it." When that's the case, his subconscious mind and foreign energies or signals might interfere with him. There are so many planes in each dimension, and information from any of them might try to disturb him. And it's possible that his soul did wrongful things in a past life, and so there would be creditors who would want to harm him. A range of things might come about. So this is what we understand genuine mental disorders to be and what causes them. It should now be apparent why I can't readily treat these for people. As for what you can do in these cases, you could try speaking with him very seriously and help him to become more mentally present. But that's not easily done. If you watch what happens when a physician at a psychiatric hospital is preparing to administer electroshock therapy, with the electrodes in his hands, you will see that the patient goes quiet with fear. What happens is that the fear of the shock makes his soul alert right then.

People who give spiritual practice a try usually find it agreeable and like to continue with it; everyone has divinity within them, after all, and on some level wants to grow spiritually. So practice becomes a lifelong pursuit for many who try it. They have spiritual aspirations and may practice regularly, even if they don't ever learn the Way through their practice or progress very far with it spiritually. The people around them such as co-workers, neighbors, and community members might know that they practice. But bear in mind that a few years back, few people who were doing energy practices were making true spiritual progress—which *could* change their lives. So they would still be regular people who just benefit from their practice in terms of health; nobody would be re-engineering their lives for them. And since they are still regular people, they might unexpectedly develop some condition, become mentally ill, experience other problems, or even pass away. That's just how things go for ordinary people. And even though others might have seen them doing energy exercises publicly, it was not true spiritual development that was happening. Or even if they did have genuine spiritual goals, they wouldn't have learned a true teaching or have attained much. So despite their spiritual aspirations, they would have been mired in the basic stages of practice, and their lives would not have been re-designed for them. This would mean that illness was inevitable for them. Only a life of virtue can free you from illness. Energy practice alone can't achieve that.

A person has to do sincere spiritual practice and focus on his character for healing to occur. That's because these practices differ from regular physical exercises in that they reach beyond this world. So adherents have to live by higher principles and standards to achieve the goal of practice. But many people don't do so and are just like everyone else. And so at the appointed time they will still fall ill. They might unexpectedly suffer a stroke one day or come down with something, or become mentally ill. And others who know that they practice might blame it for their woes. But I think you would agree that it's not warranted. Outsiders to energy practice do that only because they don't know what actually happened; even insiders to it aren't likely to know. It's less of an issue if a mental disorder ensues while someone is at home, in private, though others might still blame his practice. But it's very serious if an episode occurs while someone is practicing publicly, as people will attribute it to the practice. And public opinion about it would be hard to change. The media might even run stories about how practicing made this person lose his sanity. Some people find nothing but fault with energy practices, and in scenarios like these they highlight how the person was fine not long ago, before taking up practice. But the fact is that the individual who experiences those kinds of issues is an ordinary person and so would still encounter whatever life had in store for him. It makes no sense to blame his practice for whatever ailments or problems he experiences. No one would expect a physician to never again get sick after becoming a doctor, so why would they expect that from someone who does an energy practice? That expectation isn't fair.

From the irresponsible things that are said about energy practices, we can tell that many people don't understand their realities or how they work. They are quick to label them negatively whenever there are problems. Practices like *chi-gong* haven't been known to the public for very long, and a good number of people are closed-minded toward them; they never see them as valid, and always dismiss them and shun them. One almost wonders what's going through their heads, given how annoyed they are by these, when such things shouldn't be of their concern. And they are quick to write off energy practices as imaginary. But these practices are a science, a higher science. It's just that their critics can't realize this, because their minds are so closed and they know so little about them.

Yet another scenario that confuses people involves what is called the "*chi-gong* syndrome." It refers to when someone gets into a hypnotic kind of state. But it's not that something has gone wrong in his practice, or that he's gone over to the dark side. The person will still be very rational. I can explain what it's about. Your innate foundation is important in *chi-gong*, as we know. A common belief among people of faith everywhere, which includes Buddhists and Daoists in our country over the millennia, is that good is rewarded and evil punished. Yet some people no longer subscribe to this. In China this was especially so during the era of the Cultural Revolution, which saw traditional beliefs publicly denounced and labeled as "superstition." And so there were people who thought that nothing is valid unless it's explainable, or is something they've read about, or is known to modern science and officially recognized. That mindset isn't as prevalent nowadays, though, since a number of inexplicable things have happened in the world, even if some people would rather not think about them; and many people have witnessed or heard about the miracles of *chi-gong*.

Some people are so closed-minded that they laugh to themselves anytime someone brings up *chi-gong*. They think the person has fallen for superstition, and that it's ridiculous. And if you try to talk about certain phenomena in it, they think you are really ignorant. Though these people might be closed-minded, their innate foundations aren't necessarily poor, and so if they ever try *chi-gong* they might experience paranormal powers or have higher visions with their inner eye. So while they may be able to keep their minds closed to *chi-gong*, they won't be able to keep their bodies free from sickness. So someone like this will go to the doctor when he gets ill, naturally enough. If Western medicine doesn't prove helpful, he might give Chinese medicine a try. And if that's not effective, and folk remedies don't work, the person's thoughts may turn to *chi-gong*. After turning it over in his mind he might decide to try his luck with it. So he would come to it with reservations. Yet right from the start he might excel at it, thanks to his good foundation. And it's possible that a teacher from another dimension, or a higher being, would decide to take him as a student and give him assistance. This person's inner eye might then open or he might find himself partially enlightened. In that case his eye would likely be opened to a high plane and allow him glimpses of how the universe really is. And certain powers would come to him. As you might imagine, all of this would be hard for the mind of someone like I've been describing to take. You can just picture how psychologically trying it would be. The very things that he had always considered imaginary and simply impossible, to the point of laughing at them, would now be unfolding before his eyes and confronting him. It would be too stressful for his mind to take. And his remarks about what he sees and experiences wouldn't go over well with others, though his reasoning would be sound; he wouldn't be able to reconcile the two dimensions that he sees. He would have discovered that the way people do things here is wrong, whereas what people do in other dimensions is often right. And yet if he goes by what he sees there, people here will say he's making a mistake. So people wouldn't understand all this and might think that *chi-gong* has driven him out of his mind.

But it wasn't that he went off the deep end in his practice, and the vast majority of us will never experience what the person in this example did. Only those who are especially closed-minded possibly would. The inner eye has been opened for a sizeable number of you here, and you have indeed had otherworldly visions. It was a pleasant experience rather than shocking, and it didn't jar you in any way or lead to any kind of supposed "*chi-gong* syndrome." The people who do experience this are quite rational, in fact, and what they say is apt to be highly philosophical; the logic of their remarks is really sound. The problem is just that what they say isn't believable to non-practitioners. They might startle people by telling them that they have seen so-and-so, who is deceased, and how they were asked by him or her to do certain things. It wouldn't be something most people could believe. Later it will become evident to those experiencing this that they should keep these things to themselves. And all is well once they learn to reconcile what they see in other dimensions with this one. The people I've been describing often have psychic powers. So again, it's not that anything dark or deviant happened to them.

Another source of confusion is something that's known at higher spiritual levels as "true insanity." It is something very rare. Yet it's not about truly going insane, but rather, about *practicing what is true*. I can explain it for you. It's so rare in the spiritual arena that there might be only one case in a hundred thousand people. So it's not something widespread or that has any impact on the world.

Usually there are preconditions for true insanity: an excellent innate foundation and an advanced age. But these people's age means that they won't have the years needed to go through the full process of spiritual development. Yet this group, with their excellent foundations, have often come to this world from higher realms and have a mission. The prospect of coming to the human world is frightening to all, for a being will know nothing after arriving here and having had his memory cleared. The world and its inhabitants have a corrupting effect on people, and so those who come here learn to value worldly things like status, money, and influence. So ultimately this sort of person might fall and have no hope of escape. This setting is thus frightening to higher beings, and all dread the prospect of coming here. But some do come, like the type I'm describing. Yet they tend to fare poorly in this mortal world. Some of them commit many wrongs over the course of their lives, and really end up on the brink of falling to a lower plane. A person does much wrong and incurs many debts as he fights in life to get ahead. This sort of person's teacher in another dimension won't just stand by when he sees this and passively let this being fall, for he was once divine. But his teacher will grow worried as he anxiously searches for a solution; most likely he wouldn't be able to steer the person to spiritual practice, since chances are there would be no true teachers available. So it would be nearly impossible for him to return all the way to his heavenly home. And compounding the problem would be the fact that he'd be quite old by this point and not have enough time left in life to complete his practice, even if he did find the right kind of mind-body discipline.

The approach of making a person insane for spiritual ends won't be employed unless the person has an excellent foundation and the circumstances are truly exceptional. It's only adopted when there is no hope for the person and no chance of his returning by his own means. And so, in these rare cases, insanity is induced by deactivating certain parts of his brain. For example, the areas that make people dislike cold or filth might be deactivated, with the result that psychological problems appear and the person will start acting completely beside himself. But someone like this usually won't do wrongful things. He won't get into altercations with people, and might even do good deeds from time to time. Yet he will treat himself terribly. He might walk barefoot in the snow of winter, oblivious to the cold, wearing just a thin layer of clothes, with the skin of his feet cracked and bleeding from the cold. And he may even consume excrement or urine since he's oblivious to filth. I once knew of someone who would gnaw away at horse manure that was frozen hard like a rock, and even enjoy it; he was capable of suffering beyond what the sane could handle. We can just imagine what ordeals the insanity would have caused him. Typically these people, often older women, have psychic powers. Many from the older generation went through foot-binding, yet I know of one woman who could easily scale walls six or more feet high. At one point her family members decided to lock her inside after witnessing her frequently run off, due to her insanity. But after her family headed out, she opened the lock just by pointing her finger at it, and off she went. So then they decided to use chains. But all she had to do was give them a little shake and they fell off. They couldn't contain her. She suffered greatly with her condition. But precisely because she suffered so much, and it was so intense, she swiftly paid off the bad things that she owed. It usually doesn't take more than three years at most for people like her, and usually one or two terribly painful years suffices. Her mind returned to her as soon as the whole episode was behind her. At that point many powers that she had developed became available to her, since she had finished her practice, in effect. Cases like hers are extremely rare, yet they have indeed occurred. The phenomenon would never be possible for someone of average stock. You might be familiar with stories of crazy Buddhist monks and Daoists. There were indeed people like that in history, and there are records of them. There are many allusions to these figures, such as crazed Daoists and the mad monk who swept dirt at the wicked minister named Qin Hui.

So we can say with confidence that nobody is about to lose their minds, or "conjure fire,"* due to spiritual practice. And besides, even if someone really were to conjure fire, well, that's rather impressive. Starting a fire with your mouth or palms, or igniting things with just your fingertips would seem to mean you've got superpowers!

How Practicing Provokes Evil

To say that practicing "provokes evil" means that many of you will likely face intrusions to your practice after you start, and this topic deserves an explanation. Enormous difficulties ensue after you decide to practice, in fact. You wouldn't be able to really do this practice without the protection of my spiritual bodies. Your life would be in imminent danger without them. If the soul is immortal, as we've said, then it's possible that you might have incurred debts to others in a previous life, pushed others around, or done wrongful things, and those who were on the receiving end are going to want compensation. In Buddhism it's held that life is simply the working out of karma. So the beings you owe will come for payback; and if you overpay, the next time around it will be they who pay you. If a child isn't respectful or obedient to his parents, for example, in the next life the roles might be reversed. So turns the wheel of karma. However, we have actually observed that there are also malevolent entities at work who try to disrupt and stop your practice. But there are deeper reasons for this. They wouldn't be allowed to meddle if they didn't have grounds for it.

I'll start by describing the most common form of evil that's encountered during practice. You are likely to be enthused about practicing once you learn how, but the moment you sit down to meditate, the peace and quiet normally around you may suddenly be gone. It might be due to cars and buses beeping, footsteps echoing in the hallway, people talking and slamming doors, or even a radio that's turned on outside. So the quiet is gone. Your surroundings might be pretty pleasant normally, when you aren't practicing, yet the minute you start to, things get noisy and chaotic. Seldom do people realize what's really going on. Most just find it odd and get discouraged that it's so hard to practice. And so these abnormal occurrences might end up blocking you. But what's actually happening is that evil entities are disrupting you; they are directing people to disrupt you. This is one of the most basic forms that disruption takes, and it serves the purpose of stopping you from practicing. They do that because they can't bear the thought of your gaining enlightenment and being absolved of all your unpaid debts to them. But I should note that this only happens at a certain stage of practice; it's not allowed past a certain point. No entities will be allowed to visit you and disturb you once your debts have been worked off. You can reach that point with Falun Dafa, because our students make rapid progress and advance through the different stages of practice quickly.

There is another form of evil that might intrude upon you. As you know, your inner eye may open as a result of practicing, and what could happen is that you see frightening scenes or monstrous faces while you are practicing at home. There might be figures with disheveled hair that appear, some of which may chase you and try to kill you, or lash out at you wildly; or in some cases they might stare in through your window. It's awfully frightening. All of these things can be explained, though, as the doings of evil entities. But they are very rare in Falun Dafa. Maybe one out of a hundred people will experience them; the vast majority won't. Evil entities are generally prohibited from using those approaches on us since they don't serve any constructive purpose in our practice. But they are common in conventional spiritual practices, and might even persist for some time. They can be so frightening that some people give up practicing. You can just imagine what it must be like: someone opts to practice at night, when all is calm and quiet, and then suddenly as he practices, there is some demonic-looking creature before him that's sub-human. It's enough to scare a person out of practicing. Generally this doesn't happen in our Falun Dafa, though it does occur in a few exceptional cases. Some people's circumstances are rather unique.

Another type of evil that plagues some people is one that's specific to practices that have both martial arts and energy exercises. Mostly these are Daoist methods. I'll describe what this kind of evil typically looks like. But note that these aren't things encountered in most practices; they only come about in martial arts practices with an energy component. What happens is that someone will seek out the adherent for a contest of martial skills. As there are many Daoists in the world today, a good number do martial arts alongside spiritual practice. Those who do so have the potential to develop higher energy. It's possible for them to develop this if they can become detached from things like status and wealth. But competitiveness is harder to let go, and takes longer, and so when they are at a certain stage of practice they will be prone to getting into fights while sleeping or meditating; their consciousness might be hazy while they sleep or meditate, yet aware that a certain other person is practicing, and so their soul leaves their body to find that person for a contest of skills. These things happen in other dimensions. And there might be others who seek them out for a fight, and who will genuinely try to kill them if they don't fight back. So heated fights break out between the two parties. And the fact that this happens once they fall asleep means that it ruins their night of rest. This indicates that it's time for them to stop being competitive. But if they can't, and keep acting like that, then things may drag on for a long time, perhaps for years, while they are stuck at that stage. All of the nightly combat will leave them exhausted, with so much energy having been spent, and they will be too physically tired for spiritual practice. It could even ruin their bodies if they don't handle it right. So this is something that happens in practices that feature both energy exercises and martial arts, and it's quite common. It isn't seen in practices of a purely spiritual nature, like ours, as it's not allowed in those cases. The types of ordeals I've been describing up to this point are relatively commonplace.

There is one more type of evil that you will face, and it's one that all of you, without exception, will encounter. And this is the demon of lust, something very serious. Marital relations are normal for ordinary husbands and wives to have, as it makes successive generations possible. It allows the human race to continue on, and so feelings and emotions are basic to this world. So for ordinary people such behavior is perfectly natural in marriage. Counted among the feelings and emotions that people have are anger and happiness, love and hate, enjoyment as well as dislike, admiration and disdain, along with fondness and aversion. Ordinary people just live for feelings and emotions. Then, as practitioners who aspire to spiritual greatness, we mustn't let feelings or emotions influence how we see things. We have to break free of them. We should care little for the many attachments they cause, and ultimately, forsake them completely. Sexual desire and attraction both count as human attachments, and both should go.

Yet we aren't asking those of you who live and practice in the secular world to become quasi-monks or nuns. The young adults among us should form families as one normally would. Then what about the perils of sexual desire, you may wonder? As I've explained, our practice goes straight after human attachments and doesn't take the approach of depriving you materially. Just the opposite, we have you temper your will right here in this materialistic world, and this is truly to the betterment of your character. If you can break an attachment mentally, then you can let go of the actual thing, whatever it may be; and then you would be able to forgo it materially, of course, if you had to. But if you can't break the attachment mentally, then you won't be able to let go of the actual thing that you're attached to. The goal of genuine practice is to remove the underlying attachments. In monastic practice people are forced to let go of things materially, and the goal is the same; i.e., to eliminate the attachments behind things. It's forcibly done, making people sever all ties to things and give up even the thought of them. So while they take that approach, we don't. We instead ask that you find a way to take the material things around you lightly, and the results we get are the most solid. We don't ask that you all embrace poverty and chastity like monastics do. It would really be a problem if in the future, when our practice is widely done, everyone were to become like a quasi-monk—since our practice is done *in* the world. I tell everyone in our practice that it's a problem if your marriage to a non-practitioner ends up in divorce because of the practice. We ask that you simply care less about marital intimacy; just don't put so much stock in it, like people normally do. This is especially important nowadays, in the wake of the sexual revolution, when lewd and pornographic things are really affecting people. Some people really fall for these things, but they should have little appeal to us as practitioners.

Viewed from a higher plane, it's as if man is submerged in mud while in this world; and yet he wallows away in it, oblivious to its filth. With our practice you shouldn't be causing a big falling out with your spouse on these grounds. So it should be fine to just take it lightly at your current stage and be intimate as normal, like before. When you progress to a higher stage later on, you will experience a state unique to that phase, but for now, it is what it is, and it's fine to do as I have taught. And it goes without saying that you mustn't go in for the kinds of deplorable things that are common nowadays, which I was alluding to.

Another factor comes into play. The bodies of practitioners carry energy, as we know. Eighty to ninety percent of us will not only be free of illness after finishing these classes, but will also have higher energy. So the energy your body has will be powerful. At first, the energy that you carry will be disproportionate to the quality of your character; your energy will be higher, since we increase it rapidly for you. The process of developing your character will follow. Your character will catch up, slowly but surely, in the time to come. And so we boosted your energy for you in advance. This means that you carry a significant amount of it now. There's a palpable air of peace and compassion here, since the energy that results from following a true teaching is pure and compassionate. Those were the qualities that I developed in my own days of spiritual cultivation, and so I carry them with me. You can feel a sense of harmony as you sit in my class, and your mind is free of wicked thoughts. The smokers among us won't even give it a thought. The energy that you develop in the time ahead will have the same traits as mine, for you will have been following the ways of our Dafa. The power of your energy will keep growing, and your body will come to emit a remarkably powerful energy. And even were it not that powerful, it would still be more than enough to have sway over the typical person who is in your presence, or perhaps in your home. So your family members are likely to be positively affected and subdued by your energy. How so? People will naturally have a hard time thinking of or doing bad things around you, because your presence is one of purity, serenity, and compassion—for you exude proper thoughts. You can expect to see this.

The other day I mentioned the saying, "Bathed in divine light, conduct and thought become right," and the idea was that the energy radiating from our bodies has the power to set things straight. So it follows that when you have no lustful thoughts, the energy you give off will keep your spouse's desires in check. If you don't entertain such thoughts—and I don't think you will, being a practitioner—neither will your spouse. But this may not always be the case. It's easy to get aroused in this day and age. Things like television expose you to all sorts of unseemly images from the moment you start watching. So under *normal* circumstances, at least, you will be able to exert the kind of influence I'm describing. Later on, when your practice progresses to higher stages, you will know for yourself what to do without my having to tell you. You will then experience a different state, but it will be one which allows for your marriage to be harmonious. So you don't need to view marital relations as something so grave. Being overly worried about it is an attachment, in fact. So, while married couples don't have to worry about lusting after one another anymore, there might still be sexual desire. Just don't give it much importance, keep a balanced perspective, and that will be good enough.

Then in what forms might you encounter the demon of lust? You might be visited by it as you meditate, or, if your level of stillness isn't deep enough, perhaps while you sleep. Suddenly you will find that before you is a gorgeous woman; or, if you're a woman, the man of your dreams. And in either case the figure will be naked. If it arouses you in any way you might have an emission and the dream will become reality. But consider that in our practice we utilize the body's most vital energy and essences to change your body and extend your life. Having regular emissions would deplete these precious substances. And it would mean that you haven't passed the test of sexual desire yet, which is a problem. So I'm letting you know that each and every one of you is sure to face this test. I am sending a powerful form of energy into your brain through my teaching here. You might not be able to recall the specifics of what I said afterwards, but if and when you do have challenges with sexual desire, you should be able to recall what I've taught. The moment you regard yourself as a practitioner, you should be able to remember my teachings on this, exercise self-control, and pass the test. If you fail the test the first time, the next one is going to be harder. But if you feel sincere regret when you wake up after failing the test the first time, it might leave a deeper impression in your mind and increase the likelihood that you will exercise self-control next time and pass the test. Anyone who isn't concerned after failing the test will have a much harder time exercising control with future tests, for sure.

Episodes like these might be a matter of evil entities trying to disturb you, or a test from your master, who conjured up what you saw. Both possibilities exist, since everyone has to go through this test. This is step one when you have just begun the practice and are still somewhat worldly, and nobody will be exempted from it. One example would be what a young man, who was thirty at the time, experienced when I was holding a class in Wuhan city. He went home and meditated after hearing me teach the same material I just explained to you. In no time he entered into a state of deep stillness. He then saw Buddha Amitabha appearing out of nowhere to one side of him, and the Daoist sage Lao-tzu on the other; he relayed this in a paper he wrote reflecting on his experiences with the practice. The two looked him over but didn't utter a word. They then faded out of sight, and Bodhisattva Guan Yin appeared with a vase in hand. A white smoke issued forth from the vase. He felt happy seeing all of this unfold so vividly before him as he meditated. Then suddenly the smoke turned into stunningly beautiful, angelic figures. They danced before him, and their delicate movements were a sight to behold. He thought that these ethereal beauties were a reward from the Bodhisattva for his efforts. He was delighted at the thought of it. But then suddenly they were naked and began to act seductively, embracing and caressing him. The young man's character had grown a lot from our class, so he quickly regained his vigilance. The next thought he had was, "I'm not just anyone. I am a practitioner. You shouldn't act this way toward me, since I practice Falun Dafa." And with that thought, the whole scene vanished in a flash. It had been conjured up, as it turned out. Amitabha and Lao-tzu then reappeared. Lao-tzu gestured with his hand toward the young man, and said to Amitabha with a smile, "The lad is teachable." It meant that he approved of the young man and deemed him worthy of spiritual instruction.

The degree to which a person has sexual desire or interest has traditionally been, and still is, in higher dimensions, a critical factor in gauging whether he or she has what it takes for spiritual practice. So it's essential that we care little for these things. But, since our practice is done in the regular world, you needn't abstain completely—or at least, not in this current phase of your practice. What you need to do is value it little and change from how you may have been before, becoming more like a practitioner. Any time you experience disruptions of any sort, you should proactively think about what caused them and what you still need to let go.

How the Mind Can Lead Astray

I would like to explain how the mind can lead one astray. There are many dimensions, each physical and real, that are associated with a person's body, and in one particular dimension everything from the universe may be reflected, much like a mirror image. And while they are just reflections, they're nevertheless physical. Everything that exists in that dimension associated with your body is governed by your thoughts. This means that when you look at something with your inner eye without having any thoughts, and your mind is still, your visions will be accurate. But with the slightest thought added in, they will be false, and you might be led off track; the phenomenon is sometimes referred to as "alteration by thought." It comes about when people fail to handle themselves as practitioners or curb their longings. They might yearn for psychic powers or be attached to petty magical skills, or even the things they hear from other dimensions. These individuals are the most apt to be led astray by their minds and fall. Regardless of what spiritual heights someone may have reached, he will fall sharply and will swiftly come to ruin if this happens. It is a terribly serious problem. It's not akin to other problems, like failing to pass a single test of character; in those cases you can always get back up after a fall and keep on practicing. But someone who allows his mind to lead him astray is in serious trouble, and may be destroyed by this. This problem is especially likely for those whose inner eyes are open when they reach a certain stage of practice. Another group that's vulnerable are those whose consciousnesses are interfered with by foreign messages, energies, or images, and who put their trust in them. Some of us will be subject to interference like this from many sources after our inner eye has opened.

Let's look at some examples. It's hard to keep from being swayed by these things when your practice is still in its infancy. Suppose that you can't see your teacher in other dimensions very well, but then, one day, out of the blue, you see a towering godly figure come to you. This striking figure might pay you a couple of compliments and then try to impart instruction to you. You might be delighted by this and accept him as your teacher, and proceed to learn from him. But accepting such a being's instruction would foul up your energy. And then there's the fact that he himself wouldn't have earned true divine standing; it's merely that shape-changing is possible in the dimension where he resides. So if you allow yourself to be excited at the sight of that imposing figure before you, there's little chance you will resist his attempts at instruction. But a practitioner must be able to maintain his composure if we are to save him; failing to do so will likely lead to ruin. The lives in higher dimensions within the three realms are all heavenly beings, but they haven't earned true divine standing and are not free from the cycle of reincarnation. Then how far could that godly figure, whom you might impulsively take as your teacher and follow, really bring you? Your efforts at spiritual practice would be for naught, since figures like those aren't fully divine and learning from them would disorder your energy. It's hard to keep your composure in scenarios like these. I want you to see that this is a really serious problem, and many of us may encounter a similar episode at some point. I have made my teaching clear on this; it's up to you to put it into practice. What I just shared was one example. You should also stay composed if you see higher beings from another school of practice, and stay true to the discipline you are in. Your practice will have a good chance of success if you can disregard any supposed Buddha, Daoist deity, divinity, or fiend that tries to tempt you.

Then there are other ways in which the mind can lead

you astray. You might see deceased family members who come to plague you, sobbing or imploring you to do certain things that you shouldn't. Anything is possible. The question is, will you let them sway you? Just imagine how hard it would be if a child or parent that you loved dearly, but who has passed away, visited you from the grave and asked you to do things that would be ruinous for you. Spiritual practice isn't easy. And what's especially confusing is that now, with Buddhism "in disarray," as some people put it, you even see non-Buddhist doctrines from Confucianism like filial piety and the parent-child bond being taught. But what's the problem? What truly constitutes your life is your soul, so only the mother who gave birth to your soul counts as your true mother. You will have had countless "mothers," both human and otherwise, over the course of your reincarnations. And the same could be said for how many children you've had over all your lifetimes. Neither mother nor child recognizes the other in their next life, and any karmic debts that remain between the two will have to be settled just like with anyone else. But people can't see these things for what they are, and so they often can't move beyond their affections. Some people are inconsolably grieved at the passing of a beloved child, or mother, and long for them for the rest of their lives. But it never occurs to them that these ordeals are meant to wear them down, and are intent on making their lives difficult.

It might be hard for the average person to grasp that being attached to such things can make spiritual practice impossible, yet that's the case, and that is why things like filial piety and the parent-child bond aren't taught in Buddhism. True spiritual practice entails that you let go of human feelings and emotions. Of course, we go about our practice in the secular world, and so we should still be devoted and respectful to our parents and care well for our children; we should be good to others, not to mention our own families, in whatever setting we may be, and treat everyone with kindness. We should treat everyone well, which of course includes parents and children, and think of others first at all times. Your heart will not be selfish, then, but will be loving, kind, and compassionate. Common people, by contrast, tend to just be motivated by feelings and emotions.

Many people don't have good self-control, and this makes for trouble in their spiritual lives. For instance, some are happy and accepting if a heavenly being personally reveals something "helpful" to them. But I can tell you that it is evil beings at work anytime something is revealed to you that benefits you in worldly ways, be it your getting forewarned about adversity or your being prompted to try the lottery and being told the winning number. The only exception is cases where your life is at risk and you are told how to stay safe. If things go well in a worldly sense, thanks to that "help," you won't have had to overcome the trial that was planned for you or made the progress that you were supposed to. Spiritual growth is unlikely if your days are filled with earthly pleasures and spent in ease. How could you work off your karma then? You wouldn't have the circumstances necessary to do so, nor to develop your character. So be sure to bear this in mind. Evil entities might also resort to flattering you, telling you what great heights you have reached, or what a special or hallowed figure you are. But all of it will be false. You must break from every attachment to truly make great spiritual progress. So by all means, if you encounter any of the temptations I've described, keep up your guard!

Unique challenges come with having your inner eye open as you practice, just as challenges come with having it closed. Spiritual practice isn't easy either way. With your inner eye open, you might really find it hard to keep out all of the extra-dimensional information that you might be exposed to and that would seek to disrupt you. All of what you behold in other dimensions might be a feast for the eyes, and extraordinarily beautiful and pleasant, which might stir you. Interference might come upon you once you are stirred by it, and your energy could be thrown into disarray. Being stirred is often the trigger. Also, other problems can ensue for people who don't handle things well and allow their minds to lead them astray. They might have wrongful thoughts that prove dangerous. Suppose one day your inner eye opens and you have lucid visions. You might think, for example, that you're the only one whose eye has opened well at your practice site, which makes you think you're special and that you have learned my Falun Dafa really well or even better than others—meaning you are ahead of them. But even just thinking that way isn't right. If your mind goes further, you might even think that you're some kind of divine being, like a Buddha. And then, when you look at yourself through your inner eye, it really may appear to you that you are. That can happen because, as I mentioned, all matter in an associated dimension around one's body will transform, or be "altered," according to one's thoughts.

Any reflections that come over from the universe will be shaped by your thoughts, because everything that exists in the dimension associated with your body is under your command, and reflections are no exception; they too physically exist. So in the scenario I was just describing, if the person wonders to himself whether he's also dressed as a Buddha, then that will be what he sees. By now he'll be enthralled, thinking that he really *is* a Buddha. And if he wonders whether he might be a greater Buddha, and looks again, then that will be what he sees. And if he wonders whether he's perhaps higher than me, that will be what he sees when he looks. In other cases a person may hear voices. An evil being might interfere with the person by telling him that he's "higher than Li Hongzhi," and he falls for it. This means that he has forgotten how he got to where he is in his practice or who it was that taught him, and he hasn't thought about what will happen down the road. And regardless, any genuine Buddha or divinity that comes to the world must begin the spiritual path from scratch, with none of his original energy available to him; the only difference is that he will progress somewhat faster in practice this time. The problem I've been describing is really hard to pull out of, due to all of the attachments that tend to come up. Those attachments might even embolden someone to claim he's a Buddha and that people should just follow him, since he can guide them, as a Buddha.

That's indeed what happened in the city of Changchun. There was someone learning our practice there who was quite good at first, but who eventually landed himself in the kind of mess I was just describing. He thought he was a Buddha and ended up believing that he was above everyone else. That happened because he lost his grounding and let attachments get the best of him. Let's look at why this happens. Buddhism has taught that one should disregard any visions that are experienced, for such things are illusory; all focus should instead go to making spiritual progress through meditative trance. The reason they don't encourage visions or want people getting attached to these is that they fear the above will happen. In religious Buddhist practice there aren't any specific methods that would strengthen one's defenses against such things, and its scriptures don't offer guidance on how to break out of these snares. The Buddha didn't address this in his teachings, hoping that his disciples wouldn't have to deal with the problem of being misled by the mind, or having reality altered by thought, as they would just consider any visions that they experienced to be illusory. He knew that the presence of any attachment could turn a vision into something deceptive, which would be hard to resist. And it could send a person down the road to ruin, to the dark side, if he didn't pull out of it. Calling himself a Buddha would mean that he was already headed that way, and he might even bring possessing entities upon himself or other things, and end up in utter ruin. His heart would turn evil with all of this, and his fall would be terrible. There have been many cases of this. Even in this class now there are those who think highly of themselves and have an air about them when they speak. So even in Buddhism, attempting to figure out how you are doing in your practice is frowned upon. The episode I mentioned in Changchun was an example of someone being led astray by his own mind, or having reality become distorted by his thoughts. There have been learners in Beijing and elsewhere who have experienced this, and it has been terribly disruptive to other practitioners.

People have asked me why I don't just straighten these kinds of things out. But think about how hard it would be to make spiritual progress if we resolved for you all of the challenges you face. It is precisely when evil intervenes in your life that you can demonstrate your spiritual resolve, your discernment, your ability to stay on track, and your commitment to one practice. The spiritual journey tries men's souls, and only the most devout make it through. I would say that your journey would be too easy without the sorts of ordeals I've been describing. The divine beings in higher realms would have an even harder time with it, and would question what I'm doing, wondering how it could amount to salvation. It wouldn't seem like spiritual practice to them if your journey was unimpeded and if everyone could make it. And they would take issue if things only got easier and smoother for you as you progressed. So this was the dilemma I faced, and I had to think it over. At first I wiped out much of the evil of this kind. But even from my perspective it wouldn't have been right to keep doing that all the time. I have also heard remarks that I'm "making spiritual practice too easy for you," since you "only have small ordeals and interpersonal things to work through," and "many of your attachments go unaddressed." And they doubt whether you could "stay true to Dafa when things are tough and confusing." So in light of all this there are sure to be trials and tribulations. What I've been describing is one particular form of evil. People are so hard to genuinely save, yet so easy to ruin. Trouble is in store for you if your thinking is off.

The Importance of a Strong Mind

The wrongful things people have done over their many lifetimes result in adversity for them, or for those on the spiritual path, what are known as karmic obstacles. And it is on this account that people are born, go through aging, become ill, and pass away. Those are normal forms of karma. There is also a powerful form of karma that has a large impact on those leading spiritual lives, called the karma of thought. Thinking is a natural part of existence. But since people get lost in the secular world, they often have thoughts that revolve around things such as status and influence, power, wealth, lust, or pride, and over time, these shape into a powerful form of karma, known as the karma of thought. In other dimensions everything is alive, and karma is no exception. With any true practice one must eliminate karma. To eliminate karma means to destroy it, to transform it. Naturally, the karma won't go for it, and so you will face adversity and obstacles. The thought karma can directly interfere with your mind and cause you to silently swear at me or Dafa, or have wicked thoughts and hear abusive words in your mind. Some practitioners don't realize what is happening at the time, and even mistake those things for their own thoughts. And some think that they are suffering from entity attachment, though they are not. Rather, those are the result of thought karma surfacing in the brain. Some people are not very in control of their minds and so they go along with it and do bad things, which is ruinous for them and causes them to fall. Most people can, however, repel it and deny it by having strong, self-aware thoughts. This indicates that they are savable and can discern right and wrong; it means that their faith is strong. My spiritual bodies will then help them by eliminating a large proportion of their thought karma. What I've described is quite common. If it does occur, it is a test to see whether you can conquer the wicked thoughts. Hold your ground and the karma will be dissolved for you.

Your Thinking Needs to Be Right

When a person regularly fails to conduct himself as a practitioner, it means that his thinking isn't right. Practitioners meet with adversity as they go about spiritual practice. And the adversity might take any form, from strife with others to people scheming against you. Most often it will directly test your character. But other things will come about as well. Your body might suddenly feel unwell, since that's one of many ways that karma can be paid off. And at a certain point in time you might be made to doubt whether the teachings are true, whether you have higher energy, whether you are cut out for spiritual practice and can really make progress at it, or whether higher beings really exist. You might be made to go through this in the future, and be given a false impression that leads you to question and doubt all of this. It's done to see whether you can stay committed. If you can hold fast to the thought, "I must stay firm and not waver," then you will, with that determination, indeed do so when going through this kind of test, and naturally handle it well, for your character will have grown. Were such an ordeal brought upon you right at the outset, however, you would have no way to understand it and it would put an end to your practice since you would not yet be solid. So there is no telling what form your ordeals will take.

Ordeals like these are a necessary part of spiritual practice, and what makes progress possible. Some of you mistake the unpleasant sensations in your bodies for medical conditions, and often fail to regard yourselves as practitioners; you take those things to be health problems and wonder why you have to endure so much. I can tell you that many of the tribulations you would have had, have been taken away, and the troubles that you do experience have been greatly reduced. Had we not done this, those ordeals might have brought an end to your life or left you bedridden. So while you might find the minor troubles that you do experience hard to bear, that's only to be expected; since when was spiritual progress made with comfort and ease? There's a story that relates to this. When I was holding a class in the city of Changchun there was one individual who had an excellent foundation and was really cut out for spiritual practice. I had high hopes for him. So my plan was to ratchet up his trials a bit so that he could repay his debts and become enlightened sooner. Then one day he seemed to suffer a stroke, unexpectedly. He fell down and couldn't move, and had no sensation in his limbs. He was taken to a hospital for emergency medical care. But not long after, he was back on his feet. Had he really experienced a stroke, he never would have been back on his feet with control of his arms and legs again so quickly. Yet surprisingly, he blamed Falun Dafa for his mishap. It didn't occur to him that people normally don't recover from a stroke so quickly. He might have died right there in the street after the fall, had he not learned Falun Dafa, or he may have been paralyzed for the rest of his life, having had a real stroke.

This suggests just how hard it is to save a person. So much had been done for him, yet he didn't manage to realize it and even blamed us for his ordeal. Then there are people who have been learning for some time but who still tell me that their whole body just doesn't feel right and how they've gone to the doctor for shots or medication, but to no avail. And they weren't even embarrassed to say so. It's only to be expected that those things wouldn't help, since it is not a matter of illness. You can go for an examination and they won't find anything; it's just that you don't feel well. One practitioner who went for treatment found that the needle of the syringe wouldn't pierce his skin, and several needles even bent in the process; the contents of the final syringe even squirted out without it having pierced his skin. It then dawned on him that he's a practitioner and hasn't any business getting shots. It was only at that point that it occurred to him. So let this be a reminder that you should keep this larger perspective in mind when you meet with difficulties. Some people are under the impression that I simply prohibit going to see the doctor, and so they figure they will just see an energy healer instead. They still think it's a health problem and are hoping someone can help. But there is little chance they will find a true healer. And if it's a false one that they see, they will be ruined right then and there.

Our stance is that you would have no way to tell whether the alleged healer you saw was an authentic one. Many supposed masters are self-proclaimed. I have been verified and have on file the results of the testing done by the scientific agencies that handle research of this kind. Many masters are false, though, and have given themselves their own titles; there are all too many who put on airs and defraud people. False masters can do healings, but we should ask what makes that possible. It's because they have entity attachment. They wouldn't be able to do that otherwise. The entity that's attached can emit healing energy, since it is a form of energy itself and can readily overpower the average person. But few realize what it passes on to people when it heals them. Far below, in a realm imperceptible to the eye, all of what it emits is in its image, and there will be little that you can do about it after it has transmitted its things to your body. "The spirits are more easily invoked than dispelled," as an old saying has it. If you were just regular people who didn't practice, we wouldn't say anything, since you would just be interested in leading a normal life and finding short-term symptom relief. But you are a practitioner, and you want to continually purify your body, don't you? You have no idea how long it's going to take to clean up what those spirits put into you; their things have energy, after all. Some of you might be wondering why the *falun* or my spiritual bodies wouldn't be protecting you. But the way the universe works is that nobody will get in your way if you, of your own choosing, desire something or are trying for something. My spiritual bodies will try to hold you back, and drop hints, but they will give up if they see that you are insistent. Your doing our practice wouldn't count if you were goaded into it. No one can be coerced or forced to do spiritual practice. True growth can only come from you, yourself; nobody can help if you don't want to grow. I've laid out the teachings for you and discussed how they work. So if you still don't wish to make progress, that is your choice and you can't blame anyone else. You are the one who decides what you want, and you can be sure that neither the *falun* nor my spiritual bodies will try to bend your will. Some people go to hear other energy teachers give talks and then feel unwell afterwards, as might be expected. You might be wondering why my spiritual bodies didn't protect these people. Well, what business did they have going there in the first place? They must have been hoping to get something out of it, or they wouldn't have gone. So whatever entered their bodies and caused them to feel unwell was something they brought upon themselves, since they took it in willingly, through their own ears. Some people act recklessly and thereby injure their *falun*, deforming it, which should never happen; the *falun* is a higher being and is more valuable than your life. False masters abound at present, and some enjoy great fame. I once remarked to the head of the Chi-Gong Research Society of China about how the famous concubine named Da Ji had brought havoc to the imperial court in ancient times, and how fierce that fox spirit was. And yet, I went on to tell him, the harm that she did was minor compared to what today's false masters have done. They have been a scourge to the country and harmed countless people. It may not seem that there is anything wrong with them, yet you have no idea how many of them have bad entities on their bodies. Those things will get on your body if a false master projects energy toward you. Things are out of control now. The average person can't see these things for what they are.

Some people might be really impressed by how pro-found *chi-gong* is after attending my classes and hearing what I have to say, and so they plan to go and hear the next teacher that comes to town. But I would urge you not to do that. The bad things you hear will pour in through your ears. It's hard to save a person and bring about changes in mind and body. False teachers abound. And even those who are genuine and have received a proper training might not really be clean. Some animal spirits are fierce, and a teacher might not be able to drive them away even if he can keep them off his own body; and he wouldn't have the power to repel them on a greater scale. And it shows with his students. All sorts of bad things might be mixed in and present among them, since they might not be upstanding, even if he is.

They could be carrying various entities on their bodies.

If you are serious about practicing Falun Dafa, don't go to other spiritual or energy-related talks. Of course, if you don't want to do Falun Dafa and just want to try whatever is out there, then you're free to go ahead. Since this would mean you aren't an adherent of Falun Dafa, you would be on your own. So don't blame Falun Dafa if something goes wrong in that case. A genuine Falun Dafa practitioner is someone who aligns his conduct with our teachings on character and puts into practice what we teach. I have been asked whether it's okay to mingle with people who do other practices. My reply would be that you are practicing the Great Way, which goes far beyond what they are doing, and by the time you have completed this class your level of attainment will be far greater than theirs; you have a *falun* that took us generations of practice to form, and its power is enormous. So naturally, it won't be much of a problem if you interact with people of other practices, provided you don't take in or have a desire for anything of theirs and just remain normal friends. But that said, if the person's body does indeed carry something, it could be quite bad, in which case interaction is best avoided. But I don't think there is much cause for concern if it's a matter of your spouse doing another practice. One thing you should know is that others benefit just by virtue of your practicing, since what you practice is a true Way. Your spouse's body will also be cleansed, for your safety, if he or she does another practice and has bad things on his or her body. Everything will be cleansed for you in other dimensions, including your home. It would be awfully challenging to practice if that setting weren't cleansed and all manner of things lurked there, disrupting you.

There is one scenario, however, where my spiritual bodies cannot clean things up. One day, someone who was learning our practice saw a spiritual body of mine come to his home. He was elated by this, and invited him in. But my body replied by telling him that it was a mess inside, and that there were too many things there. And he left upon saying that. Generally speaking, my spiritual bodies will clear out any entities in other dimensions for you, however many there may be. But in this case the person's place was one big mess of *chi-gong* books. He then caught on and packed them up, after which he sold some and burned the rest. My spiritual body returned after that. This is what the person relayed to me.

Then there are people who seek out fortune-tellers. Some people are quite keen on things like the *Book of Changes* and fortune-telling, and want to know if those are still okay to use, now that they practice Falun Dafa. Here's how I view it. If you now have a considerable amount of energy, the words you say will have an impact. If something that wasn't supposed to happen, does happen, because you said it would, then you will have done wrong. Non-practitioners are quite weak. The energies and information in their bodies are not that stable and are prone to change. If you predict some mishap for someone, it might just come to be. Or suppose the person's karma is sizeable and needs to be paid off, yet you always tell him that good things are in store, which then prevents him from paying off his karma. That's a problem. Aren't you hurting him, in effect? Some people are too attached to these things to give them up, as they think that they have a knack for it. But it should be obvious that this is an attachment. And besides, even if you really do know the future, you can't just divulge divine plans to a regular person; practitioners should exercise restraint. So that's why it's a problem. When people try to make predictions based on the *Book of Changes*, for example, the predictions are bound to be a mixture of true and false, since some of what's in the book is no longer valid. And that is why it's okay for things like fortune-telling to exist in this world. But a true practitioner, who in fact has higher energy, will want to hold himself to a high standard. And yet some practitioners still seek out people to tell their fortunes. They ask to have readings done to find out how their practice is going or what troubles might lie ahead of them. They actually seek people out to predict these things. But how could you make progress if your troubles were predicted for you in advance? Your life was changed once you became a practitioner, and so the information carried by your palm patterns, your facial characteristics, your birth horoscope, and your body have changed and aren't what they originally were. The very fact that you ask someone to tell your fortune indicates that you believe them, or you wouldn't ask. What they disclose to you are just things as they appear on the surface and will be based on past designs. But things have since changed for you, in fact. If you go to them you are surely listening to them and putting faith in them, and so you will be creating a psychological burden for yourself. And that self-made burden is going to weigh on your mind, which makes it an attachment, of course, and that will take additional work to remove. So this means you have made things unnecessarily harder for yourself. Won't having a new attachment require extra suffering to remove it? With every test and ordeal there is the potential for you to either progress or regress in your spiritual development. Spiritual practice is hard enough to begin with. You are setting yourself up for failure if you make it even harder of your own doing. So you might be making added ordeals and troubles for yourself. Nobody can see what your new, reworked path of life entails. Being told what's in store for you would make it hard for you to carry out your practice, so others aren't allowed to see any of that. And this goes for both your fellow practitioners as well as for those who do other practices. Whatever they might predict wouldn't be accurate, for yours is a changed life—a life meant for spiritual practice.

I am sometimes asked whether it's okay to read the books of other religions or practices. Our take is that religious works teach people to develop their character, and Buddhist texts particularly emphasize the mind. Our practice is Buddhist, so in principle there's no problem. But that said, many passages of scriptures are inaccurate due to the translation process, and many commentaries were made with varying degrees of understanding and baseless interpretations—all of which undermine the teachings. Those who have irresponsibly interpreted the scriptures are far from the Buddha's realm of awareness, and don't know what the texts truly meant. And this is why so many interpretations exist. Coming to a full understanding of the scriptures isn't easy, especially on one's own. Maybe you are thinking that you just find them intriguing. But if you are always dabbling in the teachings or writings of another practice, you are, in effect, doing that practice. The problem is, built into any religious scripture are the energy and teachings specific to that practice, and learning anything from such a text will equate to learning that practice. And if it happens that you really immerse yourself in the text, and allow it to inform your practice, then you might have taken up that discipline in effect and no longer belong to ours.

Spiritual practice has always demanded that you commit to one approach. You should read only our books if you really wish to do this practice.

If you want to do our practice you shouldn't so much as look at the other spiritual or energy-related books out there. The books that are coming out nowadays are especially to be avoided. And older works should be avoided, too, such as the *Yellow Emperor's Classic on Internal Medicine*, *Principles of Mind-Body Practice*, and the Daoist Canon. While they don't have the bad things that contemporary books do, they nonetheless carry energies from other planes in them. Each of those works amounts to a way of spiritual practice, and so reading them adds their things to what you have and affects you. When you find a sentence agreeable to you, well then, those things will be added to yours. You will be adding in something foreign, even if it's not necessarily bad. But adding in even just a little of something else will undermine your practice and cause problems. To help you picture it, just imagine how quickly a television would malfunction if even just one extra electronic part from something else were added in. And what's more, many of today's spiritual books don't provide genuine instruction, and carry all sorts of impure things. We had one learner who was browsing through one such book when suddenly a large snake lunged forth, but I'll spare you the details. Cases like these are always a matter of practitioners getting into trouble by not handling things right; or in other words, they brought on trouble by not thinking right. It's for your benefit that we spell these things out. It should help you to see things for what they are and know how to handle them. Hopefully this will save you trouble down the road. It's critical that you keep in mind what I just talked about, even if it didn't sound that serious. Know that what I have been describing is a common pitfall. Spiritual practice is extremely demanding and a serious affair. Even just being a little careless might prove to be your undoing and ruin you in no time. So it's imperative that your thinking be right.

Martial Arts with an Energy Component

While some energy practices are purely spiritual in nature, there are others that belong to the martial arts and that are sometimes called "martial *chi-gong*." But before going into more detail, I want to first say something about all of the names and terms now going around in China that have "*chi-gong*" in them.

People are using the term "*chi-gong*" to describe all sorts of supposed practices, from "artistic *chi-gong*" to "musical *chi-gong*," from "calligraphy *chi-gong*" to "dancing *chi-gong*." But we should ask whether those are actual *chi-gong*. They seem bizarre to me. I would say they're really muddying the waters, if not ruining *chi-gong*. They have no grounds for what they're doing. They are implying that all someone has to do is get into a trance-like "*chi-gong* state" and then paint, or sing, or dance, or do calligraphy and it amounts to *chi-gong*. But that's not the case. I think anyone would agree that that's demeaning to *chi-gong*. *Chi-gong* is a far-reaching and profound body of knowledge for physical transformation. And yet people are now reducing it to some kind of hypnotic state. If it were as simple as that, and someone were to go to the bathroom while in that kind of state, then wouldn't that, too, count as *chi-gong*? It's demeaning to *chi-gong*, as I see it. A couple of years back, at the Asian Health Expo, there was something being billed as "calligraphy *chi-gong*." I went over to their booth to see what it was about. The person there picked up his calligraphy brush and proceeded to write a few words, after which he used his hand to project energy at the words. But all of the energy he sent out was dark, unlike how higher energy would be. He wouldn't have had any higher energy, in fact, as his mind was preoccupied with money and status. So his energy was bound to be bad. And he was even selling the calligraphy he had on display there at a high price, though only foreigners bought it. Whoever bought it and took it home was in for bad luck, I would say, since dark energy isn't good for anyone. Even the man's face was dark. It was money that was on his mind, and he was hungry for it. He couldn't possibly have had a higher type of energy. Yet the man's business card was loaded with titles like "International Chi-Gong Calligrapher." Gimmicks like that hardly deserve to be called *chi-gong*.

You should know that some eighty to ninety percent of you here today will not only be illness-free after our classes, but will also have formed real, true, higher energy. Your body will carry extraordinary things, beyond anything you could form on your own—even with a lifetime of practice. Even those who are young couldn't develop what I am giving you with a whole lifetime of practice; and that's assuming you could find a true teacher to instruct you. It has taken us many generations to form the *falun* and the mechanisms we use, and yet they are bestowed upon your bodies right from the beginning. So I should tell you: don't let these slip away just because they came to you easily. They are immensely valuable, simply priceless. What you will carry after these classes is true *gong*—a form of high-energy matter. If you return home and write a few words they will each have higher energy on them, even if you're not much of a calligrapher. But that doesn't of course mean that each of you is going to pick up a "master" title and become some kind of "calligraphy *chi-gong* master." That's not the right idea. The fact is simply that anyone who really does have an energy like *gong* will leave traces of it on whatever he or she touches, shining and radiant, without even consciously emitting it.

I once saw a piece in a magazine talking about an upcoming calligraphy *chi-gong* class. I gave it a cursory look to see what was going to be taught. The piece described how you would learn a breathing technique and then meditate upon the idea of *chi* at your energy center for fifteen to thirty minutes. Then you would use your mind to lift energy from your body's energy center through to your forearm, before taking up your brush and dipping it in ink. Then you would learn to move the energy to the tip of your brush and start writing, once your focus had reached the tip of the brush. But that's misleading, isn't it? It's not as simple as just moving your energy somewhere and then it becomes a new breed of *chi-gong*. By that token, at mealtime we could just meditate a bit before picking up our utensils, and then move our energy to the tips of them before we ate and we could call it "dining *chi-gong*," I suppose. And you'd be dining on energy, by that logic. It's degrading to *chi-gong* to make it seem so superficial, and that shouldn't be done.

By contrast, the kinds of *chi-gong* found in certain martial arts *are* a genuine tradition in their own right. I say that because they have been passed down for millennia and have well-developed spiritual underpinnings as well as a full system of practice. So they are comprehensive. That said, these kinds of energy practices are lower in level than the methods used in purely spiritual practice. Here's a case that makes this point, involving "hard *chi-gong*," as it's called—a type of martial practice where energy meant specifically for combat is physically amassed. In Beijing there was someone new to our practice who found that he couldn't press on anything with his hands after taking our class. When he went to the store to purchase a baby stroller and pressed on it with his hand to check its sturdiness, it broke with an audible snap. He found it odd. Another episode happened when he was at home and he went to sit down. When he pressed on his chair with his hand, it broke. He asked me what was happening. I didn't offer an explanation, as I didn't want him to get attached. I just said that anything like that is natural and that he should just let things take their course, and not give it too much thought, since it's all for the best. With the power that he had he could crush even a piece of stone to powder with just a pinch of his fingers, if he'd had a good command of it. That surely amounts to hard *chi-gong*, then, and yet he hadn't been practicing for it. It's actually common to gain powers like these while doing meditative practices; it's only that often they aren't at people's disposal since they would be hard to use appropriately. This is particularly so in the early stages of practice, when your mind has yet to elevate much; any powers that form then are sure to be unavailable. Nor will these powers necessarily be given to you when you reach advanced stages of practice later on, since by then they would serve no purpose.

Let's take a look at one example of how energy practice might factor into martial arts. Mobilizing the body's *chi* energy is a big part of it. This energy isn't so easily mobilized at first, and might not go where you want it to. To address this, a person will have to work his hands, chest, feet, legs, arms, as well as head. Training these might involve striking the trunk of a tree with your hands, or palms, or repeatedly slapping your hands against slabs of stone. You can just imagine how painful it would be for your bones to hit stone in that manner; even just light impact might result in bleeding. Yet that's not enough to mobilize the body's *chi*. For that, the person has to swing his arm so that his blood pools in the arm and causes his arm and hand to swell. They really do swell a bit, and then when he next strikes stone his bones will be cushioned. It won't hurt as much since now his bones won't be making direct contact with the stone. As he carries on practicing in this manner, his teacher will give him further instruction, and with time he will learn to mobilize energy. But that alone doesn't suffice, for in a real-life fight your opponent won't wait for you to mobilize your energy. By the time a person has learned to mobilize it, he will have gained the ability to ward off blows, as might be expected; he might not feel any pain even if he's struck with a long staff, for the *chi* he mobilized would provide a kind of cushioning. But *chi* is just a very basic thing, which belongs to the initial stage of practice; over time, with consistent effort, it will be converted into high-energy matter. It will gradually form into a dense mass of energy as this happens. An energy mass like this will have an intelligence of its own. And so it is also a mass of supernormal abilities, or a type of power. Yet this power will only be good for things like attacking and defending against blows; it won't be useful for healing. This high-energy entity is in another dimension and doesn't travel through this dimension here, so its time passes faster than ours. That's why if you strike somebody, the necessary energy will be deployed to the relevant part of your body without your having directed energy there or having willed it in any way. If someone strikes you and you move to block it, the energy will have arrived at that part of your body even before you make your move. It goes faster than you, however quick you might be, owing to the different workings of time in the two dimensions. So doing the kind of energy practice found in the martial arts can develop exceptional abilities such as Iron Sand Hands, Cinnabar Palm, Vajra Leg, and Arhat Foot—and all of these can in fact be attained by regular people through training.

The biggest difference between the martial type of energy practice and the purely spiritual, or "internal," type of practice is this: in the martial context the practice is done in motion, and so your *chi* travels just beneath the skin. And with all the motion involved, you wouldn't enter into a state of stillness or have *chi* go to your energy center; it would travel beneath the skin, instead, and just go through your muscles and tissues. And so these practices don't extend one's lifespan or develop higher powers. Energy practices of a purely spiritual sort, by contrast, require that the body be still. Typically they do have *chi* enter the body's energy center, or the lower abdomen, and they make a point of practicing in stillness and transforming one's innate body. They can extend one's lifespan and lead to higher stages of spiritual attainment.

You may have come across extraordinary-sounding *kung fu* abilities like Golden Bell, Iron Shirt, and incredible bowmanship in martial arts works. Some depict people with the ability to become weightless, who sail to and fro at great heights, and some figures even manage to cross over into other dimensions. But are those powers for real? They are, to be sure. Only you won't see regular people wielding them. Someone who really has developed advanced powers like those wouldn't readily reveal them. Powers as extraordinary as those don't come about simply by practicing martial arts; internal practice is needed to develop them. It takes being attentive to the mind and character, and a disinterest in material things. And even if someone does gain higher powers with practice, he won't be allowed to use them freely in worldly settings at any point; only when no one is around to see will it be okay to use them. Then going back to martial arts stories, something doesn't add up. The very people who they portray fighting and killing over worldly things like a swordsmanship manual, treasure, or a certain lady always have fantastic powers, coming and going like a shadow. Yet powers like those can only be gained through spiritual practice. A person must work hard on his character and become indifferent to status, wealth, and worldly things in order to get powers like those. Killing and money-lust would be the complete opposite. When you see supernormal heroes with those traits, it's the product of writers taking artistic license; they know that consumers just want whatever is stimulating and won't object. Writers often seize on this fact and do whatever they can to meet the demand. And the more incredible the story is, the more readers or viewers go for it. So it really comes down to writers taking artistic license with things. Anyone who actually has powers like those in martial arts works would never act like those characters do, much less showcase their powers.

Showing Off

Owing to the fact that they practice in the secular world, a number of practitioners have a hard time breaking many attachments, which have become second nature and aren't detectable. A tendency to show off can be a part of many actions, including even good deeds. It's common for people to build themselves up and show off a bit in their daily lives, hoping to make a name for themselves or gain from it materially. They want people to see how competent they are and to think that they're better than others. We see something like this, too, such as when someone is doing better with the exercises, has lucid visions, or does the movements a little more gracefully—and it leads to showing off.

Some people draw a crowd by claiming to have heard something from me, but what they tell people is a combination of hearsay and their own ideas. What leads them to do that is a desire to show off. And then there are people who spread gossip around, all excited and pleased with themselves, since they feel like an insider. They like to think that they're more informed than other practitioners, that no one knows as much as they do. This trait has become second nature for them, and they might not be aware of it. What's at work on a subconscious level is a desire to show off, or else they would have no motive for gossiping. Some people spread rumors about how I will stop teaching and "return to seclusion" at such-and-such date. But I didn't come out of "seclusion," so it's baseless. And there are some who have claimed that on such-and-such day I revealed something to this or that person and gave them personalized instruction. But gossiping like that serves no purpose other than to reveal their attachment—a desire to show off.

Still others want my autograph. The purpose? It's still for worldly ends, even if they just think of it as a keepsake or memento. But there is no point in an autograph if you don't genuinely practice. And what need is there for an autograph when each and every word of our books has my image and *falun* behind it, and every sentence is from me? What some people are thinking is that my energies will protect them if they have my autograph. They are still thinking about "energies" somehow, when those aren't things we dabble in. This book alone is beyond any measure of value. What more could you want? Hoping for my autograph reflects attachments, in fact. I should also mention that some people emulate the practitioners that they see accompanying me, without first thinking about whether it's appropriate to do. You shouldn't look to anybody as your example. No one is a substitute for the teachings; only Dafa itself can serve as your guide. Those who accompany me don't get any personalized instruction and are treated just like the rest of you. They are merely staff of our Association, and nothing to get fixated on. Being attached like that is harmful to our practice, even though you don't mean for it to be so. You might make things up for dramatic effect, which ends up being divisive, or you might provoke attachments in other practitioners that lead them to try to get closer to me and get extra instruction for themselves, and so on. It should be apparent that all of this goes back to the same problem.

The problems with showing off typically reach beyond what I just described. I have been teaching Falun Dafa for two years now, and it's possible that among those who are veteran to the practice, a group of you will soon find that all of your powers become available to you; and another group might find that they suddenly experience gradual enlightenment. These higher states weren't possible for you before since you still had many human attachments, and so it wasn't suitable for me to push you to such heights in one go. Your character surely had improved a great deal, yet many attachments remained, and so it wouldn't have been appropriate for you to have had higher powers at your disposal. So gradual enlightenment is in store for people once they have passed the initial phase and become solid. The inner eye will be opened to great heights with gradual enlightenment, and many powers will come to them. And I can share that with true spiritual practice, in fact, you start to develop many powers right from the outset. Some of you have now reached very advanced stages of practice and have numerous powers. Many of you might have recently begun to experience what I've been describing. There will also be some who, though not that advanced, have all of their powers freed and become enlightened—and fully so—at a lower level of attainment. That will happen because what these students' bodies have and their capacities for hardship are connected, and these won't change, since they were predetermined.

I bring this up to convey to you that you really mustn't put whoever experiences these things on a pedestal and regard them as enlightened beings. The stakes are high for your spiritual development, for only Dafa itself can guide you right. Don't start following someone or giving him an audience just because he has special powers or visions. You would be hurting not only yourself, of course, but also bringing harm to that person; he might become full of himself and end up losing all that he had, have his powers revoked, or fall. Even those who are enlightened and have miraculous powers at their command may fall if they don't exercise good self-control. This holds true even for Buddhas, much less people such as you who practice in the world. So it's vital that you exercise self-restraint, however great or many your powers may be. Recently there was someone in attendance who had the ability to suddenly vanish and then reappear a moment later. Powers like these exist, along with even greater ones. So you might ask yourself how you would do if such powers came to you. As practitioners, or adherents, of Falun Dafa you shouldn't put anyone with powers like these on a pedestal, yourself included, or yearn for such things. You will quickly experience problems if those things stir up longings in you, and your level of attainment will drop. It's possible that the person whose powers you are admiring and coveting hasn't made as much spiritual progress as you, and it's only that your powers aren't accessible to you. By admiring and coveting someone else's powers, you have, on this matter at least, slipped and fallen. I would like everyone to really be vigilant about this. I'm putting this in serious terms because the changes I described may soon take place, and it could be ruinous for you if you don't handle things well.

When a practitioner develops higher energy, has his powers freed, or becomes fully enlightened, he still mustn't think of himself as special; the visions he has are limited by his level of attainment. It's just that he has reached that point in spiritual practice, and it means that he has a corresponding level of faith, quality of thought, and amount of wisdom. So it's possible that he won't believe that still higher beings or things exist, since he will think that he has seen the ultimate reality and that there is nothing more. But that is far from being the case, since his level of attainment is limited.

Some people will have all of their powers come to them at their present stage, since they will have reached their limits in spiritual practice; the restraints will be lifted and they will experience enlightenment at their level, since nothing more is possible. Some who finish their practice in the times ahead will experience enlightenment at a lesser level within this world; some may experience it at a higher level; and some will experience it with full divine standing. And it is only enlightenment with full divine standing that counts as the pinnacle, and only such figures will be able to see, and even reveal themselves at, all planes. Even with enlightenment and having their powers freed at the very lowest of levels within this world, a person will be able to see certain dimensions and higher beings, and even communicate with them. But if and when that happens to you, you mustn't become happy with yourself, for you certainly would not have gained full divine standing. What happens next, then? They can only hope to maintain their current level of attainment and, some other day, practice to higher stages. But that would be a future matter. So there would be no point in keeping someone like that from experiencing his powers when he has reached his highest point. Any efforts at further progress would be in vain, and so his powers will be freed on account of his having reached the end of his spiritual journey. This will be the case for many people. So whatever happens, you should keep your composure as a practitioner and base what you do on Dafa, to really get things right. Keep in mind that if you gain any particular power, or if all of your powers are freed, it came to you from practicing Dafa. If you put your own powers above Dafa, or think that the insights you've gained with enlightenment are right, and that you are greater than Dafa, then I would say your fall has begun, you are in danger, and things will only get worse. You are really in trouble in that case, and all of your spiritual efforts may end up for naught. Not handling these things well could lead to your downfall and ruin your practice.

I should mention that this book combines my teachings from several classes, and every sentence comes from me. Our students and learners carefully transcribed for me every word of the audio recordings, and I personally edited the text multiple times. Everything in the book counts as my teaching, and this alone is the Way that I have set forth.

THE
SEVENTH TALK

Taking Life

THE SUBJECT OF TAKING LIFE touches a nerve with many people, who worry about what implications it has for them. For practitioners the rule is strict: there is to be no taking of life. Any true spiritual practice or tradition—be it Buddhist, Daoist, Mystical, or whatever it may be—will look upon this matter in absolute terms and forbid killing. I can vouch for this. The consequences that follow from taking life are so great as to warrant a more in-depth discussion. When the term "killing" was used in early Buddhism it mainly referred to taking human life, which is the most serious form of it. Later on the killing of large creatures such as livestock and other larger animals also came to be regarded as serious. Let's consider why religious communities have always held the taking of life to be so serious. There is a Buddhist belief that a life ended prematurely becomes a lost soul or "wild ghost," and so services have traditionally been performed to save these lives from purgatory. As the belief goes, were they not rescued from purgatory, they would have to go without food or drink and be trapped in a terrible predicament.

We hold that when a person wrongs someone he gives the other party a substantial amount of virtue as compensation. This applies to regular transgressions. But suddenly ending a life, be it that of an animal or another creature, is a sizeable sin and generates a lot of karma. Prohibitions against taking life used to mainly apply to taking human life, since the karma that's made is sizeable. But taking a regular creature's life results in significant karma and isn't trivial. It's significant, because a certain amount of adversity is allotted to each stage of your spiritual journey and they are your own ordeals, made by your own karma, and they are placed there to facilitate your progress. In each case you can overcome the ordeal so long as you work on your character. Then you can just imagine how much harder it would be to pass these, with all of the karma that comes from killing added on. Your character wouldn't suffice to get through them. And it might spell the end of spiritual practice for you altogether.

We have found that when a person incarnates, within a certain expanse of the cosmos a great many of him incarnate simultaneously; they look just like him, assume the same name, and engage in more or less the same things. So it's fitting to consider them part of the larger him. When any life (including those of larger animals) dies prematurely, the hims in other dimensions have yet to complete the lives they were ordained to lead, and may have many years of living still ahead. The life that dies early then faces the predicament of belonging nowhere, and must drift about in the expanse of the universe. So this is what people in the past thought of as lost souls or wild ghosts who have nothing to eat or drink, and who suffer terribly. And they may have been right about that. What we can say for sure is that those lives are stuck in a most frightening predicament. They must wait on and on until their counterparts in each dimension have all finished their courses of life, and only then may they go together to their next destination. The longer the wait, the greater the suffering. And with greater suffering, more karma will go onto the body of the killer, since he caused this pain. You can just imagine how much karma the killer would accrue. This is what we have observed with higher vision.

We have also seen that when a person incarnates in this world, the design of his entire life is present in another, specific dimension, and everything that is supposed to take place in his life is already laid out there. And naturally it was higher beings who planned it all out. It is owing to them that when someone is born into this world he belongs to a certain family, attends a certain school, and once he grows up he works for a certain entity, and in this manner becomes linked with society in multifaceted ways. And from this we can glean that this world, on a larger scale, is in fact well mapped out. When a life comes to a premature end, however, and no longer follows the designs that were originally in place, it means that a change has occurred. So whoever it was that fouled things up will not be forgiven by the higher being who made the designs. As persons of faith you all wish to reach higher realms, but how could your spiritual efforts take you there if beings above won't forgive you? In some cases the teacher of the person who took life will be in trouble as well, since his level won't have surpassed that of the higher being [who planned the life of the prematurely deceased]. And so he will be sent down along with the killer. So this is terribly serious, as you can see. Spiritual practice is very challenging for someone who has taken life.

It's possible that some of you who are learning Falun Dafa have fought in times of war. Those wars were states of affairs brought about by larger, cosmic events, and you were but one tiny part of those affairs. For cosmic events to unfold there have to be people carrying things out and bringing about certain states of affairs. Since those affairs had to do with larger changes, you aren't entirely to blame for what you may have done. The karma we are concerned with is the kind that stems from willfully doing wrong for selfish reasons, for your own gain, or to protect your own things. You won't be held accountable for things done owing to changes in the greater dimension or to changes in the larger designs of society.

Taking life generates a great amount of karma. Some people might be concerned about how they are going to put food on the table if that's the case, since now they wouldn't be allowed to take animals' lives. But I'm not here to address minutiae like this. I am here to teach the Way to practitioners, and I won't be giving instructions for others on how to go about their lives. You can use our teachings to gauge things and go about them however you understand to be right. Non-practitioners are free to do as they please, since that's their own business; not everyone can do spiritual practice. But practitioners should hold themselves to high standards. So the terms I'm setting forth here are meant only for people who practice.

Animals and plants count as lives, just as humans do; everything is alive in other dimensions. When your inner eye has reached the level of the *dharma* eye, you may find that stones, walls, or any object might speak to you and greet you. Some people might find it disconcerting to think that the grains and vegetables they consume are alive, and that now they might have to just passively let any flies or mosquitoes that get into their homes bite them and contaminate their food. While I am saying that we can't harm living things without reason or on a whim, I'm not asking you to be mister nice guy and fretfully sweat over every little thing, to the point that you jump around as you walk just to avoid stepping on ants. That strikes me as a tiring way to live, and it would just be a new attachment. And besides, you might still crush many microorganisms while hopping around trying to avoid ants; there are many microscopic life forms, such as fungi and bacteria, that you might unintentionally kill. Living becomes impossible if you go to such extremes. So that's not the kind of person we want to be. A spiritual life would be impossible, in that case. You should focus on the big things and practice with confidence and poise.

As human beings we are entitled to sustain our lives, and so our material surroundings should suit our life needs. While we mustn't harm any living things intentionally, we shouldn't become overly petty about things either. For example, we shouldn't stop consuming vegetables and grains just because they are alive. With that approach to life, spiritual practice wouldn't be possible. So we should be a bit more broad-minded. For example, you shouldn't be too concerned if you unwittingly step on ants or insects as you walk. Perhaps it was time for them to perish since you didn't do that intentionally. A population balance always has to be maintained in the animal kingdom and those of microorganisms, since a tipped balance would lead to a proliferation of any one species. So with that in mind we can go about our practice with confidence and poise. You can simply shoo away any flies or mosquitoes that happen to get into your home, or install screens to keep them out. But if and when you can't shoo them out and have to swat them, so be it; you shouldn't just stand by and let them bite and possibly harm people in your own home. You have strong immunity, thanks to your practice, and needn't worry about infection. But you might have family that are ordinary folk who don't practice, and are at risk of infectious disease. So you shouldn't just passively look on as an insect crawls on your child's face.

I will share with you a story from the Buddha's early years. One day he wanted to bathe while in the forest, and told his disciple to clean the basin that he used. His disciple went to do so, only to find that it was crawling with insects; were he to clean it they would be killed. The disciple returned and informed the Buddha that the basin was full of insects. The Buddha didn't bat an eye and said just one sentence, "Go and clean out the basin." But when the disciple reached the basin once again, he didn't know where to start, as doing anything would result in the death of insects. He pondered it for a moment and then returned to the Buddha. He told him, "Honorable teacher, the basin is crawling with insects. If I were to wipe it down they would be killed." The Buddha turned his gaze upon him and said, "What I asked you to clean was the basin." The disciple finally caught on and promptly wiped the basin clean. There's a point to this story. And that is, we can't cease to bathe on account of insects, start looking for new homes on account of mosquitoes, or close up our throats and cease to eat or drink just because everything consumed is alive. That's not our approach. We should keep things in perspective and go about our practice in a confident and dignified manner. All is well as long as we don't harm living things on purpose. As human beings you are entitled to have your living space and to meet your daily needs, and it's fine to ensure these. You have to maintain your life just like anyone else, and should be able to lead a normal life.

Some false masters have claimed that killing is permissible on the first and fifteenth days of each lunar month. And some have even said that killing two-legged animals is okay, as if those creatures weren't living beings. It's absurd to think that taking lives on those days is not killing. They are trying to downplay what they're doing. Some supposed masters are false, in fact, and from their words and deeds you can readily tell what they are up to and what their agenda is. Most often the figures who condone killing are plagued by entity attachment. This is apparent in how false masters who are possessed by fox spirits go about eating chicken: they wolf it down and are reluctant to give up the bones.

Taking life not only generates an enormous amount of karma, but also raises the question of compassion. Since we do spiritual practice we should have compassion in our hearts. As your compassion develops you will come to see that life is painful for all living things. This will come to pass.

Eating Meat

Eating meat is another subject that can be sensitive. But eating meat is not the same as taking life. We don't ask you to refrain from eating meat, even after you have been learning our practice for some length of time. By contrast, many who teach energy practices will tell you that meat is off limits right from day one, which catches people off guard. And that's asking a lot, as there might be a savory stewed chicken or braised fish dish awaiting them at home for dinner, which now they'd have to forgo. Abstention from meat is also required in some religious orders. Buddhist practices generally take this approach, as do certain Daoist ones. We don't ask that of you, though we do have our own approach. To understand the approach we take, you have to bear in mind that ours is a practice where the Way "works upon you," as we put it. In this kind of practice certain bodily states will be brought about by the higher energy you have, or by the Way. Different states will come about as you reach different stages of attainment in your practice. And so one day, or even today, right after I finish teaching this class, some of you might find that you can't eat meat. It will smell unpleasant to you, and eating it would make you nauseous. This, then, is a kind of abstention that's not imposed upon you, nor one that you force upon yourself. It comes from within you. It is a distaste for meat that's triggered by the higher energy that you have, and it occurs because you have reached that stage. And it's real enough that you would actually vomit if you were to consume meat.

Those who have been doing this practice for some time know firsthand that the bodily states I'm describing do come about with Falun Dafa practice, with different states unfolding at different stages. Some learners have a rather strong longing for meat and are quite attached to it; they can typically eat quite a lot of it. They're not at all put off by meat that smells or tastes strong to others, and can still eat it. So here's what is done to break the attachment. The person's stomach will be made to ache after he consumes meat, but it won't hurt if he forgoes it. It's a condition that indicates it is time to give up meat. But it won't be this way for the rest of his life, in case you are wondering. Then what's going on? His not being able to eat meat genuinely arises from within. Consider the purpose. The rules against meat in monastic orders are similar to the induced-state in our practice, where you aren't physically able to eat it, in that both seek to remove any craving for or attachment to meat.

Some people can hardly stand a meal without meat, owing to their strong human cravings for it. One morning I was passing by the rear entrance of Victory Park in the city of Changchun when three people came out of the park, talking loudly. One of them said, "What kind of practice is that? It doesn't let you eat meat. I'd rather lose ten years of my life than go without meat." What a strong desire that was. Any desire that strong should surely be let go. Spiritual practice is meant to rid you of every human desire and attachment. Then, to spell it out, if you haven't ended your craving for meat, isn't it an attachment that remains? Could you achieve spiritual perfection in that case? My point is that any attachment has to go. But that's not to say that meat is off limits from that day on. The point isn't simply to keep you from eating meat. It's to prevent attachment. If you can break the attachment during the time when meat doesn't work for you, it may well become edible again later on. At that time it won't smell bad to you or be unpleasant to consume. And in that case it's fine to eat it.

When meat becomes edible again it means that your attachment to it and desire for it are gone. And a significant change will have happened. You will experience a new state whereby meat doesn't taste that good when you eat it; you will be able to eat it along with your family when it's served, and won't miss it otherwise. It won't taste like anything special when you do eat it. But that said, it's tricky practicing in the secular world. You might reacquire a taste for meat if your family has it regularly, and the whole process will repeat itself. And this cycle could play out multiple times over the course of your spiritual journey. Suddenly, out of the blue, you might not be able to eat it again one day. If that happens, then simply don't eat it. You really won't be able to, and doing so might result in your having to throw up. Wait until you can eat it before doing so. Just take things as they come. Ultimately it's not about eating meat or not: the key is that the attachment be removed.

People make fast progress in Falun Dafa. You will advance through the stages of practice swiftly as long as you work on your character. Some people aren't very attached to meat to begin with, and it doesn't matter much to them. For them the state I've described lasts just a week or so, since it takes little time to remove what attachment there is. Some people need upwards of a few months or even the better part of a year; seldom does it exceed a year. The process takes some time, since meat is now a major part of the human diet. But it still shouldn't be eaten by those who practice in monastic settings that prohibit it.

Let's discuss how meat has been viewed in Buddhism. The earliest form of Buddhism had no prohibition against meat. The Buddha and his disciples lived a very basic life in the forest, and didn't avoid meat. Civilization was in its infancy back when he gave his teachings twenty-five hundred years ago, and many regions hadn't developed agriculture. Even those that did, had limited amounts of arable land, and many areas were heavily forested. So grains were in limited supply and scarce. People naturally depended on hunting, with civilization where it was at, and meat was a staple food in many places. The reason that the Buddha didn't allow his disciples to handle money or goods, and led them in begging for food, was to try to have them break their attachments as much as possible. So they would just eat whatever people gave them and had no business being picky, since they were leading a holy life. And the food that was given to them may have included meat.

Early Buddhism did indeed designate certain foods as taboo. Nowadays Buddhists consider meat to be what's taboo, whereas initially, in early Buddhism, it was foods like onions, ginger, and garlic that were. Few Buddhist monks today can say exactly why those foods were taboo, since most monks haven't been initiated into true spiritual practice and there is much that they don't know. The Buddha taught the three disciplines of precept, concentration, and wisdom. "Precept" was about severing all desires through moral discipline, while "concentration" was about practicing meditation and achieving complete stillness. Anything that prevented someone from experiencing that or that compromised it, was regarded as a serious hindrance. Consuming onions, ginger, or garlic results in the body giving off a strong odor. In those days, monks would meditate in circles of seven or eight people in forests or caves. Whoever ate those foods would have given off a pungent odor, which would have compromised people's ability to meditate and become centered. So it really affected practice. And this was how certain foods came to be designated as taboo and their consumption barred. It should also be said that their strong odor is highly bothersome to the many supernatural beings born of a practitioner's body.

Onions, ginger, and garlic can also lead to further cravings for these foods, and regular consumption can result in addiction to them. For these reasons they have been regarded as taboo.

Over the centuries, many monks who progressed to higher stages of practice and experienced full or partial enlightenment came to realize that prohibitions are not that vital. If a person can rid himself of a certain attachment, that material thing that he was attached to will no longer affect him, for it is the attachment that really affects you. And that is why accomplished monks throughout the ages haven't considered the question of meat to be that critical. They saw that letting go of the attachment is what's key; anything can be eaten to stave off hunger if there is no attachment at work. But at this point in time, many monks have grown accustomed to living meat-free; many religious orders have long made a practice of this. And it's not merely a single prohibition anymore, but rather, part of a larger monastic code. So, many practicing monks are used to meat being strictly taboo. But then consider the case of the "mad monk" Ji-gong. He appears in many fictional works since he flew in the face of convention and ate meat. His story has been sensationalized. The reality is that food was naturally just a pressing issue for him after he was expelled from Ling-yin Temple. He was faced with starvation, and so he ate whatever was available to him. And truth be told, it didn't really matter what he ate as long as it was just to stay full and not done out of attachment to some particular food. He progressed to the point where he was aware of this principle. And as it turns out, he hardly ever ate meat, maybe just once or twice. But writers got excited once word got out that a Buddhist monk was eating meat. The more sensational something is, after all, the more people want to read it; art and entertainment are expected to do more than just depict life, as we know. And so they have made great fanfare out of what Ji-gong did. But in reality, it's fine to eat anything as long as you aren't attached to it and it's just done to satisfy hunger.

In Southeast Asia and southern China, and this includes the two provinces of Guangxi and Guangdong, some lay Buddhists prefer to say they are "vegetarian," rather than to openly say they are Buddhist—as if it were old-fashioned to say that. So they conflate going vegetarian with practicing Buddhism, as if it were that simple. But merely following a vegetarian lifestyle could hardly bring someone to enlightenment. As we've established, meat is just one human attachment, one desire, and abstaining from it means only that one attachment has been dealt with. There are still the attachments of jealousy, combativeness, excitability, and showing off—among many others—all of which must go if you want to achieve spiritual perfection. So people are mistaken to think that simply dealing with the attachment to meat makes enlightenment possible.

Meat isn't necessarily the only food of concern. An attachment to any food is problematic; this discussion applies to other foods as well. When someone expresses an affinity for a certain food, that counts as a desire. A practitioner will have no such attachment when he or she progresses to a certain level. Our teachings are quite advanced of course, and they encompass different stages of practice; it's not feasible or expected that you become fully detached overnight. When you have indeed progressed to the point where a food attachment should go, you won't be able to eat that food, however much you may like it. If you were to eat it, it wouldn't taste right or how you would expect it to taste. Back when I was

working at a company, the cafeteria always had trouble breaking even and eventually folded. Everyone had to bring his
or her own lunch after that. It was a challenge to prepare
one's own lunch while rushing to get off to work in the morning, so I would sometimes pick up a couple of steamed buns
along with a block of soft tofu in soy sauce for lunch. Such
light fare should have been just fine, in theory. But eating it
too regularly still proved to be problematic, as any liking that
I was deemed to have developed needed to go. So at just the
sight of tofu my stomach would churn and I couldn't eat it.
This was meant to ensure that I wasn't attached. Of course,
you won't experience episodes like mine unless you have
progressed to that point. They won't happen when you have
just begun.

Buddhist practices don't permit the consumption of alcohol. Could you imagine a Buddha with a bottle of alcohol in
his hand? When I talked about not being able to eat meat,
I explained that it would be fine for non-monastics to eat it
again later once the attachment was gone. Alcohol, however,
is not something you can consume again after giving it up.
Every practitioner's body has higher energy, of course, which
takes many forms. Some powers come up to the surface of
your body and are very pure. If you consume alcohol they
will depart your body in a flash. They will leave your body
for a while, as they loathe the smell. And how deplorable it
is when people become addicted to alcohol, since it impairs
their reason. The Daoist practices that feature drinking only
do that because they don't cultivate the true soul, and want
to numb it.

There are people who really take to the bottle, and have
a great affinity for alcohol. And there are some who drink to

the point of alcoholism and just have to have it; meals without it aren't even appealing to them. A practitioner shouldn't be like that. Alcohol is definitely addictive, and the longing for it is a desire, after all. It stimulates the nerve circuits associated with addiction, and the more one consumes it the worse the addiction. A practitioner will want to be free of an attachment like that, as you can imagine. So it has to go. Some people might think this isn't feasible since at work they are responsible for entertaining clients or are often out discussing business with people, and think that it can be hard to get business going smoothly without having a few drinks together. But that's not necessarily true. Generally when people are meeting to talk business with one another, nobody is going to force alcohol on you, and you can drink however much you'd like of whatever beverage you choose, be it a soft drink, bottled water, or a beer. That's especially so when doing business or socializing with non-Chinese. And there is even less of an issue in other contexts and when in cultured company. That's generally the case, at least.

Smoking is another attachment. Some people believe that smoking can give them a lift, but I would say they are fooling themselves. Sometimes people take a cigarette break while they are at work or writing something and feel tired. After smoking they feel energized. But it wasn't smoking that did it. Rather, that feeling of being energized came from having relaxed for a bit. The mind can create a false impression and give you the wrong idea; over time, it really can form into a notion or false impression that leads one to believe that smoking is a pick-me-up, when it's really not. Smoking doesn't do the body one bit of good. Autopsies have found that the trachea and lungs of long-term smokers are black, in fact.

Then wouldn't you rather purify your body as someone engaged in spiritual practice? We want to purify our bodies on an ongoing basis and continually elevate spiritually. Yet smoking pollutes your body and does the exact opposite of what we want to do; and there are strong cravings involved. If you are someone who knows it's bad for you and have tried to quit but failed, you can take heart in knowing that it's hard to quit without the right thoughts guiding you. Now that you are doing spiritual practice, though, you can try, starting today, to regard it as an attachment to break, and see if you can manage to quit. I would urge you to quit smoking today if you are sincere about practicing, and I can guarantee that it's possible. The thought of smoking doesn't occur to anyone during my classes, and I can assure you that you can quit if you want to. As long as you have that intention, even if you do smoke again, the cigarette will taste awful. Reading this chapter of the book will be just as effective as hearing me teach this in person. Of course, we won't stop you from smoking if you don't want to do spiritual practice. But if you do, then you should quit. To share an analogy I've used before: have you ever seen a religious statue with a cigarette in its mouth? That would be absurd. So you should really quit, considering what we aspire to. I would say that you had better quit if you want to make spiritual progress. Smoking harms the body and is a craving. It's completely contrary to what we do.

Jealousy

In my teachings I often bring up the topic of jealousy. The reason is, jealousy plays out fiercely in China and it's so pervasive that it has become second nature for people, and they don't sense it in themselves. This problem of intense jealousy has roots, of course. At one time Confucianism shaped the people of China profoundly and fostered a more introverted kind of personality. Chinese people don't reveal their emotions, and make a point of self-control and patience. This has become habitual for them, and so as a whole, Chinese today have a very introverted disposition. This has its good side, of course, such as being unassuming. But it has its downside too, and can lead to unfavorable traits. The negative traits are especially pronounced now in this latter day, and they exacerbate the problem of jealousy. People nowadays get terribly envious when someone shares his or her good news. When a person gets accolades at work, or something good happens to him, he won't say a word about it when he returns to his desk lest others find out and get upset over it. People in the West sometimes remark about the jealousy Asian people have. Confucianism's influence on the Asian region runs deep, and the countries there have all been shaped by it more or less. But only in China does jealousy affect people so strongly.

This is partially due to the doctrine of total equality that was advanced in China not long ago. As the logic went, we're all in it together and so we are all equally entitled, we should all get the same wage increases, and so on. This kind of logic has a certain appeal to it, of course, with everyone seeming equal. But it's just not valid. The kinds of jobs that people do are different, and how well they do them is different too;

not everyone does his job responsibly. So as the universe would have it, people should be compensated accordingly. And that's even just common sense, since people normally believe that whoever does more should get more for it, and whoever does less should get less. But the doctrine of total equality flies in the face of all this, and claims that everybody is born the same and that any differences among people are just the product of life circumstances. I would say that's going too far, and anything so extreme is bound to be wrong. And it can't account for the fact that some people are born male and others female. Or that people have different looks, and that some are different from birth owing to congenital illnesses or deformities. We can see from higher realms that each person's whole life is laid out in other dimensions, so naturally people's lives in this world aren't the same. While people might want equality, it's not possible if that is not what life has in store for them. People's lives are different.

People in the West are by nature more extroverted, and you can readily tell how they're feeling. While this has its good points, it also has its downsides, such as a lack of self-restraint. The different dispositions that Westerners and Asians have reflect different ways of thinking, and have different consequences. People in China get upset when someone is given recognition at work or receives special treatment. Anyone who gets a slightly larger paycheck knows to quietly tuck it into his pocket and not say a word about it. Even exemplary employees have a hard time these days, as people unfairly expect them to come in early and stay after hours; or they might get jibes from co-workers, who remark about how "great" these people are, and try to offload work on them. It's hard to be a good person these days.

It's a different story outside of China. Let's say there is someone whose supervisor sees what fine work he has done and gives him more money. When he receives it he will be tickled pink, and might even look at the paycheck in front of others and remark out loud about how much he got. He can happily state the amount to everybody, worry free. In China, by contrast, if someone receives a larger paycheck, the supervisor himself might tell the person to quietly tuck it away before anyone sees it. In the West, if a kid gets a hundred at school he might joyfully run all the way home, shouting, "I got a hundred today, I got a hundred!" A neighbor might open his door and yell out, "Hey Tom, great job! That's my boy!" Or another might open her window and shout, "Hey Jack, well done!" But were the kid to do that in China, he'd be in for trouble. As he ran home from school, shouting, "I got a hundred today, I got a hundred!" people would be chastising him from inside their homes, faster than they could open the doors. "What's the big deal, it's just a hundred!" they'd quip. "So what? Who hasn't had a hundred before?" The different frames of mind in the two cultures lead to different responses. In China, it can lead to jealousy and resentment. People feel uneasy about others' good fortune instead of being happy for them. There are problems like this.

The doctrine of total equality that was pushed in China a while back really got people confused. I'll give an illustration. Suppose there is someone who thinks that nobody at his workplace is as good as he is; he excels at whatever he does and really thinks he's outstanding. He envisions himself doing just fine as a manager at the company, or even in a more senior position; even becoming head of state seems feasible to him. And his supervisor might concur that he's very able and does everything well. His co-workers might say the same, praising him for his talents and skills. But then there is someone on his team or in the office who botches everything up and never comes through. Yet one day this incompetent person is in fact promoted to a managerial position, instead of him—and even becomes his supervisor. It proves terribly trying for him. And so he goes around complaining to everyone about it, upset and consumed by envy.

The principle at work here is one that the average person isn't aware of: that you will not get what you want if it's not part of your life's design, however deserving you may seem; while someone else who is incompetent might get it, if it *is* part of his life's design. People might have their own takes on this, but their views aren't spiritually informed. As higher beings see it, things in this world unfold according to higher designs that are in place. So what a person gets to do in life certainly isn't going to be decided by how talented he is. The Buddhist doctrine of karmic rewards and retribution holds that the design of your life is based on your karma. So even someone immensely talented might end up with nothing in life if he doesn't have much virtue. Yet a person who seems incompetent may have a lot of virtue, and will thus enjoy a position of influence or have great wealth. People can't ordinarily see all of this, and so they always think that they should get whatever position or role they're fit for. As a result they spend their lives competing with others and end up hurt, believing that life is painful and tiring; they never know peace or contentment. These sorts of people are so anxious they miss meals and lose sleep over it, and feel distraught. And by the time they reach old age they will have ruined their health and will suffer all sorts of ailments.

As people engaged in spiritual practice we have all the more reason not to be like that. We believe in letting things happen naturally. We know that we won't be deprived of what is rightfully ours, and shouldn't labor to get what is not. But not everything is completely set in stone, of course. And that is what makes wrongdoing possible—the very fact that some things may be subject to change. You, however, follow Dafa, and so you needn't worry about people taking what is rightfully yours, for my spiritual bodies will be looking after you in the normal course of events. So we believe in letting things happen naturally. There might be instances where something seems to be yours, and people might say so too, and you believe it is yours, when in fact it's not and in the end it goes to someone else. From this it will be seen whether you can let it go. If you cannot, it means that you have an attachment. We use this approach to rid you of your worldly wants, for *that* is what's most important. Everyday people lack this perspective and so they contend over things.

While jealousy can play out fiercely among regular folk, it has always been quite prominent in the spiritual arena as well. Different groups often show little respect to one another, and seize upon one another's faults. But often these combative people and their practices are only interested in health and are a mess, since they came about due to entity attachment; few of them see character as important. In some cases, people who haven't experienced any special abilities, even after decades of practice, get worked up if they see a newcomer get them. And so they'll be dismissive about it. Or they might even be irate about it, and claim that it's the devil's work or that this person has gone mad. You also see people being dismissive about another person's teachings, and they convince themselves that the person is nothing special and not worth listening to. It's true that the person may not speak in a way that's impressive, but that is because he is speaking strictly about what his own practice entails. These naysayers, on the other hand, might be people who study everything and have long lists of credentials to show for it. They attend whatever teachings are being given, and know a lot—perhaps more than the figure at the podium. But what good does it do them? All that knowledge of energy practices that they have is limited to merely the most basic, physical level. And they only make things worse for themselves by taking in more teachings and complicating their energy. This makes spiritual progress less likely for them. They don't understand that you need to commit to one practice if you want to avoid problems. And even among people who *are* sincere about spiritual practice, you sometimes see people being disrespectful of one another. It's easy for jealousy to creep in if you are still competitive.

There's an episode in the novel *The Appointing of the Gods* that illustrates this. In one scene, the figure known as Honorable Divine of the Origin is choosing someone from among his disciples for the honor of appointing new deities, and selects one, named Jiang Ziya. The decision proves vexing to another disciple, however, named Shen Gongbao. Shen can't believe it, since he views Jiang as old and inept, while he himself is so powerful that he can sever his own head and put it back on. Jealousy consumes him so badly that he constantly makes trouble for Jiang.

Miraculous powers were part of early Buddhism, back in the Buddha's time. Yet nowadays almost nobody in Buddhism openly talks about them for fear of seeming crazy. People are dismissive of them. This happens because today's monks have little insight into these powers. Among the Buddha's ten main disciples, one monk, named Maudgalyāyana, was known for having greater powers than all the others. And among his female disciples the same was said to be true for a woman named Uppalavannā. Similar figures emerged after Buddhism came to China, with there being generations of "eminent monks," as they've been called. Bodhidharma himself was said to have miraculously crossed the Yangtze River by floating on a single reed. Yet the idea of powers like these has been cast aside with the march of history. The primary reason is that the figures in positions of religious authority, such as the priors, abbots, etc., are not necessarily the ones with great innate foundations. The ranks they hold are merely job titles in this world. They are still developing spiritually, just like others, only for them practicing is a vocation. You practice out in the world, by contrast, and in your spare time. Yet whether one's practice comes to fruition depends on how much heart is put into it; this holds true for everyone, and there is no way around it. There is nothing innately inferior about a novice monk who tends the hearth or cooks the meals at a monastery, and his hardships make it all the more likely he will achieve spiritual enlightenment. Senior monks, on the other hand, will find it all the harder to achieve since they enjoy comfort and ease, and do fewer things that would rework their karma. A novice monk leads a hard and tiring life, which allows him to pay off karma and enlighten more swiftly. Awakening might come to such a monk unexpectedly one day, and with it, even if not full enlightenment, will come great powers. His brothers at the monastery will seek his counsel and treat him with great respect. But this might prove too much for the abbot, who would worry that someone like this undermines his authority. And so he will be skeptical about the person's enlightenment and write it off as self-delusion, and perhaps even try to get him removed. And he might even manage to. With time, it's now come to be that virtually no one in Chinese Buddhism openly discusses supernormal powers. Just consider what became of the remarkable monk Ji-gong. His powers allowed him to miraculously transport logs from Mt. E'mei to the well at Ling-yin monastery, and then get them out of the well, one by one. And yet in the end he was expelled from the monastery [as a result of jealousy toward him].

Jealousy is a serious problem since it directly bears on whether a person can achieve spiritual perfection. If you can't rid yourself of jealousy it will undermine all of the work you have done on your character. There is a rule: anyone who doesn't free himself of jealousy while practicing cannot attain true divine standing. No exceptions. You may have heard at some point that Buddha Amitābha allows people to be reborn into his paradise with karma. But that will *not* happen in the case of jealousy. Those who fall short in some minor regard or other may be able to carry on with spiritual practice after being reborn there with karma, but *not* those who harbor jealousy. Now that I've explained this to you, who are practitioners, you really need to stop this folly. You must be free of jealousy if you want to ever achieve real spiritual progress. And it is for this reason that I've singled it out.

Healing

By bringing up this topic I don't mean to suggest that I will teach you how to heal people. No true practitioner of Falun Dafa would heal people. Were you to do that, all that has been given to your body by Falun Dafa would promptly be taken back by my spiritual bodies. The reason we take this so seriously is that it violates Dafa and harms your body as well. Some people just yearn to do more healings once they have done some, and leap at the opportunity to show off. It is clearly an attachment in that case and would severely hinder one's spiritual development.

Many false masters have preyed upon people's tendency to want to do healings after learning energy practices, and they teach them how. They make outlandish claims such as that you can heal someone by emitting your energy. But it's not even logical to think that one person could heal another just by emitting energy, when the other party has energy in his or her body as well. And who knows, their energy could even end up healing *you*. One person's ordinary energy can't exert influence over another's. A person at more advanced stages of practice develops higher energy, and what he or she emits at that point is high-energy matter. It is something that can treat and suppress disease, and have a controlling influence. But it can't uproot someone's illness at the source. Certain powers are needed in order to truly and thoroughly cure an illness. There is a specific power for curing each illness that exists. I can share that there are over a thousand such powers—as many as there are illnesses. And without these powers, healing simply cannot be done, no matter how much of a show some people might make of it.

Certain people have sown much confusion about healing among the spiritually inclined in recent years. Yet earlier on, when the true pioneering teachers of energy practices like *chi-gong* and *tai-chi* were promoting health and wellness, none of them gave instruction on how to do healings. They would either heal you themselves or teach you how to practice so that you could improve your health by exercising. Later on, false masters came about and really confused things. Whoever wishes to do healings is bound to bring entity attachment upon himself. So while there were authentic masters who did healings, they did so only in keeping with larger cosmic designs. But they were not using ordinary human means, and so they couldn't keep at it indefinitely. It was the result of cosmic shifts that were happening and a product of the times. So it was wrong for people later on to begin teaching healing. No regular person could possibly gain the power to heal after taking a class for just a few days. I can tell you that whoever claims he can cure all sorts of illnesses is under the influence of entity attachment, only he's not aware that something has latched onto his back. But something has. And so he mistakenly thinks that he is powerful and that it's a good thing that he can heal.

A true teacher must go through many years of grueling spiritual discipline before he or she can accomplish something like healing. Yet some people go about doing healings without ever pausing to consider whether they have the powers necessary to rid people of their karma, or how it's possible to do healing without having received the kind of authentic instruction normally required. And yet somehow they think that they can heal after just a few days of classes, using just their ordinary hands. False masters exploit these kinds of attachments and flawed thinking. That yearning to heal is an attachment, isn't it? And so they're happy to offer classes on healing, with fancy protocols and sophisticated names for what they do, ranging from the "energy needle" to the "illumination method," to "expulsion" and "supplementation," to "pressing vital points" and the "single grabbing method." In each case their motive is to make money off you.

Let's talk about what's being called the "single grabbing method," as an example. In our observation, the deeper reason people fall ill or experience misfortune is karma—a field of black matter. It is negative, or *yin*, by nature and something bad. Evil entities are *yin* natured as well, and dark, and they can enter a person's body when conditions suit them. And they are the root cause of the ailments that people suffer, the main source of illness. But there are also two other ways that illness comes about. One involves extremely small, negative entities that are high in density and resemble clumps of karma. The other, which is less common but does exist, is where it is piped in from one's ancestors.

Let's look at some of the more common problems, such as tumors, inflammation, and bone spurs. In another dimension, deeper than this one, there is a negative entity at the site of the ailment. Yet it can't be perceived with typical extrasensory powers or by most teachers; they can only see dark energy in one's body. And while they are right about illness residing wherever they see dark energy, that energy is not the root cause of the ailment. Rather, it is the negative entity in another, deeper dimension; the dark energy is merely the field that it exudes. People sometimes claim that they can expel and purge bad energy, but even if they can, the dark field will quickly regenerate afterwards. In some cases the entity involved is powerful, and no sooner does someone purge its field than it pulls it back. It has the capacity to draw the energy back. So treatments that are only superficial don't work.

Sickness, as seen with extrasensory powers, resides where there is dark energy present. As viewed by Chinese medicine, the energy channels, or "meridians," of the body are blocked at that place, and energy and blood are failing to pass through; i.e., the channels have been clogged up. As viewed by Western medicine, the place presents an ulcer, tumor, bone spur, inflammation, etc., and those are the forms that it takes in this dimension. If one can manage to knock out the negative entity that's behind the condition, the body here in this dimension will be problem-free. The ailment will instantly vanish once the entity has been taken out and the field is cleared, regardless of what the issue may have been—including for a herniated disc or bone spur. An X-ray will confirm that it's resolved. The root cause is the entity and what it does.

Some claim that you can do healings after just a few days of learning, and offer to instruct you in things like the "single grabbing method." I'm not exactly convinced. A human being is very weak compared to a formidable negative entity. An entity like that can control your brain, easily play tricks on you, and even end your life with little effort. It's far-fetched to think that you could grab one of those. Your human hands can't so much as touch them. You might flail your hands all around, trying to grab one, only to have it ignore you or even laugh at you. Your random grabbing would be comical to it. And even if you were to actually reach it, your hands might be instantly hurt, and seriously so. I have seen people whose hands were lame, though doctors couldn't find anything wrong with them. Yet their hands just dangled there, lifeless. I have met people like this. What happened was that their bodies in other dimensions were injured, resulting in genuine paralysis here. An injury to those bodies does indeed result in paralysis, as you might imagine. I've been asked by people who had a sterilization procedure done or had something surgically removed whether they can still do this practice. I always assure them that that's of no consequence, since your bodies in other dimensions didn't undergo the procedure, and those bodies are what's involved when we practice. So, back to what I was saying, that negative entity won't care if you can't reach it; but if you can, it might well injure your hands.

I twice brought practitioners with me to participate in the Asian Health Expo in Beijing to lend support to these national-level activities that had to do with energy practice. Our group really stood out both times. At the first expo we attended, our Falun Dafa was honored as the "Star *chi-gong* School." At the second there were more people approaching us than we could handle. Our booth was crowded with people, in contrast to others. Three lines were formed. The first had registered at the outset for morning treatments. The second was waiting to register for afternoon slots. And the last was waiting for my autograph. You might wonder why we were giving treatments, since that's not something we do. We joined in the expo and did that in order to support what was a large, national event related to energy practices, and to do our part for the cause.

I allotted a portion of my *gong* energy to each of my students who came with me to the expo; they each received a mass of energy composed of over a hundred powers. And though I sealed their hands, some were still bitten, with blisters and bleeding, and this happened regularly. That's how fierce those entities were. Then would you really want to catch them with your human hands? Even if you tried, you wouldn't be able to grab them without having the powers needed. The reason is, they know from another dimension what you are thinking and will flee even before you make your first move, only to return right after you've finished treating the person. And so the ailment returns. You need a specific power to deal with that kind of thing, such that you can pin it down right then and there when you extend your hand. And then you need another power, one tremendously strong, known as the "great way of soul extraction," to pull the entity's soul out of the body and immobilize it. This power is meant for use with specific targets, and that's what we used at the expo. You might be familiar with the story of how the Monkey King, who was full-sized, was shrunk down by the Buddha when he aimed his bowl at him. This power is capable of doing that. Any entity, big or small, will be shrunk the moment it's grasped in the hand.

Another thing is, it's not an option to extend your hand into the physical body of someone ailing and take something out. To see something like that would be far too jarring for people, and so it's forbidden, even if possible. What is done when using the single grabbing method is to extend the hand of another dimension into the ailing person. Suppose the affected person has heart disease. When one reaches toward the heart to seize the problematic entity, it is the hand in another dimension that enters. And instantly, at an extraordinary speed, it will seize that negative entity there. When the hand in the outer dimension grabs, the two hands [of differing dimensions] come together, and the entity is seized. Those things are fierce, though, and sometimes they will flail about once grabbed and burrow into the hand, biting or screaming. And small as it is while trapped in the hand, it will return to its original size if released. It's not something that just anyone can tackle; none of this is possible without the necessary power for it. Doing this kind of healing is nowhere near as simple as people might imagine.

Of course, this form of treatment might still be allowed in the future, as in the past. But restrictions would apply. The person using it would have to be someone on the spiritual path and be using it out of compassion. And it could only be used on a few good people. But whoever used it wouldn't be able to fully dissolve the karma that's involved, as his spiritual powers would fall short. So the person's hardship would still be present; it would just be that the physical ailment was done away with. Your typical, lesser energy healer is not exactly someone who has achieved divinity, and all he can do is to postpone people's ailments or change them into other forms of adversity. And he might not even realize he has done so, since it would most likely be done by his subconscious. Many acclaimed spiritual figures or teachers don't have higher energy, since it went to the bodies of their secondary souls. The only reason they can do healings throughout their lives is that they go for years, or even decades, without ever making much spiritual progress themselves. They are allowed to do healings because their practice remains at the same, limited stage. Those who practice Falun Dafa, however, are strictly forbidden from healing others. You can read this book to someone who is sick if you wish, and he might be healed if he's receptive to it. But the results will vary according to how much karma the person has.

Modern Medicine
and Energy Healing

Let's look at two modes of treatment side by side: those of modern medicine and energy healing. Most doctors of Western medicine don't consider energy healing to be valid. They reason that we should be seeing hospitals getting replaced by centers for energy healing if it really is all that people make it out to be—with people miraculously using just their bare hands to heal, and not resorting to injections, drugs, or inpatient services. But that argument is based on a misunderstanding of energy healing, and it doesn't hold up. The fact is that energy healing isn't going to resemble normal modes of treatment, since it's not an ordinary means. It is a higher means. And as you can imagine, higher things are not allowed to intrude upon the secular world in any sizeable way. It's akin to why divine beings don't wipe out the diseases of mankind when it would take them but a wave of the hand, and it's fully doable. You would think that at least one of them would do so, simply out of mercy, given all the higher beings there are. But they don't. And that's because the human condition is what it is, and birth, aging, sickness, and death are simply a fact of life. There are karmic reasons behind each of these; the debts that people have incurred have to be paid.

Were you to heal someone it would amount to violating that law. You would be allowing the person to get out of paying for his wrongdoings, which is a problem. Spiritual adherents might be allowed to do basic healings if they are moved to do so by compassion and their powers can't fully resolve the issue. But it has to be on grounds of compassion.

And even those who do have the power to actually resolve people's problems wouldn't be permitted to do so on a large scale. That would be a major breach of the human condition, which is not allowed. So we can see why energy healing will never manage to supplant the regular methods used in hospitals; it is a higher means.

Some people in China may have imagined something like a hospital dedicated to energy healing being set up, staffed by accomplished healers. But it would never work out, even if it were logistically possible. That's because higher beings will always ensure that the human condition isn't undone. So even if a hospital for energy healing were to be established, or even if energy healing clinics, centers, and resorts were set up, the effectiveness of the healers' treatments would drop significantly. The reason is that they would be acting in the secular world, and so their effectiveness wouldn't be greater than that of regular treatments; it would have to be in keeping with the human condition. The effectiveness would need to be on par with that of the treatments used in hospitals. This is why the medical use of energy healing typically doesn't go very well and multiple rounds of treatment are needed.

But even if hospitals for energy healing aren't feasible, there's no denying that energy practices can lead to healing. Energy practices like *chi-gong* have been popular in China for years, and a large number of people really have managed to gain wellness through them. People's ailments *have* disappeared, even if they were just postponed by a healer or by whatever means. There's no denying that energy healing can work. Most people who seek out healers have complicated and difficult conditions that conventional medicine couldn't remedy. So they seek out an accomplished healer to try their luck and, much to their surprise, the problem gets resolved. Generally people wouldn't seek out an energy healer if conventional means could deal with it. Healers used to be seen mainly as a fallback. But the point still holds that energy healing can be effective. The difference is that it can't be used in the same manner as conventional approaches. It is prohibited from having a broader impact on society. It can only be utilized on a small scale and without much influence, with people quietly going about it. So while it does work, you can be sure that it isn't healing on a deeper level. The best way to address your ailment is to put in the time to do an energy practice yourself.

There are some energy healers who claim that conventional medicine doesn't do much and has limited effectiveness. It's a complicated issue they raise. There are naturally many reasons for why that might be the case, if you ask me. As I see it, the principal one is humanity's moral decline. This is what has led to the emergence of all sorts of unusual diseases that medical means can't treat and that drugs are ineffective against, as well as the proliferation of counterfeit drugs—which doesn't help things at all. These problems reflect the terrible state of the world today, which man has brought about. Everyone has had a part in it, so you shouldn't try to pin the blame on anyone. And this is why whoever gives spiritual practice a go will meet with ordeals.

In some cases doctors can't identify what's wrong with someone, though the person really is sick. In other cases they might figure out what's wrong, but don't know what to call it, since the ailment is altogether novel. The medical profession categorizes these as "modern diseases." This doesn't mean that conventional medicine isn't capable of curing disease, of course. It can. People would lose confidence in it otherwise and avoid it. So it can heal people. It's merely that its methods of treatment are at the human level, while people's diseases reach beyond—with some being downright serious. And this is why doctors emphasize early detection; once an ailment progresses too far it can't be dealt with. At high doses, pharmaceuticals can be toxic. The level of today's medical treatments is the same as that of modern technology, with both being on the human plane. And so their effectiveness is limited. Something that should be clarified is that the usual means of energy healing and medical treatments only serve to postpone someone's underlying ordeal, which is the source of his suffering. It gets delayed until a later time in the person's life or even further off, without the karma being addressed in any way.

Let's revisit the topic of Chinese medicine. Chinese medicine is similar to energy healing. In ancient China many physicians had extrasensory powers, be it Sun Simiao, Hua Tuo, Li Shizhen, or Bian Que. The annals of medicine testify to the powers of these accomplished medical scientists. Yet today those powers of theirs, which were the best of the practice, often meet with cynicism. It turns out that Chinese medicine has preserved only the herbal formulas and clinical experiences of the past. Yet back in ancient China it was quite advanced—even more so than the medical science of our day. Some people may tout how advanced medicine is now, with its CT scans that can see inside the body, ultrasounds, imaging, and X-rays. And today's facilities are indeed cutting edge. But in my opinion they have yet to match the medical science of ancient China.

Consider that the physician Hua Tuo was able to perceive that there was a tumor on the brain of a minister named Tsao

Tsao, and sought to open up his skull to remove it. Tsao mistook it for a plot to kill him, and had Hua imprisoned, where he eventually passed away. Tsao later did have symptoms of a tumor, and sought out Hua, but it was too late; Hua had passed away. And in the end the condition claimed Tsao's life. So what Hua saw was real. He had an extrasensory power that people are capable of, one that the great physicians of yesteryear had at their disposal. With their powers of seeing they could perceive all four sides of the human body from just one side, looking from the front and seeing the back, left, and right. And they could even see the body layer by layer, slice by slice, and see beyond this dimension to the root cause of an illness. Modern medicine is far from being able to match that; it could take another millennium. CT scans, ultrasounds, and X-rays can see inside the body, but the equipment involved is large and terribly unwieldy. And without electricity it simply doesn't work. The inner eye, by contrast, goes with you everywhere and doesn't rely on electricity. There's no comparison.

Some people extol the virtues of modern pharmaceuticals, but these may be no better in fact. The herbal medicine of ancient China was very effective. While many formulas have been lost over the centuries, a good number haven't been and are still in use. I remember how when I was in the northeastern city of Qiqihar to give a class, I spotted a street vendor who was offering to pull bad teeth. I could tell at first glance that he was from the South, as he didn't dress like a northeasterner. He wouldn't turn anybody away and would pull teeth for whoever approached him. He had there a whole pile of teeth that he had pulled. His goal wasn't to pull teeth but to sell his herbal tincture, which emitted a thick yellow vapor. When he wanted to pull a tooth, he would uncap the bottle and place it against the person's cheek at the spot where the bad tooth was, and have him or her suck in several mouthfuls of the tincture's yellow vapor. Little of the tincture was used up in the process. Then he would cap the bottle and set it aside. Next he would take out a matchstick from his pocket, and while singing the praises of his medicine, flick the matchstick against the tooth and pop it out. It didn't cause any pain and there would be just a few flecks of blood, with no bleeding. Just imagine it: he was extracting teeth with something as fragile as a matchstick.

I would say that Western medicine's precision instruments are no match for some of the folk remedies handed down in China. Just compare the results each gets. On the one side we have a man who could pull teeth with just a matchstick. While with Western medicine, by contrast, you first need injections of anesthetics, which tend to hurt an awful lot. You then have to wait for the anesthetics to set in, and then it's time for the forceps. The dentist has to do a lot of pulling, and if things go wrong, the tooth's root will remain lodged in the gums. Then he will have to take out the hammer and chisel to chip it out, and the process is enough to strike fear into your heart. Then he brings out the precision instruments for drilling, and it hurts so much that your body might jerk in response. You bleed a great deal and have to spit out mouthfuls of blood. So, which approach would you say is better? And which is more advanced? Things shouldn't be judged by their appearances—like the tools in these two scenarios. What should be looked at is the results. The medicine of ancient China was very advanced, and Western medicine isn't likely to catch up with it anytime soon.

The science of ancient China was different from modern science, which comes from the West. It took a different course and brought about a very different mode of life. It's not appropriate to judge ancient China's science and technology with today's ways of looking at things, for the science of ancient China went a different route, honing in on how the body, life, and universe work together. Meditation and good posture were part of one's education, and when writing, people were mindful of their breathing and directed energy to different areas of the body. And in each of the trades and professions people sought to empty the mind and breathe properly. This was simply the way of things throughout society.

People have questioned whether we would have cars and trains as we do today if we had gone with the science of ancient China; they believe modernization wouldn't have been possible. I would respond that it's not appropriate to judge a different way of life based on one's own, present circumstances; an accurate assessment is only possible with a drastic shift in thinking and concepts. Perhaps in a world without televisions you would have unimagined powers, such as being able to see whatever you wish through your own forehead. Or in a world without trains and cars, you might have the ability to levitate as you sit, without the help of a lift. Taking a different scientific course would result in the world being a different place, one perhaps quite different from the world around us. The UFOs of extraterrestrial beings travel at unbelievable speeds and have the ability to enlarge or shrink. The course they have taken is even more radically divergent, as it involves an altogether different approach to science.

THE
EIGHTH TALK

Inedia*

I HAVE BEEN ASKED about the topic of inedia (*bi-gu*), or "living without food and drink." There is such a thing, and it's not unique to those leading the religious life or devotees of *chi-gong*. A good number of people throughout the world have experienced it, with some going years or even decades without food or drink, and have been just fine. Much has been said about the phenomenon, from it being an indicator of spiritual progress or purification to it being a part of advanced practice.

But it's none of the above. Inedia is simply a special method of practice that's adopted under certain circumstances. This takes some explaining. Many who renounced the world in ancient China did spiritual practice in secrecy or isolation; this was in the days before religious institutions had come about. They might have gone deep into the woods or have found a cave in which to practice, and would separate themselves from the world. And so having a source of food naturally posed a problem. Without inedia they wouldn't have been able to carry out their practice, and would have faced death from starvation or dehydration. I still recall seeing caves used for these purposes when I was traveling eastward down the Yangtze River, heading from Chongqing to Wuhan to give a teaching; the caves were situated midway up the cliffs in the Three Gorges area. Many of China's most famed mountains have similar caves. People would lower themselves into caves like these with a rope and then sever it, committing themselves to practicing inside. Death awaited them if they didn't succeed at it. So it was only in the exceptional circumstance of having no food or water that the special approach of inedia was used.

There are many practices that have been passed down from those times and that contain an element of inedia, but there are many that don't. The latter is the case for most practices that are now taught publicly. We believe that you should commit to one practice and not just do whatever suits your fancy. If you're someone who thinks highly of inedia and are hoping to experience it, then you would do well to examine your motives. There could be a range of motives at work, from admiring it to being tempted by curiosity, to wanting it because it would give you a sense of achievement as well as a way to show off. Even if it were to be used in your practice, you would still have to consume your own energy to sustain yourself, which wouldn't be worth it. And of course it's not even necessary now in this era of organized religion; now there are people who will furnish you with food and drink if you are on a spiritual retreat or practicing in a monastery or convent. And nourishment is even less of a concern for those of us who practice in the regular world. There is simply no need for inedia then. And besides, people shouldn't freely add it into their practice if it's not part of it. But if you really want to experience it, then you might as well go ahead and look for a practice that includes it. To my knowledge, a person typically experiences inedia when he is being authentically guided by a teacher to a higher stage of practice and it is part of that practice's heritage. But it would not be something shared with the public. Inedia usually happens when a disciple is somewhere secluded and being guided in secrecy.

With spiritual figures now teaching inedia to members of the general public, you might wonder whether anyone has succeeded at it. No one has in the end—none. But many have ended up in the hospital and at risk, from what I've seen. Hearing this might be confusing, as I just explained that inedia is for real. But you have to bear in mind that the human condition mustn't be undermined or tampered with. Imagine if all of the health enthusiasts nationwide, or even just all the residents in a major city like Changchun, no longer needed to eat or drink thanks to inedia. It would definitely make life easier! Nobody would need to go through the hassle of preparing meals anymore, and no one would have to labor in the fields; people would be able to just go about their business with no need for eating. But that would be wrong, as it would be changing the face of the world. It would never be allowed to happen. Nothing that upsets the world so dramatically is allowed.

Many people are put at risk when certain individuals teach inedia. Problems come up when they are set on experiencing it but still attached to food and many other things. Once they start inedia it's going to be tough when they see tasty food that stirs up their appetite, but which they can't eat. They will get anxious and want to eat. And they will feel starved if they don't. Yet if they do try to eat, they will throw up, and find that nothing stays down. So it's both frightening and unsettling. Many people have ended up hospitalized this way and really been at risk. I have had people come to me hoping that I would clean up these messes for them, but I am hesitant to get involved. Nobody would want to clean up the messes that certain teachers have recklessly made.

Another thing people should know is that the problems they run into with inedia are in fact of their own making. We do believe there is such a thing as inedia, but it's by no means some kind of higher spiritual state that comes about at advanced stages of practice, or a marker of progress. It is merely a special method of practice that's adopted under special circumstances, and it's not something to be popularized. Yet many seek to experience it, and it's even believed that there are different types of it, with it being classified into things like "full-on" versus "partial" inedia. And so you have people who will tell you that they consume fluids or fruit as part of it. But that doesn't amount to true inedia, and over time those approaches surely won't prove sustainable. Instances of true inedia have occurred when people who were deeply committed in their faith or practice settled into an isolated spot, like a mountain cave, and went without food and drink altogether.

Stealing Energy

Many people find the hearsay that surrounds energy practices so unsettling that they want nothing to do with them; they are scared away by the possibility of someone stealing their energy or of even losing their sanity. We might expect that more people would be practicing if it weren't for all of the hearsay. Part of what has made things so confusing and murky is that there are teachers of energy practices who have poor character and who teach things like stealing people's energy. But this shouldn't be as frightening as it may sound. As we see it, the kind of energy they take, called *chi,* doesn't amount to much, even if people call it fancy names like "primal energy." Anyone who still has *chi* in his or her body is merely at the stage of practicing for health, and has yet to make real spiritual progress. The presence of *chi* indicates that the person has not reached a high degree of bodily purity, and he or she is sure to have sick energy. Those who steal *chi* from people are at the low level of *chi* in their practice, and anyone who really knows what they're doing would never want to take impure energy from another person. The *chi* of people who don't practice is cloudy and impure, as it turns out, and the only way for them to make their energy brighter and clearer and remedy things is by doing an energy practice like *chi-gong.* Once the energy becomes clearer, it will be evident that there are large, dense masses of dark energy in their bodies wherever they have a disease or ailment. Practicing on a regular basis will gradually turn one's *chi* to a subtle shade of yellow as the body becomes genuinely healthy and strong. And with further practice, there will no longer be *chi* in the body and one will become truly free of disease, and experience what's referred to as a "milk-white" body.

What this suggests is that you won't be free from disease if you still have *chi. Chi* serves no purpose for us since we do true spiritual practice and need to purify our bodies.

It would make no sense to try and take impure *chi* from people. Whoever wants *chi* is at the level of *chi*, and wouldn't have the capacity to tell good energy from bad. Nor would they have the power to remove the true primal energy that is present in your body's energy center, as only someone with exceptional powers could remove that. So if someone wants to steal any impure *chi* that's in your body, you might as well let them. There's nothing great about it. I used to find, back when I was practicing, that *chi* really wasn't anything special, as I could fill my abdomen with it at just the thought of it.

Daoist practice often incorporates things like holding special stances, while Buddhist ones often use the hands to channel *chi* into the head. There's enough *chi* in the universe for someone to spend all day channeling it in, and that's possible to do once the acupoints known as the Palace of Toil and Hundred Convergences have been opened. A person can use his hands to channel *chi* if he focuses his mind on the body's energy center, and in no time he will be filled with it. But that still doesn't accomplish anything, no matter how much is stored up. Nor do I see anything impressive about accounts of people who harness so much *chi* that they can feel their fingertips or bodies swelling with it—even if others might be wowed when they sense *chi* emanating from them, since it's thought to be a sign of achievement. But these people don't have any higher energy. Their practice is still on the order of ordinary energy, and no amount of that is a substitute for the higher kind known as *gong*. The goal of practicing with *chi* is to purify the body by replacing the *chi* inside of it with better *chi* from outside of it. So simply storing it up doesn't achieve much. At the *chi* level of practice a person has yet to undergo fundamental changes, so no higher energy is involved. A person can steal as much *chi* as he'd like and still amount to nothing more than a big bag of energy. So it's meaningless. The *chi* isn't being changed into high-energy matter, after all. This means that you can set your fears aside and not worry about energy being stolen from you.

Bear in mind that as long as your body has *chi* in it there will be sickness present. So if someone steals *chi* from you, he will be taking sick energy from you in the process. He has no way to tell the two apart, since whoever wants *chi* is operating at the level of ordinary energy and isn't all that powerful; he surely wouldn't be interested in *chi* if he had higher energy. A simple experiment would bear this out, if there's any doubt. What you would do, would be to simply allow whoever really wants to steal your *chi* to do so. You could have him stand behind you and steal your *chi*, while you visualize your body being filled with *chi* from the universe. This would turn out to be great for you, as the other person would only accelerate your body's purification and save you the trouble of having to move your arms up and down to flush the *chi* through your body. And since it would be bad intentions that drove him to take your *chi*, and he would be stealing from you—even if he was stealing something bad—it would cost him virtue, which would go to you. Nobody would think of doing that if they knew what was going on: that they were giving you virtue in another dimension while taking your *chi*, and forming an exchange loop between the two of you, as it were.

The faces of those who steal *chi* tend to look unwell. This is only to be expected, given the poor physical health of their targets, who are typically out in public doing practices like *chi-gong* or *tai-chi* to try to get healthy. Those who steal *chi* don't understand that sick energy needs to be expelled from the body for the body to become healthy. What they are doing is filling their bodies with all manner of unhealthy *chi* that they've stolen, and it turns even the insides of their bodies terribly dark. And if they squander their virtue enough, they will also look dark on the outside. Their karmic field expands while their virtue shrinks, turning their bodies dark, inside and out. People wouldn't steal *chi* if they realized what they were doing to their bodies or that they were foolishly giving away their virtue.

Some of the claims that are made about *chi* come across as a bit incredible. For example, it's been claimed that *chi* can travel through walls and be projected from here all the way to America. But even if certain individuals, who are sensitive, can tell that energy did travel to them from afar, it doesn't mean much. The energy would have traveled in another dimension, not this one, and there may have been no barriers along the way for it to go through. And by the same token, this explains why sometimes people *don't* sense anything when *chi* is sent to them across an open expanse: it's because a barrier *was* present in another dimension, in that case. So this suggests that the penetrative power of regular energy isn't as great as people sometimes claim.

Higher energy, or *gong*, is what's really powerful. Those who can project higher energy no longer have *chi*; what they emit is a type of high-energy matter. When seen through the inner eye it appears as light. It gives a sensation of heat when projected onto the body and can keep a regular person's illnesses at bay. It can't fully heal people, however, in the absence of higher powers, as every ailment requires a specific power to heal it; higher energy by itself can only suppress illness. But each particle of it assumes the image of its host on a deeper, micro level. It is alive, has its own intelligence, and can tell one person from another since it is a form of higher energy. So if someone wanted to steal it from you, that would never work out; the energy belongs to *you* and so it wouldn't cooperate. And besides, a true student of spiritual practice who has higher energy will have a teacher looking after him, and no teacher would ever let anyone take energy like that.

Amassing Chi

Stealing *chi* and amassing *chi* aren't topics I would normally go into when teaching an advanced practice. I'm discussing them because I want to help restore the reputation of energy practices and do something good by calling out these unhealthy things, which nobody has done. My hope is that by exposing them, people will stop doing these awful things and those who are uninformed won't be scared away by it all.

Chi is abundant in the universe, be it the "positive (*yang*) *chi*" of the heavens, as it's called, or the "negative (*yin*) *chi*" of the earth. People are every bit a part of this universe and are welcome to take in its *chi* as they please. Yet some people don't do that, and instead are always teaching people to take *chi* from plants, and sharing their supposed findings, like how the poplar tree's *chi* is white and the pine tree's is yellow, or how and when to take it from them. Someone once even boasted that the tree in front of his house died after he drew *chi* from it. But how is that something to brag about? Wasn't that something bad that he did? As we've established, in true practice you want positive things, and to become one with the universe's qualities. Then it follows logically that you should try to be kind and compassionate (*shan*). You have to make a practice of this if you want to become one with the universe's qualities of *zhen, shan, ren.* And this is why people who often do wrongful things never develop higher energy or get their health back. So what that person did is the exact opposite of what a practitioner should do. It amounts to taking life and doing wrong, after all. It might seem that I'm stretching credibility to say that felling trees or taking a creature's life counts as killing, but that is the truth. Just consider the Buddhist teachings on reincarnation, which hold that a plant could well be the reincarnation of a human being. While we won't go into such things here, we *can* say that trees are alive and even endowed with advanced cognitive abilities.

A telling case is the work of an American polygraph researcher who instructs people in the use of lie detectors. One day he was struck by an impulse to connect the two electrodes of a polygraph to a dracaena plant. He did so and proceeded to water the plant. Afterwards he witnessed the lie detector's needle rapidly drawing a curve—exactly the type of curve seen when the human brain is momentarily excited or happy. He was amazed, thinking, "Could it be that plants have feelings?" He practically wanted to shout in the streets, "Plants have feelings!" The episode inspired him to do a lot of research in this area and many experiments.

On one occasion he placed two plants next to each other and had a student of his stomp on one of them and destroy it, right in front of the other one. He then removed the surviving plant to another room and connected a lie detector to it. Next he had five students enter the room in succession.

There was no reaction from the plant as the first four students entered the room. But when the fifth student—the one who had crushed the plant—entered, before he even got close to the surviving plant, the needle of the lie detector immediately and rapidly drew a line that in humans is specifically associated with fright. It was a great surprise to the researcher and raised profound questions, since it had always been held that only advanced life forms like human beings are capable of identifying things and making distinctions, due to their sensory organs, and are capable of analysis on account of their brains. People at one time were even accused of pseudoscience for claiming that plants have senses, thoughts and feelings, or can identify people. And yet here was a plant recognizing people and telling them apart, which would suggest that plants *do* have senses. And there have been other discoveries, still more incredible, that imply that plants even surpass modern man in some ways.

One day this same researcher connected a lie detector to a plant and wondered to himself, "What kind of experiment should I do? I know, I'll burn its leaves and see what its reaction is." With just that thought, before doing any actual burning, the needle of the lie detector started to rapidly draw a curve—the kind of curve seen in human beings when they are in distress and crying for help. This type of supersensory ability, known as "telepathy," is a latent human function and innate ability, only it has been lost with humanity's decline. It's now something that can only be had when a person recovers his or her original purity through spiritual practice. And yet here was a plant with these powers. While it might sound far-fetched, findings like this have been borne out by real and actual scientific experiments. The person I was describing carried out a range of experiments, including some that involved telekinesis. When his findings were published they caused quite a stir internationally.

Botanists around the world as well as in our country have since taken up research in this area, and such ideas are no longer dismissed as pseudoscience. As I've indicated, the things that man has discovered, observed, and invented are grounds enough to warrant rewriting the established scientific literature. But old beliefs die hard, and so there is reluctance about acknowledging such things, and nobody has attempted to systematically piece them all together.

I once saw a grove of dead pine trees in a park in northeastern China. A group of people had been practicing some kind of *chi-gong* there, where they would roll about on the ground and then use their hands and feet to take in *chi*, and in a short span of time the grove of pines had withered and died. It could hardly be said that they were doing something good. A real practitioner would consider that to be killing. If you are a practitioner, you have to change your bad traits and become a good person who strives to live by the qualities of the universe. Even in the eyes of a non-practitioner what those people were doing in the park wouldn't be considered good. It was damaging to public property, undermining the city's greening efforts, and ecologically harmful. It wasn't good by any measure. They could have just helped themselves to the universe's abundant supply of *chi* instead. When some people reach a certain stage in their practice, they may have the power to take in the *chi* of a large swath of shrubs and trees with just a swipe of the hand. But all they are getting is *chi*, and no amount of it will do them much good. Some people go to parks for the sole purpose of amassing *chi*, and figure that they don't need to do any systematic energy exercises, since they can get *chi* by waving their arms about as they stroll around. They are content to just get *chi* since they mistake it for something it's not, i.e., higher energy. You might sense cold emanating from the body of someone who does that, if you go near him or her, since the *chi* of plants that they've stored up is negatively charged (*yin*) by nature. Those who do energy practices normally seek to balance negative (*yin*) and positive (*yang*) energies in the body, whereas the people I've been describing feel good about what they are doing even when it leads to their smelling like pine oil.

The One Who Practices Achieves

There is an extremely important feature of spiritual practice that I want to reveal: that the one who actually does the practice is the one who gains the achievement. And this is another regard in which Falun Dafa is unique, among several. One, as I've mentioned, is that our practice has managed to reduce the time that you need to do exercises for, and alleviated any possible time shortage; this is done by having energy mechanisms work upon you. Another is that our physical bodies undergo dramatic changes, since ours is an authentic practice of mind and body. Then there is Falun Dafa's greatest feature, which only now, for the first time ever, am I disclosing. I hadn't revealed it before because it involves something major and that goes far back in history, and has significant bearing on those engaged in the religious life or spiritual discipline. Nobody has ever disclosed it, nor were they allowed to. Yet I have no alternative but to tell you.

Some of my students feel that with almost every sentence I am revealing the great mysteries of life for them. However, it's not that I am freely divulging things. What we are doing is saving people from this world by guiding them to greater spiritual heights, and that entails taking responsibility for them, which I can do. Haphazardly disclosing life's mysteries would, of course, amount to freely divulging them. What I want to make clear today is this: the spiritual achievement goes to the one who practices. Yet in my observation, all methods of practice now known to us, whatever tradition or lineage they may be, have historically been working on the secondary soul (the subconscious mind), and the fruits of spiritual labor have always gone to it alone. By contrast, what we call the "true" soul refers to your conscious mind—the mind through which you are aware of what you are thinking or doing. And it is this mind that truly represents you. But what a secondary soul does is always unknown to you. And although it was born at the same time as you, has the same name, presides over the same body, and looks like you, it is not you in a strict sense.

It is a law of the universe that whoever bears the costs of effort should reap the rewards, and this holds true in spiritual practice. For centuries it has been taught that during meditation or spiritual contemplation one should set aside all awareness of one's surroundings, blunting all thought, and becoming altogether lost in a state of trance or rapture. Three hours pass for some people in what seems like no time as they meditate or engage in contemplation, and they might be admired for their focus. But nobody, themselves included, has ever realized that they were not the ones in fact practicing. A telling example is that of Daoist disciplines, where it has been taught that the "knowing soul" is to die and the "original soul" be born. But what they refer to as the "knowing soul" is what we call the "true soul," and what they mean by "original soul" we call the "secondary soul." Were your knowing soul really to die you would in fact perish, for your true soul would be dead. Someone from another practice once told me that when he practices he lets his mind go, to the extent that even the family members at hand aren't familiar to him. Another person told me that he doesn't have to practice hard like others do, at dawn or late into the night, since all he has to do is recline on the couch when he gets home and go out of his body to practice, and he can just watch himself practicing as he lies there. I felt sorry for him to some extent.

But why would others save the secondary soul? The Daoist saint Lü Dongbin once stated, "I'd rather save an animal's soul than a human being's." And it really is hard to get people to spiritually awaken, for the average person is under the spell of ignorance here and finds it hard not to be selfish. Believe it or not, some people will lapse into worldly ways as soon as this class is over and they are back out in the world, and they might not put up with it if someone provokes them or pushes their buttons. And with time they will no longer regard themselves as practitioners. Many spiritual figures in the past realized that man is hard to save, for his true soul is terribly lost. Some people do have good discernment, though, and will recognize the wisdom in what someone may say. And yet others, no matter how you explain spiritual things to them, still disbelieve and think you are making things up. People like that lapse into their old ways once they are back in an ordinary setting after these classes, despite our best efforts to get them to work on their character. Worldly things seem very much real, tangible, and attainable to them, and they can't pass them up. So they have a hard time following my teachings, even if they find them agreeable. The true soul is really so hard to save as compared to the secondary soul, which can perceive other dimensions. This has led people to conclude that there is little point in trying to save a person's true soul when, after all, the secondary soul shares in the person's identity and so the outcome would appear to be the same. It wouldn't seem to matter which one the spiritual achievement goes to, as long as one of the souls gets it, since that would mean you are getting it.

Let me describe more specifically how past approaches to practice work. Someone with clairvoyant powers might see something like the following. When he meditates and enters into a state of rapture or trance, he may see an identical version of himself leave his body at that moment. If he tries to make out which of the two is really him, he will sense that it's the one who remains seated in place. After exiting the body, the other version of him is guided to practice in a dimension conjured up by his master. That dimension may take the form of a bygone society, contemporary society, or the society of a parallel world. There, in what amounts to an hour or two a day here, he is guided in practice and endures a great deal of hardship. The person here then comes out of trance when the other version of him finishes and comes back. This is as much as those with visionary powers have been allowed to know.

It is even sadder for those who can't perceive what is happening. When they regain awareness after perhaps two hours lost in trance or rapture, they will know nothing of what happened. There are also some who sleep for two or three hours as a means of practice, turning everything over to another. These are approaches that involve incremental practice, with meditation or contemplation being done for a certain length of time each day. There are also approaches where everything is completed in one stretch. For instance, there is the case of Bodhidharma, who meditated facing a wall for nine years, as you may know. And there have been many monks who sat for decades on end, with the longest span recorded being over ninety years; others have sat even longer. They would remain there, seated and still, even as dust formed into a thick layer on their eyelids or grass grew upon their bodies. Certain Daoist practices utilize these methods, as well. Some Mystical Way practices are notable for practicing via sleep, with meditation sessions that last for decades without the person waking even once. But who is it that practiced in these cases, then? The person's secondary soul. Those with the power to see things observe that [during the person's long-term meditation] a master is guiding his secondary soul to practice. The master instructs it to practice in earnest and to wait for his return, and then departs and remains away until it works off the large karmic debts that it may have incurred and that the master can't fully absolve it of.

This sort of master has to go about things in the following way, even though he is well aware of what will happen upon his departure. He leaves, and then fiends come along and try to scare the secondary soul, or morph into attractive women who try to seduce it, among other things. But they find that it really doesn't respond to their advances since spiritual practice comes rather easily to a secondary soul, as it can see through such ruses. The fiends then grow enraged and vengefully seek to kill it. And they may do just that—end its life. But once it dies, its karmic debts are paid off. So the soul is released and emerges like a wisp of smoke, and wafts about. It then reincarnates, perhaps into a poverty-stricken household, where it has a hard life. Then, when it comes of age and is old enough to understand things, its master comes again, though he likely isn't recognizable at first. The master then uses his powers to unblock the part of the secondary soul's memory that has been sealed off. This allows the soul to recall the past and recognize the master. The master then lets it know that the time is ripe for practice. And so finally, after many years, the master teaches the secondary soul.

Afterwards, the master might inform the secondary soul that it still has many attachments to remove and that it should set off on a period of roaming. There is a lot of hardship involved in roaming about, since it means that one must wander about the world and beg for food, and one might experience ridicule, verbal abuse, or mistreatment from all sorts of people. Anything can happen. But the secondary soul will conduct itself as a practitioner at all times, and handle its interactions with others well, being mindful of and perfecting its character, and never falling for the many worldly temptations it encounters. Only after many years of wandering about does it then return home. Its master may say that it has gained enlightenment and been spiritually perfected, and that now is a good time to go back [to the physical body it began from] and prepare for its final departure, since its practice has been completed; he will tell it to settle any remaining affairs it may have back in the human world. And so the secondary soul returns after years of being away. Once it does, the true soul of the person in this world comes out of its hypnotic state or rouses from its slumber.

Yet the person seated there is not the one who engaged in practice, but rather, it is his secondary soul that did; and so the achievement, the higher energy, goes to the secondary soul. The true soul did go through a lot, however. He spent what would have been his prime of life just sitting there, after all, and much of his life in this world had passed him by. And so the person is compensated accordingly. After he comes out of his hypnotic state he will detect that he now has higher energy and paranormal powers, and he will find that he can do healings or whatever else he may attempt. But it's because his secondary soul is granting his wishes—in deference to his true soul, which is in charge of the body and has the say. The reason it grants his wishes is because this person sat there for so many years that his life has passed by. But when this person eventually dies, each goes their own way; the secondary soul leaves him. What Buddhist teachings would say is that someone in this scenario is still subject to reincarnation. Yet in cases like this one, the person's body did give rise to a higher being, which is a most meritorious act. And so the person might enjoy great wealth or a position of power and influence in his next life. And this is the only way it can be handled. So the person's spiritual efforts are ultimately in vain.

We had to go through a great deal to get consent to disclose this. I have revealed a secret that stood for ages, what was regarded as the secret of secrets and never to be divulged under any circumstances; I have laid bare the basis of countless spiritual practices throughout the ages. Now you know why I said that the matter reaches far back into the past. You would be hard pressed to name one school or discipline that hasn't taken that approach. And yet it's tragic, isn't it?—after all of that effort practicing, the person has no higher energy, or real achievement, to show for it. And yet there is no one to blame. The human condition is one of ignorance and there is much that people fail to discern, even if hints are given. Higher teachings will seem like a stretch to people, yet more basic and accessible ones won't take them very far. There are even those who still hope for me to treat their ailments, in spite of all I have said. I am really at a loss for what to say to them. We are teaching spiritual practice and can only watch over those who seek to transcend this human world.

With our practice the achievement belongs to your true soul, and it is this soul that will gain higher energy for it. But this isn't something that comes about simply by deciding so. Certain conditions have to be met. Remember that our practice doesn't try to avoid the secular world, nor should you try to avoid or escape from its challenges. Rather, you are to practice while part of this world and stay alert to all of its pitfalls around you; to knowingly get shortchanged and be indifferent to it; to not fight with people when they try to take what's yours; to keep your composure when people do things that are trying; and to, in this adverse setting, strengthen your will, perfect your character, and rise above all of the bad and worldly tendencies of thought that you are exposed to.

Then it is surely you, the true soul, that is consciously enduring unpleasant things, making sacrifices, and letting go of worldly things. So the spiritual achievement should go to you, as whoever pays the costs should reap the rewards. And that is why our practice doesn't involve secluding oneself from this complicated, secular world. We want to practice amidst it and all of its problems, for we want to be the ones who gain spiritually. Even when one day there are monastics counted among us, they will still need to go out and roam about the secular world.

I have been asked why other energy practices that are done in the world don't also result in the true soul gaining spiritual achievement. The reason is, those practices are just about health or wellness. Authentic energy practices that lead to higher realms have traditionally been taught to only a single disciple, and not the general public. They will have taken their students elsewhere to practice, and will teach them in seclusion. In all these years nobody has taught something like this to the broader public. We do so because this is exactly the way of our practice and how we develop higher energy, our spiritual achievement. We take the additional step of planting numerous things onto your true soul so that it will be *you* who is really gaining the spiritual fruits. I would venture to say I've done something unprecedented by making this practice as accessible as we have. And I am not exaggerating, as you might have realized. While some of my words might, understandably, sound grandiose, the truth is that I generally reveal just a fraction of what I know. What I've disclosed is just a small part of all that could be said. I can't reveal to you any higher or profounder facets of Dafa at this time, as they would be far too advanced.

By taking this approach to practice, our discipline enables the real you to have the spiritual achievement. This is truly a first. You wouldn't find anything like it in all of history. So while this has the advantage of the fruits of spiritual labor going to you, it also comes with its challenges. It is terribly hard to rise above a complicated, worldly setting like this that tests your character with interpersonal things. The challenging part is that you have to remain unmoved when you knowingly get taken advantage of by people, when things that mean a lot to you are on the line, when people around you are contending over things, or when those you love suffer. You have to learn to see these things in the proper light. Being a practitioner is by no means easy. Someone once said to me, "Mr. Li, doesn't it suffice to just be a good person in the usual sense? It's hard to imagine going much further than that with the practice." I was really saddened to hear that, and didn't reply. Character varies widely from person to person, and each will go as far as his ability to believe takes him. But what faith you do have will be rewarded.

The Daoist sage Lao-tzu once wrote that, "The Way may be spoken of, but it is not a common way." The Way wouldn't be precious if it were something so readily available it could be found in the streets, and anyone could take it up and succeed at it. In our discipline you are the one who gains spiritually by working through challenges, and it follows that we should fit in with ordinary people as best we can. So you needn't be poor or impoverished. Your task, rather, is to develop your character while being part of the material world. In this sense the practice is convenient—the most accommodating of any, in fact—in the sense that you can fully do the practice among regular people and needn't become a monastic. But this is also what's most difficult about it, in that our practice is done in the terribly complicated secular world. Yet at the same time this is our practice's greatest virtue, for this approach enables the true you to gain the achievement. And that is the most crucial aspect of our practice, as I disclosed today. When your true soul gains this spiritual achievement, this higher energy, so too will your secondary soul, naturally enough. It only follows that it, too, will get higher energy when all of the other aspects of your body, as well as its intelligent beings and cells, are developing it. However, at no point will the secondary soul's energy be as high as yours, for you are the principal being while it is but a guardian being.

Having said this much, there is something I should share. There are a number of people engaged in spiritual practice who have always longed to progress to higher stages. They have traveled far and wide and spent a great deal, hoping that a renowned teacher might show them the way, but to no avail; a person's reputation is no guarantee of true insight, after all. So their journeys were for naught, despite all the effort and costs entailed. Here we have a wonderful practice to offer, and we have made it available to all, virtually handing it to you, right at your door. The only question now is whether you can make good on it. Those who can will have spiritual progress in store for them, while those who cannot would do well to set aside the thought of doing spiritual practice; only deceptive entities would teach you hereafter, and so I would discourage you from trying. If I can't save you, no one can. The truth is that it's now exceedingly hard to find an authentic teacher of a true practice who will instruct you, for no one is doing that anymore. Even higher realms are now in the latter days, or "end time," and the beings there can hardly concern themselves with regular people. Ours is not only the most accessible practice, but is also attuned precisely to the qualities that underlie all of existence. It allows you to make the fastest and most efficient progress, since the practice is all about your heart and mind.

The Cosmic Orbit

I would like to explain what in Daoist practice is known as "the cosmic orbit," both its "greater" and "lesser" forms. Normally the term is used by people to refer to the linking up of two of the body's energy channels—the front side's Conception Vessel and the back side's Governing Vessel. This kind of cosmic orbit is quite shallow, however, and doesn't amount to much; it only serves to bring health benefits. It is what's called a "lesser" cosmic orbit. There is another form of cosmic orbit that's considered neither lesser nor greater, which occurs when one practices meditation. It begins from inside the body by going through the Niwan Palace and then proceeds downwards, traveling internally to the energy center, where it passes through and then proceeds upwards again. It is an interior circuit and a true cosmic orbit that forms through focused meditation. Once formed, this circuit becomes a powerful energy current that drives into motion all of the body's energy channels. Daoist practices utilize cosmic orbits, while Buddhist ones normally don't. You might be curious what approach Buddhist ones use, then. The Buddha didn't mention a higher energy like *gong* during his teachings, but Buddhist practices do have their ways of transforming the body through spiritual practice. In these practices there is an energy conduit that runs from the fully opened Hundred Convergences acupoint, at the crown of the head, downwards in a spiral-like pattern and that ultimately activates all of the body's channels.

Esoteric Buddhism achieves this through what is called a "central conduit." Some may question how it's possible for them to have this conduit, since it is not something normally found in a person's body. So let's take a look at how they develop one. The body's energy channels number over ten thousand when all are taken into account, and they crisscross just like blood vessels and even exceed their number. While blood vessels don't run between internal organs, energy channels do. A web of channels stretches throughout the body from the crown of the head on down, crisscrossing horizontally and vertically. When the channels first begin to merge [in these Buddhist practices], they won't have formed a straight conduit yet, and so it might take work to push energy through them. With time they gradually widen and merge to form a straight vertical conduit. This conduit then serves as an axis upon which the *chakras* of the body rotate, with the multiple horizontal *chakras* that run through one's body being driven by the mind. And the purpose of this is to fully open up all of the body's channels.

Falun Dafa doesn't opt for the approach of using one conduit to drive open all of the body's channels. Our practice dictates that right from the outset all the channels be connected and circulate simultaneously. We begin our practice from an advanced stage and bypass more rudimentary ones. With others' approach, where one conduit is used to drive open all of the body's channels, even an entire lifetime might not be enough to fully open them up; it could take decades of difficult practice. A number of practices thus hold that one lifetime isn't enough to finish the spiritual journey. And this is why many of the more advanced and demanding of practices try to extend one's life, and many followers experience this; the person's life is extended so that he may continue his practice for a great length of time.

"Lesser" cosmic orbits are basically for health, while "greater" ones are for true spiritual practice. The greater cosmic orbit discussed in Daoist practice doesn't resemble ours, which comes on with vigor and connects all of the body's channels so that they circulate together. Theirs involves the cycling of energy through several channels, such as the three *yin* and three *yang* ones, which loop around the body by running along the hands and down to the soles of the feet, and then pass from the legs up to the hair atop the head. For them, that counts as cycling energy through the greater cosmic orbit. Some *chi-gong* masters don't offer instruction in the greater cosmic orbit, since higher practice ensues once it has been formed; they limit their instruction to the realm of health. Then there are some who do try to teach it, but don't bestow followers with any of what's needed for it. These students have no chance of success since they aren't given what they need; they might try to use their own powers of mind to form it, but it's not possible. That's no more likely to make it happen than, say, going to the gym would. Remember that you only need to do your part practicing, and your teacher will handle the rest. The greater cosmic orbit can only start to form after all of the necessary internal mechanisms for it have been planted in you.

Daoists have always regarded the human body as a microcosm, and hold that this inner universe is as large as the outer one and faithfully reflects it. The idea might seem a bit of a stretch and hard to fathom; there doesn't seem to be grounds for likening the human body to the universe, given the latter's size. But there is a logic to it that can be explained. Contemporary physics is engaged in research on the composition of matter, and it has progressed from molecules to atoms, electrons, protons, and quarks, reaching all the way to neutrinos. At these levels microscopy doesn't have the power to see what exists or know what sizes of particles lie yet further below; researchers don't know what exists at even more micro of planes. Physics today is still nowhere near reaching the tiniest particles of the universe. Nevertheless, the invisible, miniature realms of those particles might be perceptible to someone who has gone beyond normal physical form, for he would see, with magnified vision, subatomic worlds that are still greater, in keeping with his level of spiritual attainment.

The Buddha described the vastness of the universe after having witnessed it at his level of attainment. His teaching implied that there are other beings in the Milky Way galaxy with physical bodies similar to ours, and that even in just a single grain of sand a great many worlds can be found. This is consistent with modern physics, as the orbiting of electrons around a nucleus is really no different from that of the Earth around the Sun. And so the Buddha taught that in smaller, invisible realms a great many worlds can be seen even in just a grain of sand; meaning, a grain of sand is similar to a universe where lives and a multitude of things exist. Then assuming that's valid, within the worlds inside a single grain of sand, there would again be sand, presumably. And within that sand we would expect to find yet more worlds. And then in those worlds inside the sand we would expect to again find still more sand. It could go on endlessly. And so even the Buddha, with his level of spiritual awakening, concluded that the universe was both "infinitely large and infinitely small." This suggests that it is so large he couldn't see its perimeter, and so small that he couldn't determine what the tiniest elemental substance is at the origin of matter.

There are masters who have said that a city can be seen in a single pore of the skin, complete with moving cars and

345

trains. While that might sound far-fetched at first, it proves reasonable if it's considered in a scientific spirit and with a genuine intent to understand. While I was talking about the opening of the inner eye, I mentioned that many who have experienced it have had visions where they are moving along a seemingly endless tunnel in their forehead region. And each day as they exercise or meditate they see themselves moving forward, with mountains and rivers to the sides; and they pass through cities and see a number of people. They are apt to think it's a figment of their imaginations. I can dispel any doubts and tell you that those things were *not* imagined; what they saw was very clear. Things like those shouldn't be written off as imaginary, if the world within the body is as vast as masters have seen with their inner eyes. Remember that Daoist thought has long maintained that the human body is a universe unto itself. It's only to be expected, then, that the distance from your forehead to the pineal gland, [where the inner eye is located,] is going to be enormous in that inner universe—making it feel like a really long way.

If the greater cosmic orbit becomes fully formed in the course of someone's practice, it will bring about an extra-sensory power. But before going into that, we should note that the greater cosmic orbit is variously referred to as the Meridian Orbit, the Revolution of Heaven and Earth, and the Revolution of the River Channel. The orbit will give rise to an energy current when it begins flowing, even at a low level of attainment. With time, its density will increase and it will become something of a higher order, becoming a very dense belt of energy that revolves. If someone's inner eye has opened at a lower plane he might see that the belt, while revolving, has the ability to transport the various energies of the body from one location to another. The energy of the heart might be moved to the intestines, for example, or the energy of the liver might be moved to the stomach. Those who can perceive the microcosm might observe that what's moved is quite sizeable. If the energy belt is brought outside of the body it is what people call the power of telekinesis. Those with stronger powers can exercise greater telekinesis and move large objects, while those with weaker powers can exercise lesser telekinesis and move smaller objects. These are the forms that telekinesis takes and how they come about.

A person enters right into true spiritual practice with the forming of the greater cosmic orbit; with it will come different miraculous experiences and expressions of one's energy. One such experience that comes about might be familiar if you've read traditional religious works like *Lives of Divine Transcendents* and *Principles of Mind-Body Practice*, or the Daoist Canon and various alchemical manuals. These works tell of individuals who experienced levitation, and speak of people "soaring in broad daylight"—or in other words, floating up into the air in plain sight. And I can vouch that people *are* capable of it once the greater cosmic orbit has been formed. It's a simple fact. Many people have formed these orbits, as you might suspect, with all the centuries of history that spiritual practice has. I don't think it's a stretch to say tens of thousands have, since it's really just one of the first developments in a person's practice.

Then why haven't all those adherents been seen floating about? It's because the human condition is not to be upset; the secular world mustn't be violated or altered without due reason. It would be a problem if all of those people were seen flying about. The human world wouldn't be what it is.

So this is one primary reason. Another is that the people of this world are not here to be human but to become pure again and return to their true heavenly abodes, which entails faith. Everyone would want to practice if they actually saw with their own eyes people levitating, and there would be no question of faith left. So you aren't allowed to be seen levitating or just freely show people if you have the power. People still need to practice by exercising faith. And this is why once your greater cosmic orbit has formed, you won't be able to levitate if even so much as the tip of your finger or toe is locked.

When the greater cosmic orbit is on the verge of being formed, some people find that their bodies lean forward as they meditate. This is due to the energy of the back of the body flowing well, and so it feels quite light while the front feels heavy. In other cases people may tend to lean backwards instead, as the back feels heavy and the front light. You might spring upward if energy is flowing well throughout your body, and feel as if you were being lifted upward off the ground. But only in exceptional cases is this allowed to happen. Those who experience such powers tend to be at two ends of the spectrum: the very young and old, and especially older women. Both of these groups tend to have few attachments and are more likely to experience powers like levitation and be able to retain them. Men, on the other hand, and especially young men, would have a hard time not showing off and might even try to gain from their powers. That is forbidden, however, and so their powers are typically sealed up after being developed. If even so much as one part of the body is sealed up they won't be able to levitate. But it's not that people are never allowed to experience levitation. You might be allowed to have a taste of it, with some of you being allowed to continue to experience it.

Instances of levitation have occurred wherever we have offered classes. When I held a class in Shandong province there were learners from the cities of Jinan and Beijing there as well, one of whom asked me, "Teacher, do you know what's happening to me? I often start floating as I walk, and it's the same when I lie down at home to sleep—even when I have a blanket over me. I'm always floating up, like a balloon." There was a similar case involving an older woman in Guizhou province who attended my class in the city of Guiyang. At home there were two beds in her room, one next to each wall. One time she was meditating on one of the beds and had the sense that she was levitating. She opened her eyes and realized that she had floated over to the other bed. She had the thought, "I should go back," and with that, she floated back to the initial bed.

Another example involves a student in the city of Qingdao who meditated on a sofa in a room at his workplace; it was during his lunch break and nobody was around. He began to levitate while meditating, and really floated up—over a yard high. He floated up and dropped down with a loud thud, multiple times. A blanket that was folded next to him was even bounced off, onto the floor. He was both a bit excited and frightened. It carried on like this, up and down, for the duration of the lunch hour. Eventually the work bell rang and he thought to himself, "I shouldn't let people see this. They wouldn't know what to make of it. I'd better stop this right away." And just like that, it stopped. So you can see how older people exercise better self-control. Were it someone younger, they probably would have hoped that everyone would see them levitating when the bell rang and know how well they were doing at their practice, since they could fly. The temptation to show off isn't easily overcome. If you do show your powers off they will be lost, for that's not what they are meant for. Experiences like these have been recounted by learners everywhere.

We want all of the body's energy channels to be opened up right from the outset. Eighty to ninety percent of you will find that your bodies have now become light and illness-free. But in this class we do more than just boost your body to the point of being completely purified; we also plant many things in your body so that you can develop higher energy during the course of the classes. What I am doing amounts to lifting you up and putting you far ahead. Your very character is changing as I give my teachings during these sessions. Many of you will feel like a new person after the classes are over. I guarantee that your view of the world will have expanded and you will know what it takes to be a good person; you will no longer be confused about life. I'm confident of this. What this means is that your character will be keeping pace [with the physical changes that occur].

Returning to the topic of the greater cosmic orbit, though you may not be allowed to levitate, you will find that your whole body feels light and as though you are walking on air. If walking even a short distance tired you out before, now you will be able to comfortably go however far you'd like. When riding a bike it will seem as if you are getting a push, and no amount of stair climbing will tire you. I can assure you of it. Those who can't attend a class but learn the practice by reading this book will experience whatever benefits they are meant to, just the same. I'm the type of person who if he speaks must tell the truth. It would be teaching evil on my part if I were to speak falsely, say baseless things, or speak loosely and without a purpose when I am supposed to be teaching the Way. What I am doing is not easy; the whole universe is watching. There would be consequences if I misled you.

Spiritual adherents normally never come to experience more than the familiar greater cosmic orbit that I've been describing. But that orbit isn't sufficient if you want your body to be replaced by and converted into high-energy matter as efficiently as possible. For this, there needs to be another type of cosmic-orbit circulation that sets all of your body's energy channels into motion. And it is called the Prime Vertical Orbit. Very few people know of it. The name might surface occasionally in books, but nowhere is it disclosed or explained. People have skirted around the subject by keeping any discussion of it at the level of theory, since it's been a closely guarded secret. But here I am going to spell it out for you. The orbit might begin from either the Hundred Convergences acupoint at the top of the head or the Meeting of Yin point at the perineum. So, supposing energy comes forth at the former point, it will travel along the borderline between the *yin* (front) and *yang* (back) sides of the body, and move down from the ear and past the shoulder, going downwards. It weaves its way over each of the fingers and then travels along the side of the body, passing underneath the foot and then up the inner side of the leg. It then goes down the inner side of the other leg, passes under the other foot, and travels up the other side of the body. It weaves its way around each of the fingers again and completes a circuit by arriving at the top of the head. This is what constitutes a Prime Vertical Orbit. So there you have it in just a few sentences; it needn't take a full-length book, as is sometimes done. I don't consider it a great secret even if knowledge of it has been carefully guarded and only been revealed when a lineage is being genuinely passed down to a disciple. Though I have explained what it is, you shouldn't use your mind to try to bring it about or exert any control over it while practicing. That's not how we go about things in Falun Dafa. You don't need to will anything to happen when you are following an authentic spiritual discipline that leads to higher levels of attainment; all that you need will be given to you, ready to use. So in our case, the orbit will be automatically generated by the mechanisms inside you, which are working constantly to transform you. This orbit will naturally circulate on its own when the time is ripe. You might notice one day while practicing that your head is swaying to one side, which would mean that the Prime Vertical Orbit is moving in that direction; or if your head sways to the other side it means that the Orbit is moving in the other direction. It moves in both directions.

Once a greater or lesser cosmic orbit has been formed in a person, his head may nod during meditation, and it indicates that energy is coursing through. The fourth exercise that we do, called Falun Cosmic Orbit, cycles energy through the body in the same fashion as these orbits; and in fact, it will continue to cycle by itself even after you have finished doing the exercise. What the exercise does is to strengthen the mechanisms inside you, and this is what allows the orbit to continually cycle. In our practice the Way works through you. And so you will normally find that your cosmic orbit is circulating nonstop. The layer of energy mechanisms that has been placed outside of your body is equivalent to a layer of major, external energy channels, and it will guide your body to do the work automatically—even when you aren't doing the exercise. The external channels may also reverse their direction, cycling energy in one direction or the other, working at every moment to promote the flow of energy in your channels.

At this point you might be wondering what the larger goal of forming cosmic orbits is. Forming them in and of itself isn't the purpose; just having a connected orbit isn't that special. The purpose of it, as one progresses further in spiritual practice, is to fully open up all of the body's energy channels via one circuit, and the cosmic orbit does help you to achieve this. Yet [opening the channels] is something we've already begun doing for you. And as you continue on, if you track the circulation of your greater cosmic orbit, you will sense your channels broadening inside and widening, perhaps becoming as wide as a finger. This happens because a stronger energy current results in wider and brighter channels. But this still doesn't amount to much. You need to go further with your practice, to the point that all of your body's energy channels are widening and the energy is becoming stronger and brighter, until finally all of the myriad channels are merged into one whole. At that point the body will no longer have energy channels or acupuncture points, for it will be connected as one piece. And that is the ultimate goal of fully opening your channels: to transform your entire body into high-energy matter.

If you have reached this stage in your practice, it means that your body has basically been remade with high-energy matter. It means that you have reached the highest phase of practice that can occur in the human realm, and your mortal body has reached the pinnacle of its development. Your body will experience a new state, which I'll describe in a moment. At this point you will now have a substantial amount of higher energy, or *gong*. And by now you will have developed all supernormal powers (innate abilities) possible of the human body, while working on your body during the stage of human-realm practice. But since we do our practice in the world, most of your powers will have been sealed up and won't be available to you. Your energy column will have grown to a sizeable height, and the different forms that your energy has assumed will have been strengthened greatly by your powerful energy. But any powers you have at this stage will only function in this immediate dimension; they will have no impact in other dimensions since they were born of a mortal body. Yet they will still be quite substantial. These powers will be part of your bodies in other dimensions and will have metamorphosed in dramatic ways; they will be diverse and abundant, and they might even be startling to behold. Eyes will cover some people's bodies, filling each and every pore of the skin as well as the dimensions associated with their bodies. Some individuals could have images of divine beings like Bodhisattvas or Buddhas all over their bodies, since this is a Buddhist practice. The higher energy you have might assume any of many appearances and give rise to many supernatural beings.

At this point you will experience atop your head what is referred to as "three flowers gathered at the crown." It's dramatic and striking to behold, and can be seen even by those whose inner eyes aren't at a very high plane. Three flowers will appear on top of your head, one of which is a lotus flower—though not the lotus of the human realm. The other two flowers similarly belong to other worlds, and each is simply wondrous. They rotate in succession atop the head, turning clockwise and counterclockwise; the flowers turn independently. Each flower will have a tall pole accompanying it, equal in diameter to the flower and reaching to the heights of the heavens. The poles are not energy columns, however. Rather, they just happen to assume that shape and exude an otherworldly feel. You will really be startled if you see them. When your practice reaches this stage your body will be pure and fair, with skin that's supple and youthful. You will have reached the highest phase of practice in the human realm, but it doesn't mark the end of your journey. You need to continue practicing and progress still further.

What comes next is a transitional phase between that of the human realm and that which is beyond, where you will have what is referred to as a "crystal-clear body." At this point your body will still be a mortal one, even if transformed, but it will have reached the highest form possible while practicing in this realm. It is referred to as crystal clear for having achieved the greatest degree of purity and being made entirely of high-energy matter. Your whole body will be transparent if seen with higher vision, and look similar to glass, as if nothing were there. This means that your body is now a holy one, for it consists of high-energy matter, unlike the body you began with. All of the powers and magical things developed by your body will now be promptly discarded. They will be unloaded into a deeper dimension, since they serve no further purpose and couldn't be drawn upon again. Their only use might be that some day, once your practice has come to fruition and you have gained enlightenment, you will wish to look them over as you reflect back upon your spiritual journey. Just two things will remain then: your column of energy and your angelic body, which will be great in size. But both of these will exist in a deeper dimension and be imperceptible even to most people who have higher sight, since their sight is usually limited; your body will just appear transparent to them.

With further practice you will progress beyond this interim phase where you have a crystal-clear body, and begin the stage of practice that lies beyond the human realm. In this new phase you will be developing your body further, a body which will already be divine. This will be a body that's composed only of higher energy, and your character will be one that is unwavering. In this phase of practice you will be forging new powers that are befitting the title of "divine." They will be infinitely powerful and able to command any dimension. As you carry on persistently with your spiritual efforts, you will come to know what it takes to practice at still higher stages and what to expect.

Getting Carried Away

I would like to discuss the problems that stem from being overly enthused. There are many people, both spiritual and not, who have long been seeking the truth and pondering the meaning of life. With Falun Dafa they find answers to their many lifelong questions, and it's only natural that they would be excited by all the new insights they gain. I know that those who are sincere about practicing will realize the significance of the teachings and cherish them. Yet a problem is apt to follow. Namely, people are so happy that they go overboard, and come across as abnormal when they interact with people, or seem odd compared to others. But that shouldn't happen, as I see it.

Most of you practice in the secular world, and so you

should be mindful of this fact and not distance yourselves from the world. You should have relationships with others like people normally do. The only thing different about you is that you come across as someone of excellent character and who is positive, who strives to be a better person and grow spiritually, and who always tries to do the right thing. Yet some of you come across as abnormal, or apathetic about the world, and people can't relate to what you say. This could lead people to wrongly conclude that doing Falun Dafa made you that way, as if you've gone off the deep end. They wouldn't realize that you were simply too excited and not being rational, and had a lapse in judgment. I think you would have to agree, that's not the right way to be and it is extreme—which means attachment is involved. You should get over it and instead go about your life and practice in a normal way around people. People won't think well of you and will distance themselves from you if they think you are obsessed with Falun Dafa. And then you would no longer be presented with opportunities to perfect your character. It's really a problem if people think you're not normal. So keep what I said in mind and be sure to exercise good judgment.

Our practice isn't like others where the adherent is oblivious to the passage of time, lost in a state of rapture or trance, and completely absorbed as he or she practices. With our practice you have to stay mentally present. I often hear from people that they start swaying involuntarily after they close their eyes to do the exercises. But that shouldn't happen, as I see it. The problem is that you have grown used to letting your conscious mind drift off while your eyes are closed, and it's become a habit. And yet you don't sway while listening to me speak. You surely wouldn't do that while exercising if you tried to maintain the state of mind that you have when your eyes are open, and just closed them lightly. The problem is that you think that that's how practicing is done, and the idea has become ingrained; so you disappear shortly after closing your eyes and lose yourself. We teach that your conscious mind has to stay alert and aware. These exercises are meant to work upon the true you, and you should make progress through them while staying mentally present. Our practice includes a meditation. With ours, you have to stay aware that you are practicing, however focused you may be, and not let yourself slip into a hypnotic state where you're aware of nothing. Instead, you should expect to experience a very pleasant sensation as you sit there, much like sitting inside an eggshell would be, where you're aware that you are practicing but feel as if you can't move a muscle. This is necessary in our practice. Another experience that you might have is as follows. As you sit in meditation it will seem as if your legs have disappeared and you don't know where they are; and your body will have disappeared as well, including your arms and hands, and only your head will seem to remain. And as you go on, even your head will seem to disappear, leaving only your mind—with just a little awareness left that you are practicing there. It will suffice to achieve this state, as this provides the optimal conditions for your body to be transformed. And that is why you need to enter into such stillness. But don't let yourself doze off or muddle through it, lest the fruits of your efforts be gained by another.

It is essential that all of us avoid seeming abnormal to non-practitioners. You will be giving Falun Dafa a bad name if you come across the wrong way and lead people to think that Falun Dafa makes people odd. I really want you to keep this in mind. You should be careful not to get carried away in any sense or at any point as you practice. A mind that's prone to such extremes is susceptible to evil.

Guarding Your Speech

Various religious traditions have made a practice of silence, and it is something done by a specific segment of the religious community; namely, the brothers and sisters who have renounced the world and who live in monastic settings. For them, the practice entails refraining from speech altogether. They dedicate themselves to the spiritual life and are set on becoming as detached as possible, and believe that even one single bad thought might generate karma or amount to a sin. And while you may have heard of karma being referred to as "good" as well as "bad," either way, it's not something you would want to have as someone who aspires to become "empty" to this world, and have, in a sense "nothing"—as the Buddhist and Daoist traditions have put it. Adherents in certain monastic traditions have even tried to refrain from all actions. They have taken this approach since they couldn't perceive the reasons behind things or know whether something was good or bad to do; there would always lurk the question of what factors were involved. Most adherents would not have been that advanced or able to perceive such things. So if they took action, they would have to worry that what seemed like a good thing to do might turn out to be bad. Their solution was to practice non-intervention as much as possible, in the hope that by refraining from all unnecessary activities or actions they would avoid making karma. They knew that any karma they made would have to be painfully worked off. The day of a believer's spiritual perfection or enlightenment is something preordained, and any karma added along the way will only make the whole journey that much more difficult. So this explains the aversion to action.

In the Buddhist tradition the practice of self-imposed silence is based on the idea that whatever words someone utters are dictated by his thoughts, and behind those thoughts there is bound to be intention. And it's very possible that it is an attachment at work when a person's consciousness leads him to form a thought, make a comment, do something, or use his senses or limbs out in the secular world. To shed light on this, consider the issues that people sometimes have with one another, where they speak well of one person while speaking ill of another, or comment on someone's having practiced well in contrast to someone else. Comments like those reflect issues between people. Or take something commonplace, such as your expressing that you want to do something or see something done in a certain way. What you say might result in someone being unwittingly hurt or undermined. And so your words or actions might unknowingly be making karma for you, given how complex things can be between people. This is why some monastics have been so strict about refraining from speaking altogether. So guarding one's speech, or practicing silence, has always held an important place in religious traditions, and so far I've been describing the approaches others have taken.

The vast majority of people who do Falun Dafa, however, carry out their practice in the secular world (the exception being those who previously took monastic vows or were ordained), and so we inevitably lead normal lives in the world and are part of society. We have jobs and should be doing them well. Some lines of work entail verbal communication, which might seem at odds with the goal of practicing silence. But there is no conflict, as the guarding of speech that we practice is quite different from the past approach of silence. Our discipline is different from those of the past, and so too is what it asks of you. When we speak, we should simply speak in a manner befitting a practitioner, and not say anything bad or divisive. As practitioners we should gauge what we intend to say with the teachings and see whether it's appropriate. And if it is, then it's fine to speak. And besides, if we always kept silent we would have a hard time introducing the practice to people and sharing it with others. What we do is to simply exercise restraint in situations where you might be speaking out of attachment, such as talking about worldly things above and beyond what's required at your job; chitchatting with other practitioners about meaningless things; saying things that are self-aggrandizing; sharing the latest gossip that you heard; or discussing worldly things that you're fond of and find stimulating. It's in these regards that I believe we should guard our speech, and this is our version of practicing silence. Monks used to believe that even just one inappropriate thought could result in karma, or sin, and they used to take things like this very seriously. And this is why there were teachings about limiting physical, verbal, and mental activity. Physical action was limited in order to avoid doing anything wrong. Silence was practiced in order to limit all verbal activity. And mental activity was restricted so as to keep the mind clear of thoughts. These strictures have been quite central for some monastic communities. In our practice, however, it's sufficient to have a good sense for what's appropriate to say, and to live up to the expectations for your character.

THE
NINTH TALK

Energy Practices Versus
Regular Exercises

MANY PEOPLE READILY MISTAKE energy practices, or exercises, for being essentially a form of physical exercise. And it's only natural to think that way, since the two *are* comparable on a superficial level, as both promote physical health. But it turns out the two differ greatly if you get into the specifics of the techniques and approaches they employ. Physical exercise aims to foster health, and so those who do it need to engage in physical exertion and go through training routines that condition the body. The opposite holds true with energy practices. One needs to be still when doing them, and any movement that does take place is to be gentle, slow, and fluid; sometimes one is even completely motionless. So this differs much from physical exercise. And speaking at a higher level, energy practices go beyond mere health benefits to include higher and more profound facets. They involve more than the little bit about them that's familiar to people. They are higher things, and vary in form depending on how advanced they are. These practices are far from ordinary.

Physical exercise is by its very nature quite different from energy practices. Athletes, and especially competitive athletes today, need to constantly try to push their workouts to the next level; they have to consistently keep their bodies in top condition to meet the physical demands of competition in this day and age, and stay competitive. To this end, they have to increase the intensity of exercise and ensure that there is maximal blood flow. Doing so boosts the athlete's metabolic capacity and means that he is getting in better shape. Athletes seek to increase their metabolic capacity since their bodies need to always be in top competitive form. The human body is made up of countless cells, all of which are subject to a process which, in rough terms, goes as follows. A cell that has been newly produced through cellular division is full of vitality and ready to develop. After reaching its peak of development it will have nowhere to go but down, and it will do so until the very bottom is reached, at which point it will be replaced by a new cell. We can illustrate this with an analogy, using the twelve hours of the clock. A cell that is generated at six o'clock in the morning via cellular division would develop steadily up through eight, nine, or ten o'clock, with things progressing well all along. But by twelve o'clock the cell would have no further capacity to develop, and could only decline. So while the cell would still have half of its life remaining, it would be ill-suited for the competitive form that an athlete needs to be in.

So athletes respond by raising their level of physical exertion and increasing their blood flow, with the result that new cells are generated to replace the older ones earlier than is normal. This means, then, that the cells that are replaced don't complete their entire life cycle and are replaced midway through. This ensures that an athlete's body is always strong and his or her level of fitness is improving. But the fact remains that a person's cells cannot divide indefinitely; there is a limit to how many times a cell can divide. Suppose, for example, that a single cell can undergo a total of one hundred divisions (though the actual number far exceeds a million) and that under normal conditions a person would be able to live one hundred years. Then the cells of athletes, on the other hand, would only be able to complete half of their life cycle, and so these individuals would live only to be fifty. Even so, this hasn't had significant consequences for professional athletes so far, since the level of competition today forces many into retirement by thirty. And then they go back to a more normal routine, basically no worse for wear. The bottom line is that while physical training can make you fit, it comes at the cost of a shorter life, in principle. And this is why a competitive athlete who is in his teens may well look like someone in his twenties, or one in his twenties may look like he's in his thirties. Athletes often give the impression of having aged prematurely. There is a consequence for every action, and we should be aware that things have both pros and cons. What I've described are the consequences of regular exercise.

Energy practices, on the other hand, are just the opposite. They don't involve vigorous movement, and what movement there is tends to be relaxed, fluid, and slow, sometimes to the point of being motionless. And it's known that the body can become so still during meditation that every aspect of one's physiology slows down, such as heart rate and blood circulation. Many yogis in India can sit submerged in water or be buried underground for days at a time; they make their bodies completely still, controlling even their heart rates. So, if we suppose that a person's cells normally divide once a day, then a spiritual practitioner might be able to slow his cell division to just once every two days, or once per week, half month, or even longer. This would mean that he is extending his life. And this is possible even with practices that just cultivate the mind, but not the body; even they can achieve gains in longevity. This might seem to beg the question of how someone who doesn't transform his body could extend his life, when one's lifespan is normally something that's set in stone. The explanation is, it becomes possible when one achieves a level of spiritual attainment surpassing the three realms. But the person will look quite old.

Then there are practices that truly change the body. They do so by constantly storing up high-energy matter in the cells of the body. And as the density of the stored energy steadily increases, it gradually comes to inhibit, and ultimately replace, one's normal human cells. This will lead to a qualitative change, such that you become youthful, and stay that way. Of course, spiritual development is a long process that involves significant sacrifices. Both the body and mind must be tempered, which is very trying. For example, are you grounded to the point where no one ever "gets to you"? Do worldly things hold no sway over you? It's hard to reach that point; it isn't something you can just will. Your mind and your virtue have to reach a certain point first.

People have long confused energy practices with regular

physical exercises, when in fact the two diverge widely and are different at their core. Energy practices are only similar to regular exercises when they are practiced at their most basic level, for health and fitness, where the focus is on basic *chi* energy. But energy practices are altogether different at their more advanced stages. The bodily purification that happens in them has a greater purpose behind it, and higher principles have to be followed. Physical exercise, by contrast, is just an ordinary endeavor.

Thoughts and the Mind

When people discuss "thoughts" they are talking about mental processes. Here I would like to offer a spiritually informed perspective on thoughts and the mental processes that go with them, and look at the different forms that those processes (or thoughts) take, as well as how they come about. Many questions about the brain are still unanswered by the medical sciences, for the brain is not as easily understood as the outer, more superficial layers of the body. Thoughts exist at deeper planes of reality and vary in form across dimensions. But they are not as some teachers of energy practices have imagined them. These persons haven't been able to offer a good explanation of how thoughts work since they don't fully understand it. They believe that by generating a thought with their brains they can accomplish certain things, and believe that what then unfolds is done by their minds, or thoughts. But that isn't in fact the case.

Let's start by looking at where thoughts come from. In ancient China there was an expression, "thinking with the heart." It's a curious phrase, but there were reasons behind it. The science of ancient China was very advanced, since the connections among the human body, living things, and the cosmos were the focus of its inquiry. There were people back then who could actually sense that their hearts were thinking, while others might have sensed that it was their brains doing so. What accounts for this? They were onto something, in fact. The soul of a regular person tends to be quite small, yet ideas originate from it and not from the brain. And the soul doesn't always remain inside the head, at the Niwan Palace— or "pineal gland," in medical terminology. When the soul is at the Niwan Palace, a person might sense that his brain is thinking or sending out signals; and when it is at the heart, he might in fact sense that his heart is what's doing so.

The human body is a micro universe, as I've said, and in the bodies of practitioners there are abundant supernatural beings, any of which might change locations. If it is your soul that changes locations, by going, for instance, to your stomach area, then you might sense that you are actually thinking with your stomach; or if it goes to your calf muscle or heel, then you might sense that you are thinking with your calf or heel. This is fully possible, as far-fetched as it may sound. And this is something you might be able to sense even before your practice has progressed very far. The presence of the soul together with your temperament, nature, and personal traits are what make you a full-fledged, unique individual, rather than just flesh. Then what does the brain do? I regard the brain of this physical dimension as simply a processing plant. The thoughts that you have actually come from your soul, though not in the form of language. What happens is that your soul conveys to the brain a type of cosmic signal, which carries with it a certain idea. This signal, once received, acts as a prompt that the brain translates into some form of expression, such as the language you speak, a gesture made with your hands, the look in your eyes, or your overall body language. And that is the role of the brain. The prompting or thought actually comes from your soul. People usually think that the ideas they have are simply the result of the brain working on its own. But the truth is that the soul is very much involved, and when located at the heart, it might give the sense that you are thinking with your heart.

Those engaged in human biological research believe that the brain issues something akin to electrical waves. Without going into what those actually are, I will note that they believe there *is* a physical component to thought, which suggests that what I just talked about isn't far-fetched. Then we might ask what the purpose of the brain is. Various masters have claimed that they can use their minds to do superhuman things like moving physical objects, opening the inner eye, or doing healings. They say that because they aren't aware of the powers they have. They only know that things happen for them at the thought of it. What's actually happening is that their *powers* are acting at the command of their thoughts, which are in the brain; the mind alone isn't making anything happen. So some of the things practitioners accomplish are due, in fact, to the powers they possess.

Supernormal powers are innate abilities of the body, only they have declined as the world has developed and people's minds have become more complicated, with the "here and now" becoming increasingly valued and people relying more and more on the latest technology. To recover your innate powers you must strive for authenticity as you practice, become pure as you once were, and restore your original nature—or what the Daoist tradition refers to as "returning to one's original, true self." So what are now thought of as psychic or supernormal powers are in fact the innate abilities of man. The world is not experiencing "progress" quite as it seems, but is in fact regressing. It is drifting away from the qualities of the universe. I have mentioned the well-known image of Master Zhang Guo riding a donkey seated backwards, which might be hard to make sense of. But Zhang did that only after realizing that going *forward* was in fact going *backward*, and that man was growing further away from the qualities of the universe. Many people have become morally corrupt amidst larger changes in the universe, with people in China, as it grows increasingly commercialized, being a prime example; they are drifting further and further from the universe's qualities of *zhen, shan, ren*. Yet those who have become caught up in these secular trends can't sense how badly values are changing. Some even think things are great. Only those whose minds have elevated through spiritual refinement can recognize the woeful state of people's values today.

Teachers of energy practices have claimed that they can "free" or "unblock" your psychic powers, which is misleading. That's because psychic powers won't work without first being powered up by one's own energy. Nothing can be done for a person if that hasn't happened. They have to first be developed by a person's own energy and brought to maturity. And even in cases where it does seem that a teacher has activated someone's powers, that's not what happened. It was merely that he connected the person's mind with whatever powers he or she had already developed, so that now they respond to his or her mental commands, and work. So those teachers have no grounds for claiming that they freed anyone's powers. It's just that a link-up was made, and nothing more.

The thoughts of those who do spiritual practice can summon powers to do things, while a regular person's thoughts direct the limbs or sensory organs to do things. These activities resemble how the operations department or president's office of a business issues directives that are then carried out by various divisions of the company. Or it's like how in the military a commanding office might issue an order via its command post, and then troops will be mobilized to execute the mission. This is a topic I've discussed on many occasions with the heads of local *chi-gong* organizations while on the road giving classes. They have been surprised by my remarks, as they had always been trying to tap into the "potential energy" and "consciousness" of the mind; they didn't realize that there is nothing there to tap. Their efforts had been based on a wrong assumption all along. Research into the higher functions of the human body would benefit from a change in thinking and approach, as the usual means of deduction and analysis aren't well suited to dealing with things of a higher order.

There are several forms that thoughts might take, as indicated by all of the different terms people use, such as the unconscious, the subconscious, inspiration, and dreams. Let's take up the topic of dreams. Spiritual teachers are reluctant to try to explain how they work. These are exceptionally complex phenomena, for at the time of your birth other parallel versions of you were born simultaneously in multiple dimensions of the universe, and together they form a complete body with you, linked via the mind; you also have inside your body a true soul, a secondary soul, and a wide array of supernatural beings, each with its own appearance; and every cell, along with your internal organs, reflects your appearance and energies in other dimensions. There has always been a question as to what accounts for the apparent randomness of dreams. The medical sciences attribute it to alterations in brain waves, which is the measurable form that it assumes here. But those waves are actually responses to signals from other dimensions. Whatever the case, you needn't concern yourself with what happens in dreams where everything is hazy and confused, since those dreams aren't significant. There is, however, one class of dreams that *is* significant and that shouldn't be thought of as "just dreams." These are the dreams where your own mind—i.e., your true soul—saw that you were approached by a family member, or something vivid took place, or you witnessed or experienced something first-hand. In those instances your true soul really did experience something in another dimension, since your mind was lucid and things were lifelike. What you experienced did indeed happen, only it happened in another physical dimension and space-time. And so such things shouldn't be written off as just dreams, even if your body here in this world was asleep and doing what would be considered dreaming. But only in these cases are dreams significant.

It's worth noting that terms such as inspiration, the sub-conscious, and the unconscious were arrived at not by scientists but by other intellectual figures, and they were basing their ideas on merely common mental phenomena that were familiar to them. So they aren't very scientific. Consider what's meant by the unconscious. The term can't be readily explained and the concept is ill-defined, due to the fact that the energies and information from other dimensions that affect people are so complicated, and so they are often mistaken for memory traces. The subconscious, on the other hand, is something more easily explained. As the term is defined, it generally refers to a person's doing something while not cognizant of it, or doing it "subconsciously"—i.e., not intentionally. We sometimes use the term "subconscious mind" as well. It's easy for the subconscious mind (i.e., the secondary soul) to dictate a person's thoughts when he relaxes his conscious mind or isn't controlling his brain, like when he's dreaming or seems to zone out. And it is at these times, when he isn't fully present mentally, that the subconscious mind might act through him. Usually things won't go wrong, as the subconscious mind isn't under the spell of this world and can see things as they really are; it resides in another dimension, after all. When the person wakes up or snaps out of it, he might think, "Wow, I really botched that up," or "I wouldn't have done that if I were paying attention." But if he revisits the matter a few days or weeks later, he might be pleasantly surprised by how well he handled it or did it. And this is common. It was done excellently because the subconscious mind wasn't thinking about the immediate, short-term impact; it knew that things would turn out for the best in the long run. In other cases, where there is no question of long-term impact and only the present matters, what the subconscious has the person do will likely be done in a manner that's excellent right at the time.

Then there is another form of ["subconscious"] mental activity, one that's usually found in people with excellent innate foundations. It is when a person does things at the command of higher beings. But this is of course a different scenario altogether, and we won't go into it here. I want to focus on the forms of consciousness that come from our own selves.

"Inspiration" is another term or concept that was arrived at by intellectual figures. Generally, inspiration is said to have occurred when knowledge that someone has accumulated comes forth unexpectedly and spontaneously, like a spark. But this doesn't make much sense in light of materialist theory, since it would say that an individual's brain should become increasingly sharp as he gains knowledge and puts his brain to use throughout life, and the knowledge he has accumulated should be at his disposal at all times; there shouldn't be any need for what people are calling inspiration. Typical examples of inspiration might involve someone pondering something until he is at his wits' end; experiencing writer's block, or running out of ideas while composing a song; or getting stuck while engaged in scientific research. The person might be flushed with exhaustion from having wracked his brain, with cigarette butts littered all around, and yet he will still be stuck. Then finally, he might decide in a moment of frustration to take a break, and it is usually at times like this that inspiration springs up. While taking a break he relaxes and sets the matter aside, only to find that afterwards, without any effort, a solution comes to him from somewhere in the mind. [What blocked his effort previously was that] his conscious mind had been in charge, and the more that is the case, the less likely it is for other entities to come into play. And so it is under circumstances like I just described that most inspiration comes about.

Let's look at why inspiration comes then. When a person's brain is governed by his rational, conscious mind, there is little chance for the subconscious mind to get involved. The harder that someone thinks, the tighter the control that the conscious mind exerts. The subconscious mind is part of his body and was born along with him from the womb, and governs a portion of the body. If the person is thinking so hard about something that his head hurts, he's out of ideas, and it's trying for him, his subconscious mind will likewise find it hard to bear and might have a headache too. But if and when his conscious mind relaxes and loosens its grip, the subconscious can relay whatever insights it has on the matter to his brain. It can see things as they truly are, since it resides in another dimension, and so its help will allow the person to make a breakthrough and complete what he was working on.

Some people might take this to mean that they should be making use of their subconscious, as in the note that someone just passed up to me asking how to connect with it. But that's not something you can do when you have only just begun your practice and have limited powers. At this point you'd best not try to connect with it, since it is likely an attachment that's motivating you. Or it might be that you are thinking the subconscious could be utilized to benefit humanity and the world. But that too is out of the question, since what your subconscious knows is still limited—limited to the dimension it exists in. Its knowledge doesn't reach beyond its own dimension. And yet the universe is extraordinarily complex in structure, with highly intricate dimensions and numerous planes of existence, among which are vertical planes containing still many more dimensions. The developments in this world are under the control of higher beings that dwell in realms above, and what happens here on earth follows predetermined patterns that have been put in place.

The events of this human world unfold according to historical patterns. So while you might wish to foster progress in some form or other, or realize a certain goal, your wishes might not tally with those of the beings above [who decide such things]. For example, it's quite likely that the ideas of modern planes, trains, and bicycles were similarly arrived at back in the ancient world, only they couldn't come about because it was not yet the right moment in history. By contrast, people conventionally think that the reason those inventions never came about was due to the limitations of science in the past. But the truth is, the pace of scientific development is itself subject to history's designs. All of which is to say, things won't necessarily go as you hope for. There are of course cases where an individual's subconscious does play an active role in his or her life. For example, there is a writer who says that he can write ten thousand words a day, without fatigue; the words just come to him and his work is well received. As you might guess, this is the result of his conscious and subconscious minds working together, with the latter shouldering half the task. But this is rare. In most cases a person's subconscious won't get involved in any way. Any attempts on your part to have it do so won't go well, and might turn out the opposite of what you intended.

A Pure and Serene Mind

Many people have a hard time calming their minds when they do meditative exercises, and seek out teachers in hopes of figuring out why their minds are so active. Their minds are really like stormy seas, with all sorts of things churning up. And that makes it impossible for them to become still and centered. And when they don't know the cause of it, they might think that they just need to find the right technique for it, and look for a teacher who will share his or her secrets and hopefully bring them the calm they seek. So they are pinning their hopes on others, as I see it. Yet true progress comes by looking at *yourself* and focusing on your mind. It is the only way to make true progress and experience serenity in meditation. And that is an achievement. Your ability to center yourself and still your mind reflects your spiritual progress.

Only those with excellent innate foundations can just quiet their minds at will; for the average person it's simply not possible. The real reason why you can't quiet your mind is not due to your technique, or because you haven't found the secret to success; but rather, that your mind, or what's inside of your heart, is not pure. It's going to be hard to still your mind if you don't get along with others in daily life and you do selfish things for emotional reasons, or out of worldly wants and attachments, and you can't get over those things or take them lightly. And yet some people try to just battle through all of the errant thoughts that keep arising as they practice, and try to just will them away, rather than believe that it's about purity. But that is what it comes down to.

One objection might be that certain teachers *do* teach methods that allegedly quiet the mind, such as "guarding the one," visualizing, focusing or gazing upon the body's energy center, or reciting a Buddha's name. But those are more than just methods; they also involve mastery. And such mastery comes from refining the mind and progressing to higher stages of practice; achieving stillness isn't as simple as using some technique or other. Naysayers are welcome to give those methods a try and see how far they can get while still saddled with numerous desires and intense attachments that they haven't let go of. I'm skeptical when I hear people claim that they can still the mind just by reciting a Buddha's name. If people think, for example, that Pure Land Buddhism is as simple as reciting Buddha Amitabha's name, I doubt they've tried it. I would say that stillness is a matter of mastery, and not as easily found as people claim. It doesn't come easily in any spiritual discipline.

While it's well known that the Buddha taught the practice of meditation, less known is what preceded it in his teaching: the following of precepts, which are meant to bring an end to one's desires and obsessions. And only then, by emptying oneself of everything, would focused meditation become possible. So there's a logic to it. Meditation is a matter of mastery. His followers weren't expected to have fulfilled the precepts on day one, however. Rather, they would gradually come to renounce all that is bad, and as they did so, their powers of meditation would rise. Chanting a Buddha's name similarly requires undivided attention and a blank mind. As a person repeatedly chants a Buddha's name, all other regions of his brain are numbed; he becomes oblivious to everything else, with that one thought supplanting all others; and each letter of the Buddha's name appears before his mind's eye. That of course takes mastery. It's not something achievable right at the outset, and neither is quiet of mind. Anyone who doubts this is welcome to try otherwise. But they will find that their minds run amok even as their mouths are actively reciting. They might be thinking about how poorly their supervisor treats them at work, or how they got slighted with their most recent bonus. And they might get worked up as more thoughts like those go through their minds, even as they are chanting the Buddha's name. Then that hardly achieves the intent of the practice. This means that even the act of chanting a Buddha's name involves mastery, and it won't go smoothly if the mind is impure. Another example would be those who gaze with their open inner eye at the body's energy center, in the lower abdomen, where things will be bright if the energy cluster is pure, and dark if not. But here again, stilling your mind isn't as simple as gazing at your navel. It's not a matter of technique. The crucial thing is whether your mind, or thoughts, are pure. Suppose someone uses that method and peers inside at his energy center, and sees a glistening cluster of energy, much to his liking. Yet shortly after, perhaps his thoughts turn to a new home and he starts thinking about which room will go to his son, which to his daughter, which to his wife and him, or how they might share the room in the middle as a living room. It's exhilarating to him, and he might even start thinking about how to turn this dream into a reality. But calm of mind is hardly possible if your mind is preoccupied like that. Contrast that with the following view: coming to this world is like staying over at a hotel, which we quickly leave after a short stint. Yet some people are so caught up in this place that they have no interest in leaving. They have forgotten their true homes.

True spiritual practice means cultivating your mind, working on yourself, and reflecting on your role in things rather than blaming your circumstances. There is a school of practice that has taught that "Buddha is in the mind," and there is truth to that. But some people have misinterpreted this as meaning that *you* are in fact Buddha, since Buddha is in your mind. But they are mistaken; it couldn't possibly mean that. What it means to say is that *the key to successful practice* is the mind. It's a stretch to think that it means there is a Buddha in you. Divinity comes through spiritual refinement.

The reason you can't become mentally still or centered is that your mind is not empty or your practice not advanced enough. Concentration progresses from shallow to deep, and is closely linked to spiritual progress. When you manage to break an attachment, you advance in your practice and your stillness deepens. So I would say that relying on some method or other equates to looking *outward*. And that is precisely what leads people astray on the spiritual journey and brings trouble. Buddhism goes so far as to say that you are "lapsing into evil ways" when you look for outside help or blame your circumstances. True practice is about working on the mind, and only with an elevation of thought will you be able to achieve a state of pure serenity and detachment. Only by refining your character will you become attuned to the qualities of the universe; rid yourself of all bad things such as wants and attachments; expel the bad substances from your body; and move upward. With these changes you will no longer be held back by the qualities of the universe, and your virtue, which physically exists, will be converted into higher energy. It should now be clear how closely these all go together.

So, what I just described is the internal reason why people can't achieve quiet or stillness during practice: they can't will themselves to do what a practitioner should be able to do. There are also external factors nowadays that stand to severely affect practitioners and compromise their progress. China has loosened policy restrictions in recent decades in an attempt to invigorate the economy, and has implemented reform programs meant to "open up" the country. Many new technologies have been imported and the standard of living has gone up. Ask just about anyone and they will tell you that it's a good thing. But there are pros and cons to everything, and we should look at both sides of the matter. Bad things of every sort have entered China in conjunction with the reforms and opening up. Books and magazines now have sexual content added in to boost sales, lest publishers have a hard time selling them. And viewership for movies and television programs seems to suffer if there aren't any bedroom scenes, and so they're included out of a concern for box office sales or ratings. Much of what passes as "art" today leaves people scratching their heads as to how it could qualify as that. There was certainly nothing of the sort in traditional Chinese art, which dates back to antiquity. And I should add that the cultural traditions of China are not things that someone invented or put together. As I suggested in the discussion of cultures that predate history, everything traces back to a greater source. But now people's values have changed and been corrupted; even what counts as good and bad have changed. Yet while humankind has undergone these changes, the qualities and standard of the universe that are the sole measure of a person—*zhen, shan, ren*—have *not* changed, and never will. A practitioner has to go by *these*, rather than what's commonly held, if he is to rise above the ordinary. And along with what I just described, there are other external things that might prey upon you, such as homosexuality, sexual temptation, recreational drugs, and other unseemly things.

One can only imagine what would become of this world, having reached the point that it has, if it were to continue in this direction. But it won't be allowed to. If man doesn't set it right, the divine will. The catastrophes that have befallen humanity have always come in times like these. I have refrained from speaking about catastrophes in my classes.

But religions have taught about them, and they have become something of a hot topic. I would just raise the question of how perilous it may be for morals to have changed as drastically as they have and for people to now live with so much hostility toward one another. This means that our spiritual progress is seriously challenged by our surroundings; even out in public you are now confronted with indecent images.

The Daoist sage Lao-tzu wrote that, "When the superior man hears the Way, he will practice it with diligence." A superior person will realize how hard a true teaching is to come by, and know to seize the opportunity and start practicing. A complicated setting like today's world turns out to be a good thing, as I see it, for this is what it takes to produce someone really outstanding. You have to be truly solid in your practice to rise above others in a setting like this.

For someone who is really determined about practice, a complicated setting is, I believe, a good thing. You would have no way to make spiritual progress if there was no strife around you or chances to work on your character. It wouldn't be possible if everyone got along just fine. Lao-tzu also wrote about "the average man who hears the Way." That would be just an average adherent, who is fine with practicing or not, and who will have a hard time making it in the end. There are people right here today who find what I'm teaching agreeable, and yet once they are back out in the world, they may get overwhelmed by the lure of worldly things. As real as those things may seem, even millionaires and members of the ultra-wealthy have realized at the end of their lives that they in fact have nothing—that material riches can't be taken with you past this lifetime, and ultimately, are empty. By contrast, what makes higher energy so precious is that it *does* go with you at the time of death. It's carried on by your soul to the start of your next life. We believe in the immortality of the soul, and don't consider this idea to be misguided or theoretical. The cells of your physical body in this dimension may be shed at death, but in other dimensions, which are made of smaller particulate components, your body has not in fact perished. It has merely molted its shell, so to speak.

All of what I have been discussing comes down to character. The Buddha as well as Bodhidharma both noted that the land of China, which lay in the East, would give rise to the most virtuous of people. This has been a source of pride for generations of Chinese citizens and monks. But it stems from a misunderstanding: they have taken it to mean that the Chinese are spiritually gifted. Many have even been happy and smug about it, thinking they are really special and that China is home to the spiritually adept. Yet most are confused about what was meant, and haven't given thought to why it would be in *China* that you see such figures. As is often the case, few can grasp what the utterances of the spiritually accomplished, [like the Buddha or Bodhidharma,] mean, for their realms of thought and states of awareness aren't familiar to people. I don't think you need me to spell it out to get the idea: great spiritual achievement is only possible in the most complicated of settings and when surrounded by the most complicated of people.

One's Innate Foundation

A person's innate foundation is determined by how much of the material known as virtue his or her body carries in another dimension. Someone has a poor foundation if he has less virtue and more of the black matter, as it means karma is more present within him. Whereas someone will have a good foundation if he has more virtue, and thus lots of the white matter; karma has less of a presence. So people carry two types of matter, one black and the other white, and the two can be converted into one another. Remember that you can gain the white matter by going through hardships, or pain and suffering, and by doing good things; while the black matter comes from doing wrongful or bad things, and it is known as karma. So either of these might result from your actions. They can also come to you from past lives. This is possible because both of them build up over your lifetimes and reach far back, traveling from one life to the next with your soul. So we believe that both karma and virtue can be accumulated over time as well as passed down through the generations in a family. I sometimes recall how people in ancient China, or even older folks today, used to talk about previous generations in a family having stored up virtue, and would remind people to store it up and not lose it. What they said was remarkably insightful; there was a lot to it.

The quality of an individual's innate foundation can determine his ability to believe. Someone with a good foundation will tend to have more faith, thanks to all of the white matter he has. That matter is in harmony with the universe and the qualities of *zhen, shan, ren*, without any separation. And so these qualities can manifest in his body without impediment and communicate with it directly. Someone with a poor foundation, however, will tend to have less faith. That's because the opposite holds true for the black matter. It comes from having done wrongful things and runs counter to the universe's qualities, and so it separates a person from them. The black matter will encase a person's body with a field of its own if there is enough of it, and it will grow in density and thickness as it expands, and undermine a person's faith. That happens because he is being cut off from the cosmic qualities of *zhen, shan, ren* by the black matter he brought upon himself. People like this tend to have a harder time believing in spiritual practice, their faith suffers for it, and karma poses a greater obstacle for them. And the more painful it is, the less they believe. So spiritual progress is very difficult in this scenario.

Spiritual practice is easier for those with more of the white matter, for their virtue will be converted straight into higher energy as long as they embody the qualities of the universe and perfect their character. By contrast, those with more of the black matter have to go through an extra procedure. It can be likened to production at a factory. While others come to the practice with ready-made material, these individuals bring crude material, which needs an additional round of processing. And so they have to first suffer to lessen their karma and change it into white matter. And only then, once it has been remade into material virtue, is it possible for them to develop higher energy with the practice. But often these people tend to have less faith. And their faith only weakens when they have to suffer more, and they find it unbearable. So it's harder for those with more of the black matter to practice. And this is why the teachers of Daoist practices or practices with direct spiritual lineages used to search for disciples, rather than vice versa; they would select disciples based on how much karma and virtue their bodies had.

While a person's innate foundation does generally

determine his or her degree of faith, this isn't always the case. Some people have poor foundations and yet their home environment is spiritually rich, with many family members being religious or doing energy practices and believing in spiritual things. This can foster belief in a person who otherwise wouldn't have much, and strengthen his or her faith. So this means that there are other factors besides just one's foundation. And conversely, there are also cases where people with good foundations have had their ability to believe severely undermined by, most typically, the lackluster education they received in this materialistic world; it might make them narrow-minded and doubtful about anything beyond what they formally learn. And this has been even more pronounced in China in recent times, where schooling has taught people to think in black-and-white terms.

Here's a telling case. I was once teaching about the inner eye on the second day of a class. There was someone there who had an excellent foundation, and I opened his inner eye to a very high realm. He saw many things not visible to others. He was greatly surprised by it and told people about seeing *falun* floating down, like snowflakes, onto those who were present at my teaching; he talked about what my true body looked like and how my aura appeared; what the *falun* looked like; and how many spiritual bodies were present. He also saw that I was giving the teaching across multiple planes, and that *falun* were mending the bodies of those attending the class. And he even saw that as I was instructing here, my energy bodies were simultaneously teaching at many other planes, and that there were angelic fairies overhead scattering flowers, and more. The fact that he could see so much suggests that he had an excellent foundation. Yet after he described all of this, he concluded by saying that he didn't believe in such things. However, some of these things have been verified by recent science, and many more *could be* explained by what science now has to offer. And we have explained some of them here. The insights of energy practice actually surpass those of modern science. So you should now have a sense for how a good foundation doesn't always translate into strong faith.

Enlightenment

What does it mean to be "enlightened"? The term has religious origins. The Buddhist sense of it has to do with a person's grasp of the Buddha's teachings, and it is used both in the sense of one's spiritual insight into these, as well as in the sense of one's final awakening; and so it has to do with wisdom. But nowadays in China the same term is being used in secular settings for people who are clever and know how to win their supervisor's favor. Such people are said to be really "enlightened," since that's what many people think it means. But things often aren't as people take them to be, and you will discover this for yourself if you can manage to look at things from a slightly higher vantage point. When we use the term "enlightened," it's not at all in a worldly sense. We would consider somebody who is overly clever to be quite *unenlightened*. This sort of person may do his job only superficially and just be concerned with garnering praise from his superiors, and so he might end up getting himself indebted to others—who have to pick up the slack and do the real work that he neglected. His cleverness can mean that he finds ways to take credit for things and make out better, but at other people's expense; he never gets the short end of the stick, but this means that others do. And so someone like this can get more and more caught up in worldly things, and in turn, become more small-minded, believing that material things shouldn't be passed up. This might lead the person to think of himself as someone who's "practical" and who gets his way.

And somehow people admire that. But I would say there's nothing admirable about it. Living like that is more tiring than you could imagine. Someone like that has poor eating habits and neglects sleep, and probably worries about losing out even while dreaming. He is terribly petty about worldly things. It really must be tiring to live that way. What we teach, by contrast, is that you can change a tough situation just by compromising a little. But someone like I was describing won't budge, and so his life is awfully tiring. He's not someone to emulate in any way. People of faith regard someone like this as a lost soul, as he has completely fallen for ordinary, worldly things. He probably won't heed any well-meant advice about becoming more virtuous, and will respond to the idea of spiritual practice with total disbelief. He would regard it as absurd, and think it's something only a glutton for punishment—or what people call an "Ah Q"—would do, since it entails never retaliating or responding to malice in kind, and even being grateful for it. This sort of thing isn't comprehensible to someone like that, and he will probably think that you make no sense, that you're foolish. As you can imagine, it's hard for someone like that to see the light.

We wouldn't use the term "enlightened" for this kind of person, naturally. We would consider people who are "foolish"—to use his term for it—to be more enlightened than he is. But of course, there is nothing actually foolish about how

388

we are. Rather, it's just that we worry little about the worldly things that people usually can't go without and take to be so significant; meanwhile, we are still very astute with other things. We're very much conscientious and attentive with the things we do, be it scientific research or the tasks assigned at work, and we do them well. It's the trivial things like worldly gain or interpersonal stuff that we take lightly. You should rest assured that no one worthwhile is going to see you as being foolish for this.

And even someone who might indeed be considered a "fool," it turns out, is just the opposite when viewed with a higher logic. Someone who is mentally disabled isn't capable of doing major wrong in a worldly sense, nor is he capable of scheming against people; and he won't do things out of ego. So he won't squander his virtue. Others might give him their virtue, however. They might physically abuse him or make fun of him, both of which would give him virtue—something extraordinarily precious. As we've established, anything that's gained in this universe comes at a cost. So when someone mocks a disabled person or calls him names, as he opens his mouth to do so, a segment of virtue goes over to the other party. He loses that virtue because he mistreated the person for his own, selfish ends. And similarly, another portion of virtue will be sent over to the disabled person if someone physically abuses him. And while being bullied or physically abused, perhaps the disabled person just grins, almost as if welcoming it and knowing on some level that he's gaining virtue from it, and doesn't want to turn any of it down. So if we look at this with a higher logic, who's the smarter of the two? It turns out it's the mentally disabled person. He doesn't lose a bit of virtue through it all, while the other party is flinging virtue over to him, which he doesn't give back and happily takes in full. "Foolish" as he may be in this lifetime, he won't be in the next, for his soul is no fool. There is something to the religious belief that the virtuous will be blessed in the next life, for blessings come on account of virtue.

Virtue, we believe, can be converted into higher energy without needing any intermediary steps. This means that it is virtue, in its converted form, that determines your level of spiritual attainment; for it becomes higher energy. So virtue, once transformed, decides your level of attainment and your spiritual power. That means it should be cherished, doesn't it? And it goes with you from one life to the next. In Buddhism it's held that your celestial rank reflects your level of attainment; meaning, it bespeaks of your effort. And there is a religious belief that those born with greater virtue, or blessings, might enjoy abundant wealth or positions of high office. By contrast, those lacking in it might have little success even just begging for food, since they would have no virtue to exchange, and nothing in life is free, after all. And what someone with no virtue faces is true death, where both body and soul are destroyed.

There was once a master of *chi-gong* whose level of attainment was quite high when he first taught publicly. He later got caught up in fame and fortune, however, and so his teacher led away his secondary soul; his practice had been carried out by the secondary soul, in fact. Prior to this, when his secondary soul was still present, what he did was dictated by it. An example would be the time when his workplace was allotting housing. His supervisor announced that anyone who needed housing could come and describe their circumstances and needs. While everyone proceeded to do so, this person didn't say anything. Then, when it came to decision time, the person in charge concluded that he was in greater need than others and would be given the housing. Others objected and insisted that it should go to them, and went on about how great their needs were. This person's response was simply, "Then one of you can have it." People might normally call someone "foolish" for responding like that, but some who were present knew that he engaged in spiritual practice, and asked him what on earth he *would* want, if even free housing didn't appeal to him. He responded, "I'll settle for whatever people don't want." He didn't say that because he was foolish, but because he cared little for worldly things and believed in going with the flow; he had a perfectly good head on his shoulders. People pressed him for an example, as they couldn't imagine something that people "don't want." He replied, "I'll settle for the stones on the ground that get kicked around and that nobody wants." To the average person that might make no sense; his or her plane of thought, or level, wouldn't be adequate to grasp the idea. Of course, this man wasn't about to start picking up pebbles. Rather, he was stating a principle, though the common man wouldn't realize it: not to seek after worldly things. And let's talk about stones. You might be familiar with how some religious scriptures describe everything in heaven as being golden—from the trees to the ground, birds, flowers, to dwellings, with even the bodies of the higher beings there, by some accounts, being fashioned of glittering gold. There, stones are a rarity, and so it's said that stones are used as currency, in fact. Now, it wasn't that the man I was describing planned on bringing stones there with him. Rather, he was hinting at a higher truth along these lines, but which wasn't understandable to the average person.

A practitioner will surely not be occupied by the wants that normally consume people, and will place little value in worldly things. What he will have in his life, however, are higher things that people ordinarily can't have—even if they come to know about them and want them.

So this is one sense of the term "enlightened," and it has to do with the realizations people come to during their spiritual development. Yet in China the term is now being used in secular ways, the opposite of how we use it. However, enlightenment in the truest sense goes further than I've described. It has to do with whether a person of faith can, when he meets with adversity, hold fast to the guidance of his teacher—be it in whatever practice or belief—and remember that his is a spiritual life, see the situation for what it is, and embrace it and handle it in the manner set forth by his way of practice. Some people can just never believe in such things, though, and think that there's more to gain by being worldly. What makes it so hard for them to believe is that they aren't willing to open their minds. For example, some people are only here for healing and get put off when I explain that that's not what this kind of practice is for, and then the rest of the time they won't be receptive to anything I say.

In some cases people don't act very enlightened, such as when they go and make notes in my books. People whose inner eyes are open have seen that this book is bathed in brilliant colors, and emanates golden light, with each word having a spiritual body of mine behind it. And you can be sure that I am not making this up and trying to mislead you. Each mark someone writes in there is dark. I think that if you are clear on what this book is doing—that it is taking you to greater spiritual heights—you won't even consider doing that. You should be more thoughtful about certain things. Shouldn't you treasure a book that can guide your practice? And yet by contrast, you might be so reverent toward the religious images you have at home, being careful not to so much as touch them, and praying to them daily, even when all that worship doesn't amount to genuine practice. Yet you would desecrate these profound teachings of Dafa, which have the power to truly guide you in spiritual practice.

More properly used, the term "enlightened" should be referring to how well someone understands the things that happen in his spiritual development or the guidance that was imparted by his teacher. Yet this isn't to be considered being *fully* enlightened. For someone to become fully enlightened, he will have to, from the day he begins his practice, utilize the years left in his life to strive to constantly progress and remove attachments, wants, and desires. And as he does so, he will gain more and more higher energy until eventually he arrives at the final stage of practice. At that point all of his material virtue will have been converted into higher energy, and he will be at the end of the path his teacher designed for him. All of what had locked his body up until that moment will be blasted open. His inner eye will reach the highest point of whatever plane he is at, and he will be able to see into all dimensions existing at his level; see matter as well as the supernatural beings that exist in each corresponding space and time; as well as see the Truth of the universe. He will have miraculous powers at his disposal, and be able to see and have access to higher beings in many realms. I think you would have to agree that at this point he is an "enlightened" being—someone who has achieved awakening via spiritual practice. In the terminology of ancient India, he has become a "Buddha."

The form of enlightenment I just described is one type of full enlightenment, known as "sudden enlightenment." In cases of sudden enlightenment, the person is locked during his years of practice and doesn't know how much energy he has or what it's like. He will not sense anything physically, as even his cells are sealed up. Any energy he develops is locked away and kept from him. It continues like this all the way until the very last stage of his practice, at which point his energy is unlocked and his senses are opened. Practicing in this manner is extremely trying, and only someone with a great spiritual makeup can succeed at it. The person has to go from being simply a good person to someone who constantly works on his character, suffers, makes spiritual progress, and raises the bar for himself—yet never being able to perceive the higher energy he is gaining from it. His is the hardest path, practicing for so many years without any sense of his achievements, and so it takes a great spiritual makeup.

There is another form of enlightenment, which is referred to as "gradual enlightenment." Many practitioners can sense the *falun* turning in them right from the outset, and I open the inner eye for everyone, even if some can't manage to see initially; eventually they will come to have visions as well, and with increasing clarity, as they learn to use the eye over time and their levels of attainment rise. Psychic powers will also come about for this group as they perfect their character and whittle away their attachments. And they will be able to see or sense the changes they undergo along the journey, for the most part, as well as the transformation of their bodies. They will progress in this manner until the final stage, where they will have reached the highest point they were meant to, and the Truth of the universe at their level will be fully revealed to them. With this, their innate bodies will have been transformed and their powers strengthened to a considerable extent. So all of these goals were met gradually, in their case, and thus the designation "gradual enlightenment." There is nothing easy about this approach, either. For example, for those who may still harbor attachments, there is the temptation to show off and a good chance of doing wrong, given the powers at their disposal. And if they succumb to that temptation, they will lose the higher energy that they worked so hard to obtain, and they might even end up in ruins. Or those who have visions might perceive supernatural beings from other planes, who might try to goad them into doing certain things or have them become followers of their practices. But those beings would have no way to guide a person to true divine standing, since they haven't achieved it themselves.

What's even more challenging about it is that the entities in higher dimensions are all at least semi-divine, and capable of expanding to an enormous size and making impressive displays of their powers. And if you fall for it, you might end up going along with them. But doing so would spell ruin for your practice. Even if those beings *were* full divinities, you would still have to begin practicing anew, from scratch. The multitude of beings found throughout the [three-realm] heavens are just transcendent figures, ultimately. They haven't reached the highest levels of achievement or met the ultimate goal of practice; they have yet to break free of the three realms. But to a regular person they really do come across as towering, imposing, and almighty, even if they lack true divine standing. So it remains to be seen whether you can stay poised when signals or energies from other dimensions come to you, or visions that tempt you start to appear. And this is why we say that practicing with an open inner eye is difficult. The challenges to your mind are even greater then. The good news is, it's likely you won't begin gradual enlightenment and gain such powers until you reach the midway mark on your journey. Though I do open the inner eye for all of you, many powers aren't made available at first; they are blasted open only later, after your character has developed sufficiently, your mind has become steady, and you have gained self-control. Gradual enlightenment will only come to you upon a certain level of attainment, and by then you should be able to exercise self-control in regard to the many powers that you gain. And then you will carry on practicing, in this manner, until eventually all of your powers become available to you. Many of you belong to the group I'm describing—where gradual enlightenment begins midway. So you needn't be anxious if you have yet to experience visions.

You might be familiar with how Zen Buddhism makes a distinction between sudden and gradual enlightenment. The sixth Zen patriarch, Hui-neng, believed in sudden enlightenment, while Shen Xiu, of Zen's Northern school, believed in gradual enlightenment. The two approaches have long been the subject of debate among Buddhists. But the debate isn't that meaningful, as I see it, because what the two figures were referring to was just an individual's degree of insight into the teachings as he practices. Some arrive at insights in a sudden flash, while others arrive at them more slowly, over time. But either should be fine, as in both cases the person does enlighten to something. Naturally, it's better to do so instantly, but gradually is okay too; in either case the person comes to a new understanding. So neither approach is wrong.

The Spiritually Adept

It takes more than just a good innate foundation to be worthy of being called "spiritually adept." Spiritually adept individuals are rare, and historically have been few and far between. As you would imagine, for starters they have to have abundant virtue. They are sure to be individuals who can suffer beyond the normal threshold, who have superior self control, who are able to make whatever sacrifices are needed, who don't squander their virtue, and who are spiritually discerning, among other things.

Let's explore what it means to "suffer beyond the normal threshold." There is a Buddhist belief that human beings are fashioned to suffer—that as long as someone is human he must inevitably suffer. They believe that the beings in other dimensions don't have bodies as humans do, and are free of ailments as well as the routine miseries of life; so they aren't subject to the pains that we are. And as beings of other dimensions, they can float about effortlessly and are weightless, which is just wondrous. Whereas normal human beings, saddled with the bodies that they have, are burdened by heat and cold, thirst and hunger, as well as fatigue, on top of which there is the cycle of birth, aging, sickness, and death. In a word, it's not pleasant.

I recall a news report about survivors of the devastating earthquake that once hit Tangshan city. Those who nearly died but were resuscitated were surveyed and asked about any near-death experiences they may have had. Surprisingly, those who did, consistently described something extraordinary: at the time of death they had no sense of fear, and to the contrary, they had a feeling of liberation and a sense of excitement. Some described being suddenly freed from the bonds of their bodies and enjoying the incredible experience of floating about freely, and seeing their own bodies below while doing so. And some described seeing otherworldly beings in other dimensions, while some told of traveling to otherworldly places. In all cases they described how at the moment of death they became free of pain and experienced a sense of joy over the freedom they suddenly felt. This suggests that the human body is an instrument of suffering, only we don't realize it since we were all born into the world the same way.

So I would say that human beings have it the hardest. The other day I indicated that space and time are different here, in the human world, from those in other, larger dimensions. What is two hours here, for instance, might equal an entire year elsewhere. This means that whoever manages to practice here, in this painful setting, is just exceptional; it indicates that he has the Way in his heart, that he wants to develop spiritually, and is truly special. He hasn't lost the innate divinity within, even here in this trying place, and wishes still to make himself worthy of heaven. And so unconditional help can be extended to someone like this. When higher beings behold this kind of person meditating through the night, for example, they hold him in high esteem. Remember that a couple of hours here may equate to a year in another realm, and so a night of meditation might equal six years elsewhere. This is an exceptional setting.

Then consider just how hard it may be to suffer beyond what's normal. Suppose someone goes to work one day, only to find his company not doing well financially, and that there are more employees than jobs. The company has to reform and start contracting work out, and so excess employees are being let go. This person is one of them, and suddenly finds himself unemployed. We can just imagine how stressful that would be. He has no source of income to support his family now, and no other skills to land a job. So he goes home, terribly dejected. Upon returning home, he learns that his elderly parent has become seriously ill. He goes to great lengths to borrow enough money to check his parent into the hospital, and rushes them there, feeling anxious and upset. Later he goes back home to get a few things for them, only to have his kid's teacher show up at the door, informing him that his child injured someone in a fight, and that he, as the father, had better quickly come straighten things out with the other kid's parents. After taking care of all this he returns home, sits down, and then a phone call comes from someone telling him that his wife is having an affair. Now of course, you shouldn't expect to go through the same. Most people wouldn't be able to take it, and might think there is no reason to go on, or even try to take their own life in desperation. My point is that you may have to go through some of the most trying ordeals imaginable. They could take any of a variety of forms. The scheming that goes on between people, the things that test your character, and the cutthroat nature of society are no less trying than the scenario I described. Some people, for instance, find the pain of humiliation to be so great that they take their own lives. This means that to practice in a setting as complicated as this, we need to be able to weather the most trying of storms and have outstanding self-control, or *ren*.

And what does that look like, in practice? For starters, a practitioner should be able to hold back from retaliating, and patiently endure. Anyone who succumbs to retaliating could hardly be called a practitioner. Those who have bad tempers might think that this is too hard for them to do. But I think they simply need to work on their tempers, as practitioners should be able to stay composed. Some people lose their tempers when disciplining their children and get all worked up. But it needn't be like that. You shouldn't genuinely get angry. You have to be calm and rational for your child to be reared well. Do you really think you could develop higher energy if even little things get to you or cause you to lose your temper? I recall someone once telling me that he could take getting publicly humiliated as long as nobody he knew was there to see it. But that's not good enough. You might one day get slapped in the face and disgraced right in front of those whom you would least want to see it. How you handle it would be revealing and show how composed you are. To really make the grade, you would have to not only keep your composure but also not let it get to you. Remember that a holy being would never let anything affect him or her emotionally; worldly things simply don't occupy a holy person's mind. They will always be pleasant and upbeat, however badly they might be treated. If you can genuinely be like that, then you have already achieved a basic level of divinity, known as *arhat*.

People might worry that they will come across as cowards or pushovers if they exercise that much patience. But there is nothing cowardly about it. The older generation and those who are more cultured can practice self-restraint and not stoop to arguing with others. So all the more so should we, as practitioners. It could hardly be called cowardly. I would take it to be a sign of great composure and willpower. That kind of self-restraint is what defines a practitioner. There is an old Chinese saying that, "The common man will answer insult with his sword." It's only to be expected that the typical person fights back. And that's what makes him ordinary, as opposed to a practitioner. To do what I've described means that you must have good willpower and self-control.

There was a well-known figure in ancient times named Han Hsin, who was extremely able; he served as a chief general to the future emperor Liu Bang and was instrumental in creating his empire. We should note what set him apart. It's said that from a young age he was different from others, and there's a well-known anecdote about his willingly enduring the indignity of crawling, on hands and knees, between another man's legs. As the story goes, when he was young he was active in the martial arts and carried a sword on him, as was customary. He was walking down the street one day when a thug blocked his path, standing with his hands on his hips. The thug challenged him, saying, "What are you carrying a sword for? Do you have the guts to kill a man? Let's see you prove it by cutting off my head." And with that said, he bent over and stuck his neck out. But Han couldn't see any point in beheading the man. And like today, doing that would get you reported to the authorities and cost you your life, so it wasn't something to do rashly. When the thug saw that Han wasn't about to kill him, he declared, "If you want to get past me but don't have the guts to kill me, then you'll have to get on your hands and knees and crawl." And that is just what he did. We can see from Han's exceptional composure that he was different from others, and therein lay the key to his success. Thinking that honor is worth fighting for is a misguided, worldly notion. A life that revolves around pride, as you can imagine, is going to be tiring and painful, and not worth it. As people who seek spiritual transcendence, we should be still better than a Han Hsin, who led an ordinary existence, after all. Our goal is to rise above the ordinary and make strides toward higher realms. While we won't go through what Han did, we will face insults and humiliation as we practice in this world, and they might be every bit as challenging. The strife that you experience with others may really grate on your soul, and be every bit the equal to what Han went through—if not harder.

You also need to be able to forgo the things that people normally long for and are attached to. This takes time to accomplish. It's not something that can be done overnight, any more so than becoming holy. But you shouldn't take a relaxed approach just because we know it takes time. It's a problem if you take my words to be license for being lax. To follow a sacred path requires the ultimate dedication and effort.

You also need to preserve your virtue, maintain your integrity, and refrain from acting impulsively. You can't simply do whatever you would like to; you have to uphold your character. It's common in Asian culture to believe that you can "make merit" by doing good deeds. But as practitioners we strive to preserve the merit, or virtue, we have, rather than seek to gain more. People often strive to gain virtue or blessings by doing good works, and hope to secure a better next life. But from our perspective, you needn't be concerned with the next life, for you will be freed from reincarnation if you achieve enlightenment. A second reason we opt to *preserve* virtue is that the two kinds of matter carried on our bodies weren't built up over just one lifetime, but trace back over many lives. And besides, you could scour an entire city and not find even one genuinely good deed to perform—even if you did this daily.

Then there is another facet to this. The seemingly good things that people do in an attempt to gain virtue could prove to be bad things; and the apparently bad things that you see people do could turn out to be good things. That's because there are underlying reasons for events, which may not be evident. There are ordinary laws in place in this world to regulate human affairs, which is as it should be. A practitioner, however, is someone who operates on a higher plane. And as a higher being you should go by a higher logic; you mustn't always look at things with an ordinary lens. You are apt to mishandle things if you intervene, since you may not know the underlying reasons for them. So this is why we subscribe to the doctrine of "non-interference," and say that you can't simply jump in on an impulse. Someone once tried to reason with me by saying that he got involved in things because he really just wanted to "see justice served." My response was that he'd best join the police force, in that case. But I'm not telling you to turn a blind eye to life-threatening situations if you see them. I'm talking about intervening in the fights that people have, be they verbal or physical, since your stopping them might mean that the parties involved can't work out a past debt that was to be settled. And then in that case they would have to wait until another time before going through it again. So my point is, you are likely to mishandle situations and lose virtue when you can't see the reasons for things.

You can't criticize ordinary people for getting involved in other people's affairs, since they have their own ways that they follow. But you should go by a higher logic and refrain from getting involved unless you come upon something like a terrible crime. To not do anything in those circumstances would reflect poorly on your character, since a good person would respond. If you don't even care when someone is getting murdered or there's a fire, then what would you care about? But I should say that such events serve little purpose for us, and might not be part of the plan for you, or something for you to see. What we strive to do is preserve our virtue by not doing wrong. In many instances it would be wrong for you to get involved and take action, even if just slightly, and would cost you virtue. And the stakes are high. A loss of virtue will mean it is that much harder to advance in your practice and achieve your ultimate goal. So it takes good judgment to determine when to intervene in things, and this might result from a good foundation or good influences.

I believe that the world will be a better place if we can each work on ourselves and look at our character, or thoughts, to identify the source of any problems we experience, and then make a point of doing better next time and try to always be thoughtful towards others. Morality will improve, people will become more civil, and the world will be safer for it. Perhaps a police force wouldn't even be needed; people would be policing themselves, so to speak, by becoming self-reflective. What a world that would be. Yet today, even with a legal system that's become quite comprehensive, people still do wrong in the face of the law. That's because laws cannot change the heart, and so people still commit wrongful acts when nobody is there to stop them. I believe the world would be a different place if everyone were to work on themselves, like we do, and nobody would need to think about intervening and righting wrongs.

This is as far as I can go with my teaching, as anything higher must be left to you to arrive at as you practice. Nor can I spell out all of the little things in life that you might like to ask about, as then you would have nothing left to work through. You have to do your own practice and arrive at your own understanding of things. There would be nothing left to work through if I spelled everything out. But you can take heart in knowing that the teachings of Dafa I have made available can serve as your compass.

I am likely going to stop giving classes soon. In anticipation of that, I am planning to make my genuine teachings available to all, so that everyone can have them to guide their practice. From the start I've been motivated by a sense of responsibility to all of my students as well as to the world more broadly, and this continues to be the case. The public's response should be a good barometer of how we've done, so I won't say more. I made this practice public so that, for one, more people could benefit from it, and secondly, so that those who are sincere about spiritual growth would have teachings to guide them. Along the way I've also spelled out what it takes to be a good person, and hope that after my instruction at the very least you can do that, if not become a practitioner—to the betterment of the world. You now have the tools in your hands to be a better person. And I am confident that after the class you will be.

Not everything has gone smoothly while giving my teachings, as there have been a variety of disruptions. The classes have gone truly well nevertheless, thanks to the great support from the sponsoring organizations and the leaders from different segments of society, along with the efforts of our staff.

Everything I have taught has been to help you succeed in your practice, and I have disclosed things never made public before. What's unique about my teachings is that they incorporate modern science and the science of the body in order to make things more accessible, and yet the teachings are very spiritually advanced. This is done mainly in hopes that you will, with time, truly embrace the teachings and get somewhere in the practice. That is my purpose. We have come across many people that find the teachings agreeable, but think they will be hard to put into practice. But I think it really depends on the person. For the average person who isn't interested in spiritual growth, it's going to seem hard, or quite a stretch, and not like something he will succeed at. So it will seem hard for someone like that, who's not interested in spiritual development. It's like what Lao-tzu wrote: "When the superior man hears the Way, he will practice it with diligence; when the average man hears the Way, he will sometimes believe and sometimes doubt; when the inferior man hears the Way, he will laugh at it. Were it not derided, it would not be a true spiritual path." Those who are sincere about practicing will find it very much doable and not some impossible task. This has been borne out by the many among us who have progressed to great spiritual heights through the practice, some of whom are present today. I hadn't revealed this previously for fear that they might become proud or attached, which would affect the growth of their spiritual power. The practice isn't hard so long as you are sincere about spiritual growth, are willing to go through whatever it takes, and can come to look upon the material things of this world with detachment and indifference. The practice only seems hard to people because they still hold on to worldly things. So there is nothing inherently hard about the practice or advancing to higher stages; it's simply that people are held back by attachments. The difficulty lies in the allure of worldly things, which are so tangible and immediate, and hard to forsake. Another likely pitfall is the anger people experience when there is a falling out, which might get the best of them if it's not kept in check. Back in my days of practice, more than once a teacher told me, "Nothing is truly unbearable or impossible." And it really is so. It's an outlook you only stand to benefit from. So the next time you are going through a real trial or tribulation, try to keep this in mind, and see if you can bear it. Or when faced with what seems impossible, and even if others say so, try to keep this in mind, and see if it might just be possible. I believe that if you can do that, you will always find that there is light at the end of the tunnel.

It might be hard to remember everything taught here, with all that's been said. So here are my main hopes, in closing: that you will really become a practitioner and do spiritual practice in earnest; that both veterans of the practice and those new to it will one day be spiritually perfected through Dafa; and that from today forth you will really make the most of your time to practice.

Postscript

Zhuan Falun is not meant to be a literary work, and is not, as such, concerned with the literary or stylistic conventions of our day; nor does it necessarily use terms in the ways that people are now accustomed to. Were these conventions to have been prioritized, it would come at a significant cost: while the text would perhaps be more in keeping with certain expectations, or rhetorically elegant, it would be accompanied by a shallowing and limiting of its message. This is a book that offers spiritual guidance of a higher order and that speaks to multiple stages of practice, and affords insights into the Way on numerous levels. All of this is meant to foster real, substantive changes in the reader—from his body, to his energy, to his spiritual state itself—and much of this would be impossible were the approach to the text otherwise.

Hongzhi Li
January 5, 1996

ENDNOTES
from the translators

p. i **Dafa:** A Chinese Buddhist term, this can be translated as "Great Way," "Great Law," or "Great Teaching." It is used as shorthand for the practice's full name, Falun Dafa. The term also appears historically in the names of certain Chinese spiritual practices, as described later in this chapter.

p. i **zhen, shan, ren:** *Zhen* translates as true and genuine; *shan* as compassionate, good, and kind; and *ren* as tolerant, composed, forbearing, and patient. *Zhen* is pronounced as in the "-gion" of "region," *shan* with an open "ah" sound, and *ren* as spelled.

p. 2 **offering instruction:** The contents of this book were originally delivered as a course, with a series of in-person talks or lectures being given in sequence over the span of several days.

p. 6 **chi:** The term *chi* (also spelled *qi*) is often likened to, and thought to approximate, the well-known Indian term *prana* and the ancient Greek term *pneuma*. It is the same word as what in Japanese is called *ki*.

p. 10 **dharma:** The Chinese term used here, *fa*, is normally rendered by translators according to context, as it is wide-ranging in meaning and sense. In the Chinese Buddhist tradition, *fa* is itself a translation of the originally Sanskrit term *dharma* (or *dhamma*, in the Pali canon), which initially referred to the Buddha's teachings and has thus long been synonymous with "truth," "way," or "law" (in a moral or spiritual sense). The term is translated variously as "Way," "teachings," and "spiritual truths," in this book. It might be noted that this same term, *fa*, appears in the two-syllable word *Dafa*, which is part of the practice's name.

p. 10   *the Buddha, Shakyamuni:* In keeping with the conventions of English, the historical Buddha—"Gautama Buddha" or "Shakyamuni Buddha"—is referred to as "the Buddha" elsewhere in the text. His full title is used in several passages where multiple Buddhas are discussed, for disambiguation. The title "Shakyamuni" means "Sage of the Śākya clan." This is the same figure who was known as Siddhârtha, prior to his enlightenment.

p. 16   *Lei Feng:* A household name in modern China, the figure of Lei Feng has been celebrated since the 1960s for his selfless acts of service to his country and fellow citizens.

p. 26   *chi-gong:* Falun Dafa is considered a type of *chi-gong*, or "energy practice."

p. 44   *falun:* Literally translated as "wheel of law," or "*dharma* wheel," this refers to the wheel-like entity depicted in the color insert at the front of the book. It is a term used in the Buddhist tradition, dating back thousands of years.

p. 51   ***inner eye:*** The Chinese term here, *tian-mu*, is also commonly referred to as the "third eye," "spiritual eye," or sometimes, in earlier centuries, "mind's eye." The most traditional term from the Western context (i.e., "inner eye") is used in this edition.

p. 85   ***spiritual bodies:*** This is a translation of the Chinese term *fa-shen*, which is itself historically a translation of the Sanskrit Buddhist term *dharmakaya*. It should be noted that the use and meaning of the term in Falun Dafa is not necessarily the same as that in other Buddhist traditions (where its interpretation varies widely). The term is discussed in greater detail later in the book.

p. 107   ***general public:*** The Chinese term used here would typically refer to practitioners who had not previously taken monastic vows, been ordained, etc. prior to learning Falun Dafa.

p. 181   ***Mandorla:*** This is the best-established term for the circular, often almond-shaped ring that surrounds divine figures in Asian religious art as well as in Renaissance and Medieval European art. It is sometimes referred to as an "aureola" as well. The Chinese term, *xuan-guan*, which has ancient roots, translates literally as "mysterious juncture" or "obscure pass."

p. 183   ***jie-yin:*** This *mudra* is also known by its Sanskrit name, i.e., *dhyani*. It consists of resting the fingers of one hand atop those of the other, with both palms facing upward, and the two thumbtips touching so as to form an oval.

p. 193   *four sides … eight directions:* For Chinese readers, the "four sides" would be understood as referring to north, south, east, and west, while "eight directions" would be arrived at once northeast, northwest, southeast, and southwest are added to the four sides just named.

p. 213   *performing a consecration:* It might be helpful to note that the Chinese term being translated here, *kai-guang*, consists of two words that more literally mean "light opening" or "opening [with] light." This explains the otherwise curious behavior that figures in the passage engage in; they are most likely trying to "open" the statue's eyes with "light." Image consecration ceremonies are common to both South Asian and East Asian Buddhism.

p. 239   *conjure fire:* This phrase and passage can be read in Chinese as a play on two senses of the term *zou-huo*, which normally means something like "to lose one's mind" and is negatively associated with energy practices in China (as discussed throughout the section); the same term, if read strictly in a literal sense, means to exude or conjure fire.

p. 319   *Inedia:* This refers to going without food or drink for prolonged periods of time, and is a phenomenon found historically in religious and spiritual traditions throughout the world. In the 1980s and 90s in China, as the passage suggests, this had become a fairly well-known phenomenon associated with *chi-gong*, and was the subject of much debate and research.